The Complete Eurovision Song Contest Companion

★ ★

ABOUT THE AUTHORS

Paul Gambaccini, Tim Rice and Jonathan Rice were co-creators of *British Hit Singles* (Guinness). Tony Brown was the editorial consultant on many editions. They also created for Guinness companion volumes such as *British Hit Albums*, *Number One Hits*, *Hits of the Sixties*, *Hits of the Eighties*, *Top 40 Charts*, *Top 1000 Singles* and *Hits Quiz.* The combined sales of these books now exceeds 1,500,000 copies.

PAUL GAMBACCINI presents the Classic Countdown on Classic fm and the American hits on Radio 2. His ancestors came from four of the countries that compete in Eurovision. As a TV film reviewer he did actually give several movies 'nul points'.

TIM RICE (failed Eurovision lyricist 1969) has written book and lyrics for the musicals *Joseph and his Amazing Technicolour Dreamcoat*, *Jesus Christ Superstar*, *Blondel*, *Chess* and *Evita.* More recently he wrote for the Walt Disney feature cartoons *The Lion King* and *Aladdin.* He has won three 'Best Song' Oscars.

JONATHAN RICE is an author, consultant and broadcaster who has written books on bridge, football, golf, politics and Japan, as well as three books on cricket and three based on BBC TV sitcoms. He has been a member of the international jury for the Yamaha Song Contest in Tokyo, the richest of the Eurovision clones.

TONY BROWN is an expert on popular music. He writes for the music industry trade magazine *Music Week* and is a consultant for chart compilers CIN. He has acted as editorial researcher on the Guinness books listed above.

The Complete Eurovision Song Contest Companion

Paul Gambaccini Tim Rice Jonathan Rice Tony Brown

Foreword by Terry Wogan

★ ★

First published in Great Britian in 1998 by
PAVILION BOOKS LIMITED
London House, Great Eastern Wharf, Parkgate Road, London SW11 4NQ.

Designed by Nigel Partridge
Edited by Emma Tait
Picture Research by Image Select Limited

A CIP catalogue record for this book is available from the British Library.

ISBN 1 86205 167 4

Set in Bauer Bodoni

Colour reproduction by Lydia Litho
Printed and bound in England by Bath Press
2 4 6 8 10 9 7 5 3 1

This book may be ordered by post direct from the publisher.
Please contact the Marketing Department. But try your bookshop first.

PICTURE CREDITS

Associated Press: Section B: 1TR, 4BR. BBC Picture Archives: Section A: 1BL, 2R, 3T&B, 5T&B, 6TL&BR, 7B, 8TL,R&B; Section B: 1TR&B, 2T&B, 3BL, 6BL, 7T&BR, 8L&BR; Back cover: top right; Front cover: top right, bottom right.
Farabolafoto: Section A: 4B; Back cover: bottom right.
Hulton Getty: Section A: 1TL, 1R.
Popperfoto: Section B: 4T, 7BL.
Rex Features: Section A: 2L, 4T, 7T&R; Section B: 3T&BR, 4BL, 5TL, R&B, 6T&R; Back cover: top right, centre, second left, far left; Front cover: centre, second left, second right.
Universal Pictorial Press: Front cover: bottom left, far left.

CONTENTS

AUTHORS' THANKS AND ACKNOWLEDGEMENTS

The four authors would like to thank those people who have contributed their time and effort to help us create this book. In particular we must thank Sir Cliff Richard, Terry Wogan and Jonathan King for their memories, their revelations and their advice; Alex Goldberg for his help with photo research; Neil Dickinson for giving us access to his comprehensive video collection; Tom Rice for his hours of research and help with the details of hundreds of individual entries and the vagaries of the scoring systems; and Roger Houghton for keeping the faith.

We have tried to check and recheck the facts in this book, and hope to have got most of them right most of the time. Where there is some doubt over the name of a song or a performer, we have in general followed the details given on television at the time, although there are exceptions. The 1978 winner, for example, is so widely known as 'A-Ba-Ni-Bi' that we have not followed the television spelling of 'Ah-Bah-Nee-Bee', which appeared on the screen that night. There are several other examples, especially where the original name or title was written in a different script, such as Greek, Hebrew or Cyrillic. In the result tables for each year, the songs appear in the order in which the entries were sung. The example below shows you how to read the voting tables.

UNDERSTANDING THE VOTING TABLES

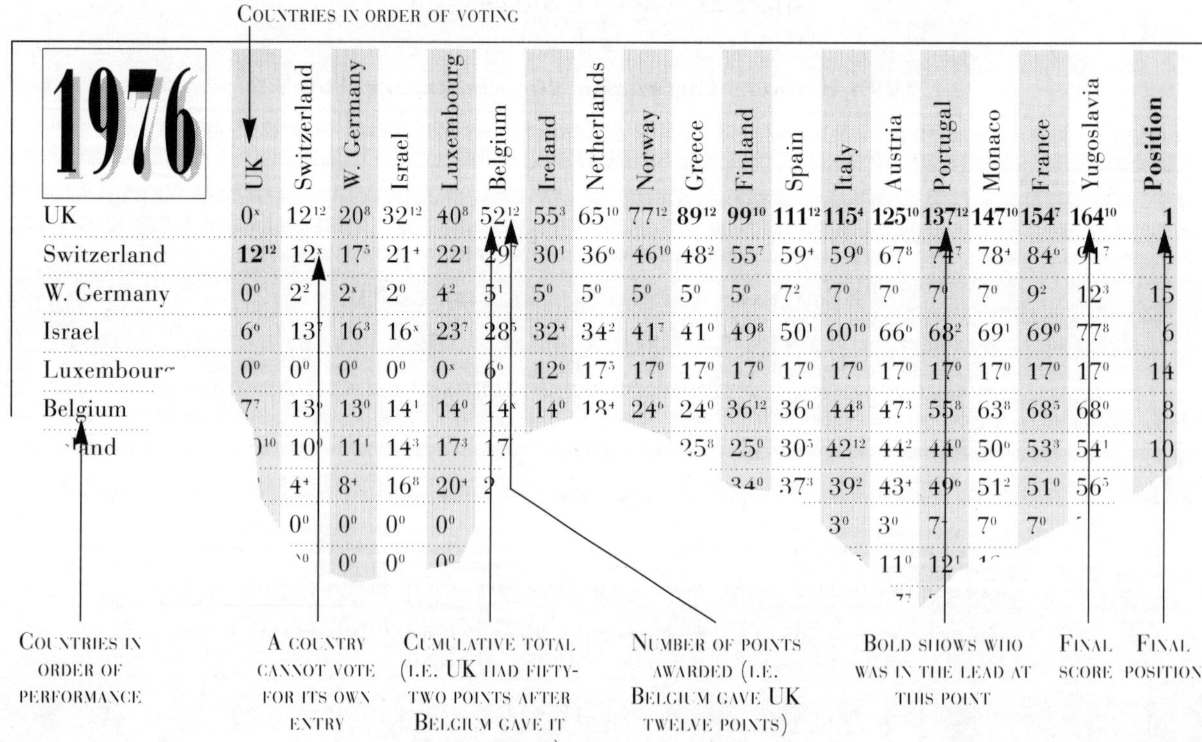

1976	UK	Switzerland	W. Germany	Israel	Luxembourg	Belgium	Ireland	Netherlands	Norway	Greece	Finland	Spain	Italy	Austria	Portugal	Monaco	France	Yugoslavia	**Position**
UK	0^x	12^{12}	20^8	32^{12}	40^8	52^{12}	55^3	65^{10}	77^{12}	**89^{12}**	**99^{10}**	**111^{12}**	**115^4**	**125^{10}**	**137^{12}**	**147^{10}**	**154^7**	**164^{10}**	**1**
Switzerland	**12^{12}**	12^x	17^5	21^4	22^1	29	30^1	36^6	46^{10}	48^2	55^7	59^4	59^0	67^8	74^7	78^4	84^6	91^7	4
W. Germany	0^0	2^2	2^x	2^0	4^2	5^1	5^0	5^0	5^0	5^0	5^0	7^2	7^0	7^0	7^0	7^0	9^2	12^3	15
Israel	6^6	13^7	16^3	16^x	23^7	28^5	32^4	34^2	41^7	41^0	49^8	50^1	60^{10}	66^6	68^2	69^1	69^0	77^8	6
Luxembourg	0^0	0^0	0^0	0^0	0^x	6^6	12^6	17^5	17^0	17^0	17^0	17^0	17^0	17^0	17^0	17^0	17^0	17^0	14
Belgium	7^7	13^6	13^0	14^1	14^0	14^x	14^0	18^4	24^6	24^0	36^{12}	36^0	44^8	47^3	55^8	63^8	68^5	68^0	8
[illegible]land	10^{10}	10^0	11^1	14^3	17^3	17				25^8	25^0	30^5	42^{12}	44^2	44^0	50^6	53^3	54^1	10
		4^4	8^4	16^8	20^4	2					34^0	37^3	39^2	43^4	49^6	51^2	51^0	56^5	
		0^0	0^0	0^0	0^0								3^0	3^0	7	7^0	7^0		
		0	0^0	0^0	0^0									11^0	12^1				

FOREWORD
BY TERRY WOGAN

I love the Eurovision Song Contest. I've loved it since Kenneth McKellar in his kilt, Pearl and Teddy, Teddy's brother Bryan, The Allisons, Sandie Shaw, Lulu, Dana, Cliff... but I must stop, to brush away the sentimental tear... I *love* the Eurovision Song Contest. I love it for its magnificent foolishness, its grand illusion that it brings together the diverse peoples and cultures of Europe on one great wing of song, when all it makes manifest is how far apart everybody is.

Because I've always treated the Eurovision Song Contest as a huge joke instead of an International Television Festival of Fine Music, I come in for a great deal of abuse, usually from members of the Eurovision Song Contest Fan Club (an international group of people who regard it as only marginally less important than The Second Coming) or my fellow commentators from foreign parts, who point the accusatory microphone: 'If you don't like Eurovision – vy do you do eet?'

They just don't get it. I sometimes wonder, when in vacant or in xenophobic mood, whether *anybody* gets it, except the man on the Clapham Omnibus, and me. On the Big Night, hundreds of millions of Europeans sit agog above their pastas, daubes, paellas and pumpernickels and watch Eurovision without the suggestion of a smile. The hundreds of international commentators yammer away reverentially as if it was Wagner at Beyreuth. To their shame, and mine, I've even noticed the Irish taking it seriously, from time to time... And another thing, what sort of an eejit would bother doing something for twenty-five years that he didn't like?

The Eurovision Song Contest is a truly wonderful idea, which doesn't bear the most casual inspection. How can anybody imagine that a Turkish jury can judge a Swedish song? How does a Croatian assess a Portuguese fado? Now, if everyone sung in English... there's the rub. After the Swedish group Abba won in 1974 in Brighton with 'Waterloo', the greatest of all Eurosongs, it was decided that each country's entry should be sung in its native tongue. There hasn't been a Eurovision winner that's been an international hit since then. It's just that popular music, 'pop', is an Anglophone thing. It has its roots in America, whence came jazz, blues, rhythm and blues, rock 'n' roll and country. It just doesn't sound right if it isn't sung in English. French pop? German? Italian pop's never left Napoli. Spain can't lose the flamenco, ditto the Portuguese with the fado. Dutch doesn't sound right, the Scandinavians and the Slavs even more so, and if those singing in Greek didn't vote for each other, who would?

If the Irish entry wasn't sung every year in English, would it have carried off the Grand Prix quite as often? Aha! I hear you cry, but if that's the case, why hasn't the United Kingdom won more frequently? Well, don't quote me, but when did Ireland last have a war with anybody in Europe? Politics, friends, politics. But that's another story, an unnecessary smudge on a great ideal, the Eurovision Song Contest.

And on a certain Saturday night in May, millions of British viewers will be watching a show that bears no relation whatsoever to their own musical tastes. They'll be watching it to sneer at the songs, jeer at the frocks, fall about at the dancing. They'll find it camp, schlocky or silly, according to taste. But they won't miss it for anything. And neither will I. This is the book for all those people out there who will be glued to their televisions on the night of the Contest. They'll have to carry me off in a box ...

★ ★

THE EUROVISION SONG CONTEST

1956

Won by Switzerland: 'Refrain'

Written by Geo Voumard and Emile Gardaz

Performed by Lys Assia

Orchestra conducted by Fernando Paggi

The Eurovision Song Contest started modestly, on a Thursday in the Teatro Kursaal in Lugano, Switzerland. It had been the idea of Frenchman Marcel Baison, who had seen the immense success of the San Remo song festival, which began in Italy in 1952. Baison thought that a song contest would be the ideal way to develop the idea of European unity and bring together many of the nations of that continent through the rapidly improving technology of television under the aegis of the recently formed European Broadcasting Union (EBU). He probably had no idea that over four decades later the contest would be still going strong, featuring some countries that were not even on the map in 1956 and others that have never been part of Europe.

The first Contest featured only seven nations, so each country was allowed to put forward two songs. Luxembourg and Switzerland decided to send only one singer to perform both songs, but all the other countries used two performers. Seven of the songs were in French, three in German, two in Dutch and two in Italian. Lys Assia for Switzerland sang in both German and French, and her French song won. It was the first of fifteen winning songs in that language, although the most recent winner to have performed in French did so as long ago as 1988 – Céline Dion won for Luxembourg that year. No other language has been so successful at Eurovision, but then again, no other language has been used as often. English is the next most successful language, but in 1956 there was no British entry, no Irish entry and no songs at all in English.

'Refrain' set no precedent in subject matter or mood by being a sad song about 'the colour of rain, the regret of my twenty years, chagrin, sadness at being no longer a child. I know that my path, my lost love, cannot cross yours, you who thinks no more of me'. Sadness does not generally sell at Eurovision, but the thirty-year-old Miss Assia was not to know that in 1956. She was probably as well known to audiences as any of the competitors that year, having introduced the world to the song 'Oh Mein Papa' in 1953. Within a year, it had topped the charts in both America and Britain, in versions by Eddie Fisher and Eddie Calvert, but Lys Assia was the first to record it.

The other songs introduced us to several long-running Eurovision themes, such as local geography ('De Vogels Van Holland'/'The Birds of Holland' and, rather more startlingly 'Messieurs Les Noyés De La Seine'/'The Drowned Men of the River Seine'), time ('Le Temps Perdu'/'Lost Time', 'Les Amants De Minuit'/'The Midnight Lovers'), and all-purpose happiness ('Im Wartesaal Zum Grossen Glück'/'Waiting For Good Fortune' and 'Le Plus Beau Jour De Ma Vie'/'The Most Beautiful Day Of My Life'). Lys Assia's other song, 'Das Alte Karussel'/'The Old Carousel' was the first of many entries to refer to fairs, circuses, clowns, puppets and the like. This has always been a powerful theme in Eurovision, as the

1956 EUROVISION SONG CONTEST

Host country: Switzerland ★ *Venue:* Teatro Kursaal, Lugano
Date: 24 May ★ *Presenter:* Lohengrin Filipello
Voting structure: 2 jury members from each participating country in the hall. There was no scoreboard as the voting was kept secret.
Total entries: 14 (2 songs from each of 7 countries)
Debut countries: Belgium, France, Germany, Italy, Luxembourg, Netherlands, Switzerland

Country	Performer	Song	Pts	Pos.
Netherlands	Jetty Paerl	De Vogels Van Holland	-	-
Switzerland	Lys Assia	Das Alte Karussel	-	-
Belgium	Fud Leclerc	Messieurs Les Noyés De La Seine	-	-
Germany	Walter Andreas Schwarz	Im Wartesaal Zum Grossen Glück	-	-
France	Mathé Altéry	Le Temps Perdu	-	-
Luxembourg	Michèle Arnaud	Ne Crois Pas	-	-
Italy	Franca Raimondi	Aprite Le Finestra	-	-
Netherlands	Corry Brokken	Voor Goed Voor Bij	-	-
Switzerland	**Lys Assia**	**Refrain**	**-**	**1**
Belgium	Mony Marc	Le Plus Beau Jour De Ma Vie	-	-
Germany	Freddy Quinn	So Geht Das Jede Nacht	-	-
France	Dany Dauberson	Il Est Là	-	-
Luxembourg	Michèle Arnaud	Les Amants De Minuit	-	-
Italy	Tonina Torrielli	Amami Se Vuoi	-	-

familiar ideas and images translate easily across all cultures.

Most of the performers were women, although Germany used two men, Walter A. Schwarz and Freddy Quinn. The German record of success in Eurovision has always been very feeble, with only one win, in 1982, to their credit. Perhaps their inability to judge the European mood, at least as far as musical taste is concerned, began at Lugano, although it must be said that the ladies who sang for them subsequently fared little better.

That first year of Eurovision no record of the voting was ever made public. What we do know is that there were two judges from each competing country, who were able to vote for their favourite song, and that Luxembourg television was obviously in a financial crisis at the time. As well as being unable to afford two singers, it decided against the expense of sending judges to Lugano, and asked the Swiss judges if they would vote on their behalf. Perhaps we should not be altogether surprised, therefore, that it was a Swiss entry that won, and the first seeds of doubt about the voting systems in Eurovision were cast.

A Thursday night in Lugano is not a typical birthplace for an enduring cultural phenomenon, but the Eurovision Song Contest soon turned into a bonny, and sometimes rather too bouncy, baby.

★ ★

THE EUROVISION SONG CONTEST

1957

Won by Netherlands: 'Net Als Toen'

Written by Guus Jansen and Willy van Hemert

Performed by Corry Brokken

Orchestra conducted by Dolf van der Linden

Eurovision was still a nervous toddler in 1957, experimenting and learning by its mistakes as much as by its successes. Nobody had yet really decided what style of song was suitable for the competition, with the result that some of the entries stretched the viewers' and juries' imaginations a little too far. Perhaps we are looking back across the years with too much hindsight, but it certainly seems that the early years of Eurovision were trying to promote not merely popular songs from Europe, but, more specifically, popular songs that were absolutely *not* American. The American influence on music in Europe after the war, with American Forces Radio heard by everybody throughout the Continent, was overwhelming, and in the early years of Eurovision, at least until the mid-1960s, any song that showed its American influences fared very badly.

The United Kingdom, competing for the first time, had a song with the same plot line as Dana's 1970 winner, 'All Kinds Of Everything', and the soprano tones of the popular musical film star Patricia Bredin, but she came and went very quickly. Her entry, timed at just one minute fifty-two seconds, was the shortest ever performed at Eurovision. It was followed by one of the longest. Italy's Nunzio Gallo and his guitarist Piero Gauzio

1957	Switzerland	Denmark	France	W. Germany	Netherlands	Austria	Italy	UK	Luxembourg	Belgium	**Position**
Belgium	1^{1}	3^{2}	3^{0}	5^{2}	5^{0}	5^{0}	5^{0}	5^{0}	5^{0}	5^{x}	8=
Luxembourg	0^{0}	0^{0}	0^{0}	0^{0}	0^{0}	3^{3}	7^{4}	8^{1}	8^{x}	8^{0}	4=
UK	2^{2}	2^{0}	2^{0}	2^{0}	3^{1}	4^{1}	4^{0}	4^{x}	5^{1}	6^{1}	7
Italy	0^{0}	1^{1}	1^{0}	1^{0}	3^{2}	3^{0}	3^{x}	5^{2}	6^{1}	7^{1}	6
Austria	0^{0}	0^{0}	0^{0}	0^{0}	1^{1}	1^{x}	1^{0}	3^{2}	3^{0}	3^{0}	10
Netherlands	**7^{7}**	**10^{3}**	**14^{4}**	**15^{1}**	**15^{x}**	**21^{6}**	**22^{1}**	**23^{1}**	**26^{3}**	**31^{5}**	**1**
W. Germany	0^{0}	0^{0}	6^{6}	6^{x}	6^{0}	6^{0}	7^{1}	7^{0}	7^{0}	8^{1}	4=
France	0^{0}	2^{2}	2^{x}	8^{6}	9^{1}	9^{0}	9^{0}	11^{2}	15^{4}	17^{2}	2
Denmark	0^{0}	0^{x}	0^{0}	0^{0}	5^{5}	5^{0}	8^{3}	10^{2}	10^{0}	10^{0}	3
Switzerland	0^{x}	2^{2}	2^{0}	3^{1}	3^{0}	3^{0}	4^{1}	4^{0}	5^{1}	5^{1}	8=

★ ★

1957 EUROVISION SONG CONTEST

Host country: Germany ★ *Venue:* Grosser Sendesaal Des Hessisches Rundfunk, Frankfurt am Main
Date: 3 March ★ *Presenter:* Anaid Plikjan
Voting structure: 10 jury members from each country, each of whom awarded 1 point to their favourite song ★ *Total entries:* 10
Debut countries: Austria, Denmark, United Kingdom

Country	Performer	Song	Pts	Pos.
Belgium	Bobbejaan Schoepen	Straatdeuntje	5	8
Luxembourg	Danièle Dupré	Tant De Peine	8	4
United Kingdom	Patricia Bredin	All	6	7
Italy	Nunzio Gallo	Corde Della Mia Chitarra	7	6
Austria	Bob Martin	Wohin, Kleines Pony	3	10
Netherlands	**Corry Brokken**	**Net Als Toen**	**31**	**1**
Germany	Margot Hielscher	Telefon, Telefon	8	4
France	Paule Desjardins	La Belle Amour	17	2
Denmark	Birthe Wilke and Gustav Winckler	Skibet Skal Sejle I Nat	10	3
Switzerland	Lys Assia	L'enfant Que J'étais	5	8

began with a guitar introduction fifty-five seconds long and launched into a mournful little tune that ran for a full five minutes and nine seconds.

Neither the long nor the short ever looked like winning. The tall, on the other hand, in the person of Corry Brokken, cruised home in one of the most one-sided contests in the history of the competition. She came on after Austria's song about riding a pony, which sounded far too much like an American cowboy tune to have any chance at all. With her big eyes, her big ear-rings and long white gloves, she poured her heart into a mournful ballad regretting that things were no longer as they were before. Halfway through her performance, she was joined on stage by a tiny man in glasses with a violin, who stood beside and virtually underneath the very tall Miss Brokken. She was not put off by this sudden apparition. The violinist turned out to be Sem Nijveen, and by the time he had finished his instrumental break, 'Net Als Toen' was threatening to take the record so recently established by Italy for the length of its performance. They finally stopped at four and a half minutes, about one minute longer than the official rule book allowed.

The German song mixed words from many European languages into its lyrics. 'Hello, how do you do, allo, grazie' and so on are lyrics that have been used over and over again, sometimes with success, in Eurovision. However, it was Margot Hielscher, complete with telephone receiver in hand as she sang, who first thought of it. The Danes went for the theatrical vote. With a song the title of which translates as 'The Ship Must Sail Tonight', Gustav Winckler entered wearing full naval captain's uniform, complete with peaked hat, and Birthe Wilke wore a white overcoat and hat and carried a handbag. It was the ending – a long passionate kiss – that we remember more than the song.

THE EUROVISION SONG CONTEST

1958

Won by France: 'Dors, Mon Amour'
Written by Pierre Delanoe and Hubert Giraud
Performed by André Claveau
Orchestra conducted by Franck Pourcel

In the week when Elvis Presley had two hits in the British top ten, sharing the top rungs with names like Danny and the Juniors, the Crickets and Little Richard, the Eurovision Song Contest sailed serenely along, with barely a sidelong glance at what was really going on in the outside music world. And thus it has always been, which is a great part of its charm. As Terry Wogan says, 'It's a good idea to bring people together on the wings of song. But pop music is an Anglophone thing. Eurovision has got nothing to do with popular music. It does not reflect young popular musical taste.' With the United Kingdom not taking part after its first abortive effort the year before, there were no Anglophone nations in the Contest, so we should not have expected any trace of 'pop' music at all. We did not get any.

The Netherlands, where the Contest was broadcast from, means tulips, and the organizers did not disappoint us. The stage was decked out with tulips to such an extent that they outnumbered the admittedly small audience, and showed almost as much emotional response to many of the songs.

As has become traditional with Eurovision, the biggest hit performed on the show did not win. Italy's entry was by Domenico Modugno, singing 'Nel Blu Dipinto Di Blu'/'The Blue Painted In

1958	Switzerland	Austria	W. Germany	Belgium	Denmark	Sweden	Luxembourg	France	Netherlands	Italy	**Position**
Italy	1^{1}	2^{1}	6^{4}	$\mathbf{10^{4}}$	10^{0}	11^{1}	11^{0}	12^{1}	13^{1}	13^{x}	3
Netherlands	1^{1}	1^{0}	1^{0}	1^{0}	1^{0}	1^{0}	1^{0}	1^{0}	1^{x}	1^{0}	$9^{=}$
France	1^{1}	$\mathbf{8^{7}}$	$\mathbf{9^{1}}$	$\mathbf{10^{1}}$	$\mathbf{19^{9}}$	$\mathbf{20^{1}}$	$\mathbf{21^{1}}$	$\mathbf{21^{x}}$	$\mathbf{21^{0}}$	$\mathbf{27^{6}}$	**1**
Luxembourg	1^{1}	1^{0}	1^{0}	1^{0}	1^{0}	1^{0}	1^{x}	1^{0}	1^{0}	1^{0}	$9^{=}$
Sweden	$\mathbf{3^{3}}$	4^{1}	4^{0}	5^{1}	5^{0}	5^{x}	8^{3}	8^{0}	10^{2}	10^{0}	4
Denmark	0^{0}	0^{0}	0^{0}	0^{0}	0^{x}	1^{1}	1^{0}	2^{1}	3^{1}	3^{0}	8
Belgium	1^{1}	1^{0}	6^{5}	6^{x}	7^{1}	8^{1}	8^{0}	8^{0}	8^{0}	8^{0}	$5^{=}$
W. Germany	0^{0}	1^{1}	1^{x}	2^{1}	2^{0}	3^{1}	3^{0}	5^{2}	5^{0}	5^{0}	7
Austria	2^{2}	2^{x}	2^{0}	3^{1}	3^{0}	4^{1}	5^{1}	8^{3}	8^{0}	8^{0}	$5^{=}$
Switzerland	0^{x}	0^{0}	0^{0}	2^{2}	2^{0}	6^{4}	11^{5}	14^{3}	20^{6}	24^{4}	2

★ ★

1958 EUROVISION SONG CONTEST

Host country: Netherlands ★ *Venue:* AVRO studios, Hilversum
Date: 12 March ★ *Presenter:* Hannie Lips
Voting structure: 10 jury members from each country, each of whom awarded 1 point to their favourite song ★ *Total entries:* 10
Debut countries: Sweden

Country	Performer	Song	Pts	Pos.
Italy	Domenico Modugno	Nel Blu Dipinto Di Blu	13	3
Netherlands	Corry Brokken	Heel De Wereld	1	9
France	**André Claveau**	**Dors, Mon Amour**	**27**	**1**
Luxembourg	Solange Berry	Un Grand Amour	1	9
Sweden	Alice Babs	Lilla Stjärna	10	4
Denmark	Raquel Rastenni	Jeg Rev Et Blad Ud Af Min Dagbog	3	8
Belgium	Fud Leclerc	Ma Petite Chatte	8	5
Germany	Margot Hielscher	Für Zwei Groschen Musik	5	7
Austria	Liane Augustin	Die Ganze Welt Braucht Liebe	8	5
Switzerland	Lys Assia	Giorgio	24	2

Blue', better known around the world as 'Volare'/'To Fly'. The song was inspired by an illustration on the back of a cigarette packet, which shows how much times have changed. Nowadays, cigarette packets no longer feature pictures of blue painted on blue; they are covered in government health warnings, which do not inspire romantic ballads. Domenico Modugno was first on and, even viewing videotapes forty years on, it is hard to understand why he did not win. Perhaps it was because the rules at the time did not allow backing vocalists (the rules about how the songs can be presented change with almost every year), and 'Volare' is the ultimate big-chorus, singalong Euro-hit. With just one voice belting out 'Volare, wo ho-ho-ho, cantare, wo-ho', it lost a certain something. The song went on later in the year to top the American charts and become the first ever Eurovision hit to reach the British top ten. It sold millions all around the world and won the very first Grammy Awards as Best Male Vocal Performance, Song of the Year and Record of the Year for 1958, but it got nowhere near winning Eurovision.

Modugno did not give up, though things did not improve. The next year he sang 'Piove (Ciao Ciao Bambina)'/'It's Raining', which placed sixth but sold by the bucketload around the world for both Domenico and his compatriot Marino Marini. The 1960 and 1961 Italian entries ('Romantica' and 'Al Di La') were both big hits around the world without coming near victory in the Contest, and there are plenty of non-Italian examples too. 'Are You Sure' by The Allisons (second in 1961), 'Warum Nur Warum'/'Why Oh Why' (sixth for Austria in 1964, but a UK top ten hit and US top thirty hit in its English version as 'Walk Away'), 'L'Amour Est Bleu'/'Love Is Blue' (fourth in

1967), 'Congratulations' (second in 1968), 'Marianne' (tenth in 1968, but covered by Cliff Richard to give him another hit later that year), 'Eres Tu'/'Touch The Wind' (second for Spain in 1973, but subsequently an American top ten hit), and of course, Gina G's 'Ooh Aah ... Just A Little Bit', which only came eighth for Britain in 1996, but sold over four million worldwide.

The vacancy created by Britain's absence was filled by Sweden. It is difficult to be sure whether or not they understood the point of Eurovision, but they produced the jazz and folk singer Alice Babs to kick their Euro-career off. She appeared wearing a Swedish skirt and apron, and began the song with several 'la la la's. The lyricists at least got the hang of Eurovision early on.

Despite technical difficulties meaning that Domenico Modugno had to perform his song a second time at the end because it 'hasn't been seen and heard in various countries', the juries gave France a clear lead almost from the beginning, and when Denmark gave nine of its ten votes to 'Dors, Mon Amour', the contest was effectively over. Lys Assia performed in Italian, the third language she had used for Switzerland in three years, having already sung in French and German. Lys Assia's up tempo novelty song about 'Giorgio from Lake Maggiore' almost caught France on the wire, but the Italians, the last country to vote, gave six points to France and only four to Switzerland. 'Dors, Mon Amour' won by three votes.

André Claveau certainly gave the song all it was worth. It was a little hard at first to relate to a man singing, 'Sleep, my love, protected by my arms around you' as he stood on stage with his hands clasped firmly behind his back, but by the time he got to the big ending ('Here comes the morning sun, the sun of eternal love'), his arms were gesticulating more like the local windmills than a man holding a baby in his arms. His frantically waving arms were to be copied by many a Euro-balladeer in the years to come.

VOTING BIAS

SWITZERLAND

Countries most likely to vote for Switzerland:

UK
Netherlands
Italy
Denmark
Belgium

Countries least likely to vote for Switzerland:

Spain
Sweden
Israel
Portugal
Greece

Countries for whom Switzerand is most likely to vote:

Israel
UK
France
Italy
Ireland

Countries for whom Switzerand is least likely to vote:

Germany
Denmark
Luxembourg
Austria
Belgium

Although German is the most widely spoken of the four official languages of Switzerland, the Swiss have shown a remarkable reluctance to vote for their Teutonic neighbours.

THE EUROVISION SONG CONTEST

1959

Won by Netherlands: 'Een Beetje'
Written by Dick Schallies and Willy van Hemert
Performed by Teddy Scholten
Orchestra conducted by Dolf van der Linden

With the return of the United Kingdom to the competition, there were eleven nations lined up on the starting grid at Cannes, the biggest field so far. As all of the competing nations apart from Italy were geographically higher up the map than Cannes, there was an obvious incentive to head for the south of France in March, rather than stay in cold, dreary northern Europe. But that was not the only reason for taking part. There are signs that, from this year, the competition really did begin to take a hold on the public imagination, and there is certainly evidence in the songs performed that people were beginning to think about what might, or might not, make a winning song. Not everybody got it right, of course.

The set showed some imagination. It consisted of three turntables, which revolved to reveal the performer and a suitable national backdrop, and which – most astonishingly – never broke down. The beginnings of national feeling, and a Eurovision that divides rather than unites the competing nations, were to be seen here. After all, that's what makes the Contest such a success forty years on. The presenter Jacqueline Joubert was hardly a trendsetter for Eurovision, though. She spoke only in French throughout, apart from a

1959	Belgium	UK	Austria	Switzerland	Sweden	W. Germany	Netherlands	Monaco	Italy	Denmark	France	**Position**
France	2^{2}	2^{0}	3^{1}	4^{1}	4^{0}	8^{4}	8^{0}	10^{2}	11^{1}	15^{4}	15^{x}	3
Denmark	0^{0}	2^{2}	4^{2}	5^{1}	9^{4}	9^{0}	10^{1}	11^{1}	12^{1}	12^{x}	12^{0}	5
Italy	1^{1}	1^{0}	1^{0}	4^{3}	5^{1}	5^{0}	5^{0}	6^{1}	6^{x}	6^{0}	9^{3}	6=
Monaco	0^{0}	0^{0}	1^{1}	1^{0}	1^{0}	1^{0}	1^{0}	1^{x}	1^{0}	1^{0}	1^{0}	11
Netherlands	**3^{3}**	4^{1}	**7^{3}**	**7^{0}**	7^{0}	9^{2}	9^{x}	10^{1}	**17^{7}**	**17^{0}**	**21^{4}**	**1**
W. Germany	1^{1}	1^{0}	1^{0}	2^{1}	2^{0}	2^{x}	2^{0}	2^{0}	3^{1}	3^{0}	5^{2}	8
Sweden	0^{0}	0^{0}	0^{0}	0^{0}	0^{x}	0^{0}	3^{3}	3^{3}	3^{0}	4^{1}	4^{0}	9=
Switzerland	1^{1}	**6^{5}**	**7^{1}**	7^{x}	**10^{3}**	**11^{1}**	11^{0}	12^{1}	12^{0}	14^{2}	14^{0}	4
Austria	0^{0}	0^{0}	0^{x}	1^{1}	3^{2}	3^{0}	3^{0}	4^{1}	4^{0}	4^{0}	4^{0}	9=
UK	2^{2}	2^{x}	4^{2}	**7^{3}**	7^{0}	7^{0}	**12^{5}**	**14^{2}**	14^{0}	15^{1}	16^{1}	2
Belgium	0^{x}	2^{2}	2^{0}	2^{0}	2^{0}	5^{3}	6^{1}	7^{1}	7^{0}	9^{2}	9^{0}	6=

★ ★

1959 EUROVISION SONG CONTEST

Host country: France ★ *Venue:* Palais des Festivals, Cannes
Date: 11 March ★ *Presenter:* Jacqueline Joubert
Voting structure: 10 jury members from each country, each of whom awarded 1 point to their favourite song ★ *Total entries:* 11
Debut countries: Monaco

Country	Performer	Song	Pts	Pos.
France	Jean Philippe	Oui Oui Oui Oui	15	3
Denmark	Birthe Wilke	Uh-jeg Ville Ønske Jeg Var Dig	12	5
Italy	Domenico Modugno	Piove	9	6
Monaco	Jacques Pills	Mon Ami Pierrot	1	11
Netherlands	**Teddy Scholten**	**Een Beetje**	**21**	**1**
Germany	Alice and Ellen Kessler	Heute Abend Woll'n Wir Tanzen Geh'n	5	8
Sweden	Brita Borg	Augustin	4	9
Switzerland	Christa Williams	Irgendwoher	14	4
Austria	Ferry Graf	Der K Und K Kalypso Aus Wien	4	9
United Kingdom	Pearl Carr and Teddy Johnson	Sing Little Birdie	16	2
Belgium	Bob Benny	Hou Toch Van Me	9	6

few words in English during the voting sequence, and held in her hand an enormous pointer with which to show us all how the scoring was coming along. This was not a prop that caught on.

France opened the show with a song that obeyed the fundamental rule of having a title that anybody could understand, whatever their nationality. 'Oui Oui Oui Oui' did not stretch anybody's linguistic abilities too far. It was also, rather more subtly, a song with a geographic theme, suggesting that yes, yes, yes, yes, I'll go in my little boat around the world. I'll see the skies over Capri, the sun in Hawaii, and so on. Mention a few famous places in your song, and you'll probably collect a few votes. Denmark went for the bouncy love song idea, complete with xylophone riffs and ladlefuls of cloying happiness. Italy's Domenico Modugno, back for another try, lost the Eurovision plot completely, pouring his heart out in a sad love ballad, complete with a spoken middle section. Lost love barely ever won Eurovision, even though he did create another enormous worldwide best-seller for himself. Jacques Pills, whose daughter would win Eurovision a year later, acted the Luxembourg entry more than sang it. Germany took the rock'n'roll route. The Kessler twins, who looked and sounded like the Beverley Sisters meeting the Chordettes, included words like 'teenager' in their lyrics, and they even danced in the instrumental break. This was much too advanced for Eurovision, which generally likes to potter along about five years behind the times. The Swiss entry was perhaps the best song, but its lyrics were full of 'Why am I so alone?' and the like, which just won't do. Austria took the novelty song route with a calypso, which also incorporated a smattering of Strauss waltzes, polkas and a bit of yodelling.

VOTING BIAS

MONACO

Countries most likely to vote for Monaco:

Italy
Germany
UK
Sweden
Denmark

Countries least likely to vote for Monaco:

Norway
Portugal
Austria
Belgium
Switzerland

Countries for whom Monaco is most likely to vote:

France
Germany
Spain
Italy
UK

Countries for whom Monaco is least likely to vote:

Ireland
Denmark
Netherlands
Sweden
Israel

Only a small minority of Monaco's 30,000 population is Monagasque, the majority are French and Italian. No surprises then when it comes to Monaco's voting.

Novelty songs have always been an integral part of Eurovision, but this early example was not one of the best. The UK went bouncy, having decided for the first time to take Eurovision seriously. They were rewarded with the first of their fourteen second places.

For the second time in the four years of the Contest, the Netherlands won the Grand Prix, and at the same time broke the coincidental sequence in which the winning performer had a surname beginning with successive letters of the alphabet. In 1956, it was A for Assia, in 1957 B for Brokken and in 1958 C for Claveau. Corry Brokken, who had performed every year so far for the Netherlands, stepped aside, and her place was taken by another lady with a big smile and an effervescent personality (aren't they all?), but without the initial D, Teddy Scholten. The letter D was not a winning initial until 1970.

The Dutch song was an up tempo number, the theme being that Miss Scholten loves you 'a bit'. This was quite the other end of the lyrical scale to Bob Benny's Belgian entry, which asserted that his love was bigger than me, and stronger than all sorts of things. Rather surprisingly, Teddy Scholten's understatement easily outscored Bob Benny's hyperbole. The voting was close even though the outcome was, in the end, clear cut. No song picked up votes from more than seven of the juries, and with three more juries to vote (Italy, Denmark and France – the countries voted in reverse order of performance), the UK was in the lead with fourteen points, with Switzerland on twelve points, Denmark on eleven points and France and Netherlands each on ten. But Italy's seven votes for the Dutch entry, with one each for France, Denmark and Germany, turned it round completely, and although Denmark then gave France four votes while ignoring the Netherlands altogether, the result was no longer in doubt. The four votes that France gave the winners were not even necessary, as 'Een Beetje' won by five votes from the UK.

THE EUROVISION SONG CONTEST

1960

Won by France: 'Tom Pillibi'

Written by André Popp and Pierre Cour

Performed by Jacqueline Boyer

Orchestra conducted by Franck Pourcel

The year 1960 marked a new stage in the development of the Eurovision Song Contest. It was the first Contest staged in Britain (1998's Contest is the eighth to be held in the UK); it was the first of four to be hosted by Eurovision's most prolific hostess, Katie Boyle; it marked the first appearance of Norway; and it was the first of six Contests to be won by the song that was performed last.

London's Royal Festival Hall is not a small theatre by 1960s' standards, but looking back over almost four decades of ever-expanding Song Contests, it seems tiny. The idea of bringing the curtain down between acts is almost quaint: in the 1990s there is no curtain to bring down, just a huge stage and sophisticated lighting to allow performers to arrive and depart with the right amount of anonymity. It is also no longer the custom to introduce all the performers at the start of the Contest, nor for all of them to wear evening dress, with many of the ladies wearing long white gloves and full evening gowns. Miss Boyle proudly

1960	France	Italy	W. Germany	Netherlands	Switzerland	Monaco	Austria	Norway	Belgium	Denmark	Luxembourg	Sweden	UK	**Position**
UK	0^{0}	2^{2}	3^{1}	8^{5}	**12^{4}**	**13^{1}**	**16^{3}**	**18^{2}**	**19^{1}**	19^{0}	**24^{5}**	25^{1}	25^{x}	2
Sweden	2^{2}	3^{1}	3^{0}	4^{1}	4^{0}	4^{0}	4^{0}	4^{0}	4^{0}	4^{0}	4^{0}	4^{x}	4^{0}	10=
Luxembourg	0^{0}	1^{1}	1^{0}	1^{0}	1^{0}	1^{0}	1^{0}	1^{0}	1^{0}	1^{0}	1^{x}	1^{0}	1^{0}	13
Denmark	0^{0}	0^{0}	0^{0}	0^{0}	0^{0}	0^{0}	0^{0}	2^{2}	2^{0}	2^{x}	3^{1}	3^{0}	4^{1}	10=
Belgium	0^{0}	3^{3}	4^{1}	4^{0}	4^{0}	4^{0}	5^{1}	5^{0}	5^{x}	5^{0}	5^{0}	9^{4}	9^{0}	6
Norway	1^{1}	1^{0}	1^{0}	2^{1}	6^{4}	6^{0}	7^{1}	7^{x}	8^{1}	10^{2}	10^{0}	10^{0}	11^{1}	4=
Austria	0^{0}	1^{1}	1^{0}	1^{0}	1^{0}	1^{0}	1^{x}	1^{0}	2^{1}	4^{2}	4^{0}	4^{0}	6^{2}	7
Monaco	3^{3}	3^{0}	**10^{7}**	**10^{0}**	11^{1}	11^{x}	11^{0}	11^{0}	11^{0}	13^{2}	14^{1}	14^{0}	15^{1}	3
Switzerland	0^{0}	1^{1}	1^{0}	1^{0}	1^{x}	1^{0}	3^{2}	4^{1}	4^{0}	4^{0}	5^{1}	5^{0}	5^{0}	8=
Netherlands	0^{0}	1^{1}	1^{0}	1^{x}	1^{0}	1^{0}	1^{0}	1^{0}	2^{1}	2^{0}	2^{0}	2^{0}	2^{0}	12
W. Germany	**4^{4}**	**4^{0}**	4^{x}	4^{0}	4^{0}	6^{2}	8^{2}	8^{0}	10^{2}	10^{0}	10^{0}	11^{1}	11^{0}	4=
Italy	0^{0}	0^{x}	0^{0}	1^{1}	1^{0}	3^{2}	3^{0}	3^{0}	4^{1}	4^{0}	5^{1}	5^{0}	5^{0}	8=
France	0^{x}	0^{0}	1^{1}	3^{2}	4^{1}	9^{5}	10^{1}	15^{5}	18^{3}	**22^{4}**	23^{1}	**27^{4}**	**32^{5}**	**1**

★ ★

1960 EUROVISION SONG CONTEST

Host country: United Kingdom ★ *Venue:* Royal Festival Hall, London
Date: 25 March ★ *Presenter:* Katie Boyle
Voting structure: 10 jury members from each country, each of whom awarded 1 point to their favourite song ★ *Total entries:* 13
Debut countries: Norway

Country	Performer	Song	Pts	Pos.
United Kingdom	Bryan Johnson	Looking High, High, High	25	2
Sweden	Siw Malmkvist	Alla Andra Får Varann	4	10
Luxembourg	Camillo Felgen	So Laang We's Du Do Bast	1	13
Denmark	Katy Bødtger	Det Var En Yndig Tid	4	10
Belgium	Fud Leclerc	Mon Amour Pour Toi	9	6
Norway	Nora Brockstedt	Voi-voi	11	4
Austria	Harry Winter	Du Hast Mich So Fasziniert	6	7
Monaco	François Deguelt	Ce Soir-là	15	3
Switzerland	Anita Traversi	Cielo E Terra	5	8
Netherlands	Rudi Carrell	Wat Een Geluk	2	12
Germany	Wyn Hoop	Bonne Nuit, Ma Chérie	11	4
Italy	Renato Rascel	Romantica	5	8
France	**Jacqueline Boyer**	**Tom Pillibi**	**32**	**1**

announced that there was a prize of a 'silver gilt vase', to be presented by the BBC at the end of the Contest on behalf of the European Broadcasting Union to the performer and writers of 'the best new popular song of 1960'.

The songs varied from light operatic, as represented by Austria and, to an extent, Great Britain, to whimsical love songs, served up by Norway and the Netherlands, among others. The British entry, written by a schoolmaster, John Watson, gave Bryan Johnson (the brother of Teddy Johnson who had sung for Britain the year before) the chance to show off his whistling as well as his singing skills, but whistling has never been a strong favourite with Eurovision juries, as Bobbejaan Schoepen had discovered in 1957. The Austrian entry had been written by its conductor, the distinguished composer Robert Stolz, who was then just short of his eightieth birthday. From major light operatic successes like 'The White Horse Inn' in 1930 to the Eurovision Song Contest thirty years later is by no means a typical career progression.

There were sad songs of broken hearts, from Monaco and Italy, and gentle ballads of true love from Belgium and Germany. Renato Rascel, who sang the Italian 'Romantica', looked anything but romantic, described by one reviewer as a 'short fat man with big ears', but his real problem was that 'Romantica' is really a woman's song. The mournful Luxembourg entry, performed by Camillo Felgen, a Radio Luxembourg disc jockey, would have become the first song ever to score no points at all, had not one Italian juror taken pity on the song. Germany used the ploy of giving the song a title in a different language, in this case French, which was to work for Udo Jürgens and Austria six years later. Austria and Switzerland had a piano playing what Stan Freberg called 'kling kling kling jazz' with the right hand, while the Belgian song tried almost every musical style in the one song. Sweden settled for a swinging big band jazz number, and Norway, making their debut in the competition, put Nora Brockstedt in a typically Norwegian fur outfit and gave her an 'I'm Happy' number to sing. Norway have done a lot worse many times since.

It was France, though, with a song that began as a children's song but was just a little more subtle than it seemed, that stormed to victory. 'Tom Pillibi' has two castles, so we were told, one in Scotland and one in Montenegro. But he also has two secrets, of which Jacqueline Boyer admitted she knew one; he was also, by the final verse, exposed as a liar. By that time we suspected that Miss Boyer was in love with him. Eighteen-year-old Miss Boyer was the daughter of Jacques Pills, who sang 'Mon Ami Pierrot' for Monaco the year before in an unsuccessful attempt on the summit of Eurovision. She was cheered loudly by the audience in the hall at the end of her song and certainly benefited from singing last, and thus being freshest in the judges' minds.

The margin of that victory was seven points, which under the scoring system working at the time seemed like a massive victory. But the result was in doubt until almost the very end, and France did not take the lead until the penultimate round of voting, when Sweden gave them four points to the United Kingdom's one. When Britain, voting last, gave France five points, the final margin seemed huge, but in reality it was a close-run thing. So it was Jacqueline Boyer who took home 'the silver gilt vase', presented to her by the 1959 winner, Teddy Scholten.

VOTING BIAS

NORWAY

Countries most likely to vote for Norway:

Belgium
Ireland
Sweden
Netherlands
Iceland

Countries least likely to vote for Norway:

Spain
Malta
France
Austria
Greece

Countries for whom Norway is most likely to vote:

Sweden
Denmark
Finland
France
Ireland

Countries for whom Norway is least likely to vote:

Germany
Austria
Italy
Spain
Luxembourg

Norway made its debut in 1960. Initially it supported the Danes (Norwegian and Danish are closely related), but by the late 1960s its love affair with its Swedish neighbours had begun in earnest.

THE EUROVISION SONG CONTEST 1961

Won by Luxembourg: 'Nous Les Amoureux'

Written by Jacques Datin and Maurice Vidalin

Performed by Jean-Claude Pascal

Orchestra conducted by Léo Chauliac

The same venue and the same presenter as 1959, the Palais des Festivals in Cannes and Jacqueline Joubert, did not give exactly the same result, although the United Kingdom and Denmark were second and fifth again. Three countries were entering for the first time – Spain, Finland and Yugoslavia – so there were sixteen songs in the largest final so far. None of the three new entrants made much of an impact, but it was left to the Spanish entry, a powerful up tempo jazz-influenced song belted out by the pearl-bedecked Concita Bautista, to get the competition under way. Monaco's entry was more typically Eurovision, a bouncy childish song all about

1961	Italy	UK	Luxembourg	Denmark	Norway	Belgium	Switzerland	France	W. Germany	Sweden	Netherlands	Yugoslavia	Finland	Austria	Monaco	Spain	**Position**
Spain	0^{0}	1^{1}	1^{0}	1^{0}	3^{2}	3^{0}	3^{0}	5^{2}	5^{0}	6^{1}	7^{1}	7^{0}	7^{0}	7^{0}	8^{1}	8^{x}	9
Monaco	0^{0}	1^{1}	1^{0}	1^{0}	1^{0}	1^{0}	2^{1}	2^{0}	2^{0}	2^{0}	2^{0}	2^{0}	5^{3}	5^{0}	5^{x}	6^{1}	10=
Austria	0^{0}	1^{1}	1^{0}	1^{0}	1^{0}	1^{0}	1^{0}	1^{0}	1^{0}	1^{0}	1^{0}	1^{0}	1^{0}	1^{x}	1^{0}	1^{0}	15=
Finland	2^{2}	4^{2}	4^{0}	5^{1}	5^{0}	5^{0}	5^{0}	6^{1}	6^{0}	6^{0}	6^{0}	6^{0}	6^{x}	6^{0}	6^{0}	6^{0}	10=
Yugoslavia	0^{0}	1^{1}	1^{0}	2^{1}	2^{0}	2^{0}	3^{1}	5^{2}	5^{0}	5^{0}	6^{1}	6^{x}	6^{0}	9^{3}	9^{0}	9^{0}	8
Netherlands	2^{2}	2^{0}	2^{0}	2^{0}	2^{0}	2^{0}	2^{0}	3^{1}	4^{1}	4^{0}	4^{x}	6^{2}	6^{0}	6^{0}	6^{0}	6^{0}	10=
Sweden	0^{0}	0^{0}	0^{0}	0^{0}	0^{0}	0^{0}	0^{0}	2^{2}	2^{0}	2^{x}	2^{0}	2^{0}	2^{0}	2^{0}	2^{0}	2^{0}	14
W. Germany	0^{0}	0^{0}	0^{0}	1^{1}	1^{0}	1^{0}	1^{0}	1^{0}	1^{x}	2^{1}	2^{0}	2^{0}	2^{0}	3^{1}	3^{0}	3^{0}	13
France	0^{0}	2^{2}	3^{1}	3^{0}	3^{0}	3^{0}	3^{0}	3^{x}	7^{4}	8^{1}	8^{0}	8^{0}	9^{1}	9^{0}	11^{2}	13^{2}	4
Switzerland	2^{2}	4^{2}	4^{0}	4^{0}	4^{0}	4^{0}	4^{x}	4^{0}	4^{0}	8^{4}	10^{2}	11^{1}	11^{0}	13^{2}	15^{2}	16^{1}	3
Belgium	0^{0}	0^{0}	1^{1}	1^{0}	1^{0}	1^{x}	1^{0}	1^{0}	1^{0}	1^{0}	1^{0}	1^{0}	1^{0}	1^{0}	1^{0}	1^{0}	15=
Norway	0^{0}	0^{0}	0^{0}	1^{1}	1^{x}	6^{5}	6^{0}	6^{0}	6^{0}	6^{0}	6^{0}	7^{1}	9^{2}	9^{0}	9^{0}	10^{1}	7
Denmark	0^{0}	0^{0}	0^{0}	0^{x}	8^{8}	8^{0}	8^{0}	8^{0}	8^{0}	10^{2}	11^{1}	11^{0}	12^{1}	12^{0}	12^{0}	12^{0}	5=
Luxembourg	3^{3}	3^{0}	3^{x}	4^{1}	4^{0}	4^{0}	5^{1}	6^{1}	11^{5}	12^{1}	13^{1}	18^{5}	21^{3}	25^{4}	29^{4}	31^{2}	1
UK	1^{1}	1^{x}	9^{8}	10^{1}	10^{0}	11^{1}	18^{7}	18^{0}	18^{0}	18^{0}	21^{3}	21^{0}	21^{0}	21^{0}	21^{0}	24^{3}	2
Italy	0^{x}	0^{0}	0^{0}	4^{4}	4^{0}	8^{4}	8^{0}	9^{1}	9^{0}	9^{0}	10^{1}	11^{1}	11^{0}	11^{0}	12^{1}	12^{0}	5=

1961 EUROVISION SONG CONTEST

Host country: France ★ *Venue:* Palais des Festivals, Cannes
Date: 18 March ★ *Presenter:* Jacqueline Joubert
Voting structure: 10 jury members from each country, each of whom awarded 1 point to their favourite song ★ *Total entries:* 16
Debut countries: Finland, Spain, Yugoslavia

Country	Performer	Song	Pts	Pos.
Spain	Concita Bautista	Estando Contigo	8	9
Monaco	Colette Deréal	Allons, Allons Les Enfants	6	10
Austria	Jimmy Makulis	Sehnsucht	1	15
Finland	Laila Kinnunen	Valoa Ikkunassa	6	10
Yugoslavia	Ljiljana Petrovic	Neke Davne Zvezde	9	8
Netherlands	Greetje Kauffeld	Wat Een Dag	6	10
Sweden	Lill-Babs	April, April	2	14
Germany	Lale Andersen	Einmal Sehen Wir Uns Wieder	3	13
France	Jean-Paul Mauric	Printemps (Avril Carillonne)	13	4
Switzerland	Franca di Rienzo	Nous Aurons Demain	16	3
Belgium	Bob Benny	Septembre, Gouden Roos	1	15
Norway	Nora Brockstedt	Sommer I Palma	10	7
Denmark	Dario Campeotto	Angelique	12	5
Luxembourg	**Jean-Claude Pascal**	**Nous Les Amoureux**	**31**	**1**
United Kingdom	The Allisons	Are You Sure?	24	2
Italy	Betty Curtis	Al Di La	12	5

happiness on a spring day. The distinguished French conductor Raymond Lefevre must have wondered whom he had offended, to be asked to wield the baton. Indeed, for much of the evening, the most exciting point seemed to come when the baton was handed with due ceremony from conductor to conductor.

The songs showed few moments of originality or musical excitement. Austria was represented by a Greek Cypriot, Jimmy Makulis, who sounded like the Italian American Dean Martin, and Finland's first Eurovision effort was a dull ballad more typical of 1940s' film music than post-Presley pop songs. The Dutch entry was delivered with gusto by a Doris Day clone, but it was Lill-Babs for Sweden who at last provided some variety, punctuating yet another song about spring and happiness by whistling a few bars here and there. By the end of the song she had proved conclusively that it is not possible to maintain a cheeky grin and whistle at the same time. Unfortunately the judges did not think much of her attempts at originality. She finished fourteenth beating only Belgium and Austria.

Germany turned out Lale Andersen, 'the original Lili Marlene of the Desert War' as she was

VOTING BIAS

FINLAND

Countries most likely to vote for Finland:
Norway
Greece
Israel
Iceland
Ireland

Countries least likely to vote for Finland:
Italy
Portugal
Belgium
Luxembourg
France

Countries for whom Finland is most likely to vote:
Italy
Sweden
Israel
Cyprus
Belgium

Countries for whom Finland is least likely to vote:
Ireland
France
Austria
Netherlands
Germany

The Italians clearly enjoyed the Finns' first entry in 1961's Eurovision. This failed to set a precedent, and, despite Finland's ardent devotion to Italy, the Italians have largely ignored its songs since.

tactfully described, but her song was very much a poor copy of Vera Lynn, with the lyrics about meeting again almost a direct translation of Dame Vera's 1952 hit, 'Auf Wiederseh'n Sweetheart', (which of course was sung in English, despite its German title; Miss Andersen sang part of her song in French to return the compliment). Twenty-four year-old Jean-Paul Mauric for defending champions France introduced a chorus of 'Binge Bong, Binge Bong' into his springtime song, setting an unfortunate and much imitated example for future Contests. Twenty-three year-old Franca di Rienzo, three-quarters Italian and one quarter Russian, sang for Switzerland wearing too much mascara and a daring strapless gown, which was probably why she came third, easily the best placing among the ten women singing that night. Belgium and Norway were represented by previous participants back for more, Bob Benny had appeared in 1959 singing 'Hov Toch Van Me' and Nora Brockstedt had come fourth for Norway in 1960. They were the fifth and sixth to sing about different times of the year (summer and September respectively).

Italian-born Dario Campeotto snapped his fingers and played air violin on behalf of Denmark, but was overshadowed by the Luxembourg entry, sung by the tallest contestant, the actor turned singer Jean-Claude Pascal. 'Nous Les Amoureux' had the virtue of not being about the weather and of having the only arrangement in which the drums played an audible part, but although it emerged as the winner on the night, in subsequent sales terms it was overwhelmed by both the songs that followed it: the runner-up, 'Are You Sure?' by The Allisons, and 'Al Di La' by Betty Curtis for Italy. 'Are You Sure?' sold over a million copies across Europe that summer and 'Al Di La' featured a year later in a film called *Rome Adventure*, sung by Emilio Pericoli. His version became the third Italian entry of the past four years to hit the American top ten, even though none of them won Eurovision.

THE EUROVISION SONG CONTEST

1962

Won by France: 'Un Premier Amour'
Written by Claude-Henri Vice and Roland Valade
Performed by Isabelle Aubret
Orchestra conducted by Franck Pourcel

The seventh Eurovision Song Contest came from a new venue – the RTL Auditorium in the Villa Louvigny in Luxembourg – and featured a new scoring system. Juries were asked to award three points to their favourite song, two to the second and one to the third. Although this system produced the clearest winner since 1957, it was never used again in exactly the same form. All told, there have been seven different voting systems, and three of those systems were tried only once. The very first contest involved undisclosed voting by two judges from each competing nation, which produced a home town result. The second (and second most successful system, used for ten contests in all) was introduced in 1957, and involved each of ten

1962	Monaco	Italy	Luxembourg	UK	Yugoslavia	Switzerland	Norway	France	Netherlands	Germany	Sweden	Denmark	Austria	Spain	Belgium	Finland	**Position**
Finland	0^{0}	0^{0}	0^{0}	3^{3}	3^{0}	3^{0}	4^{1}	4^{0}	4^{0}	4^{0}	4^{0}	4^{0}	4^{0}	4^{0}	4^{0}	4^{x}	7=
Belgium	0^{0}	0^{0}	0^{0}	0^{0}	0^{0}	0^{0}	0^{0}	0^{0}	0^{0}	0^{0}	0^{0}	0^{0}	0^{0}	0^{0}	0^{x}	0^{0}	13=
Spain	0^{0}	0^{0}	0^{0}	0^{0}	0^{0}	0^{0}	0^{0}	0^{0}	0^{0}	0^{0}	0^{0}	0^{0}	0^{0}	0^{x}	0^{0}	0^{0}	13=
Austria	0^{0}	0^{0}	0^{0}	0^{0}	0^{0}	0^{0}	0^{0}	0^{0}	0^{0}	0^{0}	0^{0}	0^{0}	0^{x}	0^{0}	0^{0}	0^{0}	13=
Denmark	0^{0}	1^{1}	1^{0}	1^{0}	1^{0}	1^{0}	1^{0}	1^{0}	1^{0}	1^{0}	2^{1}	2^{x}	2^{0}	2^{0}	2^{0}	2^{0}	10=
Sweden	0^{0}	0^{0}	0^{0}	0^{0}	0^{0}	0^{0}	0^{0}	0^{0}	1^{1}	1^{0}	1^{x}	4^{3}	4^{0}	4^{0}	4^{0}	4^{0}	7=
W. Germany	2^{2}	2^{0}	2^{0}	4^{2}	4^{0}	4^{0}	4^{0}	4^{0}	6^{2}	6^{x}	6^{0}	7^{1}	7^{0}	7^{0}	7^{0}	9^{2}	6
Netherlands	0^{0}	0^{0}	0^{0}	0^{0}	0^{0}	0^{0}	0^{0}	0^{0}	0^{x}	0^{0}	0^{0}	0^{0}	0^{0}	0^{0}	0^{0}	0^{0}	13=
France	1^{1}	3^{2}	4^{1}	5^{1}	8^{3}	11^{3}	14^{3}	14^{x}	14^{0}	17^{3}	20^{3}	20^{0}	22^{2}	24^{2}	26^{2}	26^{0}	**1**
Norway	0^{0}	0^{0}	0^{0}	0^{0}	0^{0}	0^{0}	0^{x}	2^{2}	2^{0}	2^{0}	2^{0}	2^{0}	2^{0}	2^{0}	2^{0}	2^{0}	10=
Switzerland	0^{0}	0^{0}	0^{0}	0^{0}	0^{0}	0^{x}	0^{0}	0^{0}	0^{0}	2^{2}	2^{0}	2^{0}	2^{0}	2^{0}	2^{0}	2^{0}	10=
Yugoslavia	0^{0}	3^{3}	3^{0}	3^{0}	3^{x}	3^{0}	3^{0}	6^{3}	6^{0}	6^{0}	8^{2}	8^{0}	8^{0}	8^{0}	9^{1}	10^{1}	4=
UK	0^{0}	0^{0}	0^{0}	0^{x}	2^{2}	4^{2}	4^{0}	4^{0}	4^{0}	4^{0}	4^{0}	6^{2}	6^{0}	7^{1}	7^{0}	10^{3}	4=
Luxembourg	3^{3}	3^{0}	3^{x}	3^{0}	3^{0}	4^{1}	4^{0}	4^{0}	4^{0}	4^{0}	4^{0}	4^{0}	5^{1}	8^{3}	11^{3}	11^{0}	3
Italy	0^{0}	0^{x}	2^{2}	2^{0}	3^{1}	3^{0}	3^{0}	3^{0}	3^{0}	3^{0}	3^{0}	3^{0}	3^{0}	3^{0}	3^{0}	3^{0}	9
Monaco	0^{x}	0^{0}	3^{3}	3^{0}	3^{0}	3^{0}	5^{2}	6^{1}	9^{3}	10^{1}	10^{0}	10^{0}	13^{3}	13^{0}	13^{0}	13^{0}	2

1962 EUROVISION SONG CONTEST

Host country: Luxembourg ★ *Venue:* Grand Auditorium de RTL, Villa Louvigny
Date: 18 March ★ *Presenter:* Mireille Delanoy
Voting structure: Each nation awarded 3 points to its favourite song, 2 points for the second and 1 point for the third ★ *Total entries:* 16
Debut countries: None

Country	Performer	Song	Pts	Pos.
Finland	Marion Rung	Tipi-tii	4	7
Belgium	Fud Leclerc	Ton Nom	0	13
Spain	Victor Balaguer	Llamame	0	13
Austria	Eleonore Schwarz	Nur In Der Wiener Luft	0	13
Denmark	Ellen Winther	Vuggevise	2	10
Sweden	Inger Berggren	Sol Och Vår	4	7
Germany	Conny Froböss	Zwei Kleiner Italiener	9	6
Netherlands	De Spelbrekers	Katinka	0	13
France	**Isabelle Aubret**	**Un Premier Amour**	**26**	**1**
Norway	Inger Jacobsen	Kom Sol, Kom Regn	2	10
Switzerland	Jean Philippe	Le Retour	2	10
Yugoslavia	Lola Novakovic	Ne Pali Svetla U Sumrak	10	4
United Kingdom	Ronnie Carroll	Ring-a-Ding Girl	10	4
Luxembourg	Camillo Felgen	Petit Bonhomme	11	3
Italy	Claudio Villa	Addio, Addio	3	9
Monaco	François Deguelt	Dis Rien	13	2

jurors from each country awarding one point to their favourite song. This gave Corry Brokken a massive win in its first year of operation, but after that only Sandie Shaw in 1967 really dominated. It was discredited by the ludicrous 1969 result, when four songs tied for first place.

The 1962 system originated the idea of each jury ranking its favourite songs. However, as only three songs could be voted for, several entries were left behind in the voting from the earliest stages. That year, the first ever 'nul points' were collected by Belgium, Spain, Austria and the Netherlands, while the French entry had the contest sewn up, with three countries still to vote. Seldom can the voting have been so unexciting.

The songs matched the voting: it was a year in which the technical excitement of phone lines across Europe all coming in on cue outdid the excitement of the performances, which were bland throughout. The stage was unimaginatively decorated with twinkling stars on the backdrop, and the songs, the orchestrations, the performers and their outfits vied with each other for the Conformity Prize. It was jointly awarded to everybody. Marion Rung, making her first appearance for Finland, set the scene with a song about a little bird in springtime (where have we heard that before?), before Fud Leclerc, Belgium's regular French-language performer, strolled on in a dinner jacket and launched himself into a powerful ballad about love. He looked, and sounded, very much the same as the other eight male performers who followed him, the only difference being his problem with the high notes. His was the first ever performance to attract no votes in the history of the competition, so his name is secure in the record books.

Fud Leclerc was rather less full of hand signals than those who followed him, which perhaps counted against him. Some of them put their hands in their pockets; some stood with their hands behind their backs; some emoted, arms outstretched, about the pain of love. Some did permutations of all gesticular options, but it was Isabelle Aubret who won the Contest, despite an almost total absence of arm movements and forced smiles, because she had by far the best song. In a weak field, she was not only the best-looking performer – a factor that it was not politically incorrect to use in 1962 – but she delivered a good song very well.

As soon as Mlle Aubret finished, there was a technical failure: the picture from Luxembourg was lost. However, within only a couple of minutes it was restored and the Contest continued. None of the final seven entries really challenged the French song, and the only smattering of originality came from the Yugoslav entry, which told the romantic tale of two cigarettes glowing in the night. The jurors liked the later entries, though: the final eight entries picked up a total of seventy-seven votes, compared with only nineteen given to the first eight.

The jurors were given five minutes to make up their minds – five minutes that were taken up by the musical comedy of Achille Zavatta, whose act involved falling down the steps and swallowing the mouthpiece of his oboe, before finally being dragged off by two large men dressed in black.

VOTING BIAS

BELGIUM

Countries most likely to vote for Belgium:
UK
Netherlands
Portugal
France
Spain

Countries least likely to vote for Belgium:
Switzerland
Austria
Israel
Sweden
Ireland

Countries for whom Belgium is most likely to vote:
Norway
Germany
Ireland
UK
Austria

Countries for whom Belgium is least likely to vote:
Netherlands
Italy
Greece
France
Portugal

The Belgians rarely score many points in Eurovision. The Dutch are among their few allies and yet the Belgians consistently fail to return any favours and regularly give the Netherlands lower than average marks.

★ ★

THE EUROVISION SONG CONTEST

1963

Won by Denmark: 'Dansevise'
Written by Otto Francker and Sejr Volmer Sørensen
Performed by Grethe and Jørgen Ingmann
Orchestra conducted by Kai Mortensen

The 1963 competition came from the BBC Television Centre, and was produced from two different studios. One contained Katie Boyle and the audience; the other contained the orchestra and the performers. Although nobody stated that the show had been pre-recorded, the speed with which the set was changed between songs, and the fact that the audience was not in the same studio as the performers, leads to the inevitable conclusion that several – if not all – of the performances were pre-recorded. But that was not the scandal of the night. Nor was it the ridiculously self-congratulatory speech given, in a broad Scottish accent and without translation, by the BBC's Stuart Hood, explaining how much better the BBC did these things than anybody else.

1963	UK	Netherlands	W. Germany	Austria	Norway	Italy	Finland	Denmark	Yugoslavia	Switzerland	France	Spain	Sweden	Belgium	Monaco	Luxembourg	**Position**
UK	0^{x}	3^{3}	3^{0}	3^{0}	8^{5}	8^{0}	11^{3}	14^{3}	17^{3}	17^{0}	20^{3}	25^{5}	27^{2}	27^{0}	28^{1}	28^{0}	4
Netherlands	0^{0}	0^{x}	0^{0}	0^{0}	0^{0}	0^{0}	0^{0}	0^{0}	0^{0}	0^{0}	0^{0}	0^{0}	0^{0}	0^{0}	0^{0}	0^{0}	13=
W. Germany	0^{0}	0^{0}	0^{x}	0^{0}	2^{2}	2^{0}	2^{0}	2^{0}	2^{0}	2^{0}	2^{0}	2^{0}	2^{0}	2^{0}	5^{3}	5^{0}	9
Austria	4^{4}	4^{0}	4^{0}	4^{x}	4^{0}	4^{0}	8^{4}	9^{1}	9^{0}	9^{0}	11^{2}	11^{0}	14^{3}	16^{2}	16^{0}	16^{0}	7
Norway	0^{0}	0^{0}	0^{0}	0^{0}	0^{x}	0^{0}	0^{0}	0^{0}	0^{0}	0^{0}	0^{0}	0^{0}	0^{0}	0^{0}	0^{0}	0^{0}	13=
Italy	2^{2}	3^{1}	3^{0}	3^{0}	6^{3}	6^{x}	8^{2}	13^{5}	17^{4}	22^{5}	22^{0}	25^{3}	25^{0}	28^{3}	33^{5}	37^{4}	3
Finland	0^{0}	0^{x}	0^{0}	0^{0}	0^{0}	0^{0}	0^{x}	0^{0}	0^{0}	0^{0}	0^{0}	0^{0}	0^{0}	0^{0}	0^{0}	0^{0}	13=
Denmark	3^{3}	8^{5}	10^{2}	13^{3}	17^{4}	19^{2}	24^{5}	24^{x}	24^{0}	27^{3}	27^{0}	27^{0}	32^{5}	37^{5}	37^{5}	42^{5}	**1**
Yugoslavia	0^{0}	0^{0}	0^{0}	0^{0}	0^{0}	0^{0}	0^{0}	0^{0}	0^{x}	0^{0}	1^{1}	3^{2}	3^{0}	3^{0}	3^{0}	3^{0}	11
Switzerland	5^{5}	5^{0}	9^{4}	14^{5}	15^{1}	20^{5}	20^{0}	24^{4}	24^{0}	24^{x}	24^{0}	28^{4}	29^{1}	33^{4}	37^{4}	40^{3}	2
France	0^{0}	4^{4}	5^{1}	7^{2}	7^{0}	11^{4}	11^{0}	11^{0}	16^{5}	20^{4}	20^{x}	21^{1}	21^{0}	22^{1}	24^{2}	25^{1}	5=
Spain	0^{0}	0^{x}	0^{0}	0^{0}	0^{0}	0^{0}	0^{0}	0^{0}	2^{2}	2^{0}	2^{0}	2^{x}	2^{0}	2^{0}	2^{0}	2^{0}	12
Sweden	0^{0}	0^{x}	0^{0}	0^{0}	0^{0}	0^{0}	0^{0}	0^{0}	0^{0}	0^{0}	0^{0}	0^{0}	0^{x}	0^{0}	0^{0}	0^{0}	13=
Belgium	0^{0}	0^{x}	0^{0}	4^{4}	4^{0}	4^{0}	4^{0}	4^{0}	4^{0}	4^{0}	4^{0}	4^{0}	4^{0}	4^{x}	4^{0}	4^{0}	10
Monaco	1^{1}	3^{2}	8^{5}	9^{1}	9^{0}	12^{3}	12^{0}	12^{0}	13^{1}	14^{1}	19^{5}	19^{0}	23^{4}	23^{0}	23^{x}	25^{2}	5=
Luxembourg	0^{0}	0^{0}	3^{3}	3^{0}	3^{0}	4^{1}	5^{1}	7^{2}	7^{0}	9^{2}	13^{4}	13^{0}	13^{0}	13^{0}	13^{0}	13^{x}	8

1963 EUROVISION SONG CONTEST

Host country: United Kingdom ★ *Venue:* BBC Television Centre, London
Date: 23 March ★ *Presenter:* Katie Boyle
Voting structure: Each nation awarded 5, 4, 3, 2 and 1 point to its favourite top 5 songs
Total entries: 16 ★ *Debut countries:* None

Country	Performer	Song	Pts	Pos.
United Kingdom	Ronnie Carroll	Say Wonderful Things	28	4
Netherlands	Annie Palmen	Een Speeldoos	0	13
Germany	Heidi Brühl	Marcel	5	9
Austria	Carmela Corren	Vielleicht Geschieht Ein Wunder	16	7
Norway	Anita Thallaug	Solhverv	0	13
Italy	Emilio Pericoli	Uno Per Tutte	37	3
Finland	Laila Halme	Muistojeni Laulu	0	13
Denmark	**Grethe and Jørgen Ingmann**	**Dansevise**	**42**	**1**
Yugoslavia	Vice Vukov	Brodovi	3	11
Switzerland	Ester Ofarim	T'en Va Pas	40	2
France	Alain Barrière	Elle Etait Si Jolie	25	5
Spain	José Guardiola	Algo Prodigioso	2	12
Sweden	Monica Zetterlund	En Gång I Stockholm	0	13
Belgium	Jacques Raymond	Waarom?	4	10
Monaco	Françoise Hardy	L'Amour S'En Va	25	5
Luxembourg	Nana Mouskouri	A Force De Prier	13	8

That was just patronizing and thoughtless, rather than scandalous. The scandal was the voting.

Any neutral would have said, after seeing all the songs performed, that there were only two, or maybe three, likely winners: the Danish entry sung by Grethe Ingmann with her husband Jørgen on guitar; the Swiss song belted out by the Israeli Ester Ofarim (incidentally the one hundredth song performed in the Contest); and the Monaco entry sung by the eighteen-year-old French pop star Françoise Hardy. In the event, Mlle Hardy was probably too up to date to have much real hope, but the race between Denmark and Switzerland went into extra time.

After four countries had voted, the two songs were both on fourteen points. It was now Norway's turn to vote. For no real reason, there was a misunderstanding on the phone line between Oslo and Katie Boyle, although viewers could clearly make out that the Norwegian jury had awarded the maximum five points to Britain, four to Italy, three to Switzerland, two to Denmark and one to Germany. These votes were added to the scoreboard, but Miss Boyle promised that we would go back to check the Norwegian results at the end. Incidentally, Norway's song that year was so dull that Anita Thallaug, its performer on the night, even refused to record it. There are not

VOTING BIAS

DENMARK

Countries most likely to vote for Denmark:

Norway
Sweden
Iceland
Netherlands
Israel

Countries least likely to vote for Denmark:

Yugoslavia
Switzerland
Turkey
Italy
Spain

Countries for whom Denmark is most likely to vote:

Sweden
Germany
UK
Austria
Ireland

Countries for whom Denmark is least likely to vote:

Italy
Spain
France
Greece
Israel

The northern European countries, in particular the Swedes, benefit most from Danish munificence. They tend to ignore the Mediterranean bloc completely.

many songs in the history of the Contest that have not been recorded by the performer, because a Eurovision entry will almost always guarantee at least a local hit and respectable sales, but 'Solhverv' is one of them. The world of recorded music has not suffered a great loss.

At this point, we returned to the Norwegian jury, for confirmation of its scores.When the votes were all in, and Monaco's inadvertent extra point for Luxembourg had been deducted, the final scores read Switzerland forty-two, Denmark forty. Norway (and Sweden and Finland and the Netherlands) had failed to score a single point. Finland had resorted to the traditional 'la la la la' tactic, Sweden had produced a song about the its of its capital city, and the Netherlands was represented by a song about toys, but even these well-worn Eurovision themes could not inspire a single juror to cast a vote in their favour.

This time, the scores came through loud and clear: five again for Britain, but now it was four for Denmark, three for Italy, two for Germany and only one for Switzerland. This meant adding two points to the Danish scores and taking two away from Switzerland, which neatly reversed the final result and gave the title to the Danes, Norway's close neighbour. Admittedly, Denmark had scored five lots of maximum points from the voters, while Switzerland had been given only three, but even so, the Swiss were originally ahead when all the votes were in. The analysis on page 21 shows Norway's tendency to vote for other Scandinavian countries. Subsequent EBU explanations have officially absolved the Norwegians from local favouritism, but the suspicion remains.

There have been many voting irregularities over the years, including the moment in 1993 when one head of a foreign delegation was overheard offering ten or twelve points to any country whose jury would give top marks to his country's entry. But the 1963 contest gives us the only example of a jury altering its vote publicly to change the destination of the Grand Prix.

THE EUROVISION SONG CONTEST

1964

Won by Italy: 'Non Ho L'Eta'

Written by Nicola Salemo and Mario Panzeri

Performed by Gigliola Cinquetti

Orchestra conducted by Radivoj Spasic

In terms of the margin of the lead over the second song, Italy's victory in 1964 was the most crushing ever. Gigliola Cinquetti scored almost three times as many points as the second-placed song, Britain's 'I Love The Little Things'. For the first time, an Italian song that was a genuine international hit actually won Eurovision, rather than finishing in the minor places, which had been that country's fate in the late 1950s and early 1960s. 'Non Ho L'Eta' succeeded where 'Nel Blu Dipinto Di Blu', 'Piove' and 'Al Di La' had failed. The song was aptly translated as 'I'm Not Old Enough To Love You', as Miss Cinquetti was just sixteen years and ninety-two days' old when she performed in Copenhagen.

This was the first of two Eurovision

1964	Luxembourg	Netherlands	Norway	Denmark	Finland	Austria	France	UK	W. Germany	Monaco	Portugal	Italy	Yugoslavia	Switzerland	Belgium	Spain	**Position**
Luxembourg	0^{x}	3^{3}	3^{0}	3^{0}	3^{0}	3^{0}	6^{3}	6^{0}	11^{5}	11^{0}	11^{0}	14^{3}	14^{0}	14^{0}	14^{0}	14^{0}	4=
Netherlands	0^{0}	0^{x}	0^{0}	1^{1}	1^{0}	1^{0}	1^{0}	2^{1}	2^{0}	2^{0}	2^{0}	2^{0}	2^{0}	2^{0}	2^{0}	2^{0}	10=
Norway	0^{0}	0^{0}	0^{x}	5^{5}	6^{1}	6^{0}	6^{0}	6^{0}	6^{0}	6^{0}	6^{0}	6^{0}	6^{0}	6^{0}	6^{0}	6^{0}	8
Denmark	0^{0}	0^{0}	1^{1}	1^{x}	1^{0}	1^{0}	1^{0}	1^{0}	1^{0}	1^{0}	1^{0}	1^{0}	1^{0}	1^{0}	1^{0}	4^{3}	9
Finland	0^{0}	0^{0}	3^{3}	6^{3}	6^{x}	6^{0}	6^{0}	9^{3}	9^{0}	9^{0}	9^{0}	9^{0}	9^{0}	9^{0}	9^{0}	9^{0}	7
Austria	0^{0}	0^{0}	0^{0}	0^{0}	0^{0}	0^{x}	0^{0}	0^{0}	0^{0}	0^{0}	0^{0}	5^{5}	5^{0}	5^{0}	6^{1}	11^{5}	6
France	1^{1}	1^{0}	1^{0}	1^{0}	1^{0}	4^{3}	4^{x}	4^{0}	4^{0}	9^{5}	12^{3}	12^{0}	13^{1}	13^{0}	13^{0}	14^{1}	4=
UK	0^{0}	1^{1}	6^{5}	6^{0}	9^{3}	10^{1}	11^{1}	11^{x}	12^{1}	12^{0}	12^{0}	12^{0}	12^{0}	17^{5}	17^{0}	17^{0}	2
W. Germany	0^{0}	0^{0}	0^{0}	0^{0}	0^{0}	0^{0}	0^{0}	0^{0}	0^{x}	0^{0}	0^{0}	0^{0}	0^{0}	0^{0}	0^{0}	0^{0}	13=
Monaco	3^{3}	3^{0}	3^{0}	3^{0}	3^{0}	3^{0}	8^{5}	8^{0}	8^{0}	8^{x}	8^{0}	8^{0}	11^{3}	12^{1}	15^{3}	15^{0}	3
Portugal	0^{0}	0^{0}	0^{0}	0^{0}	0^{0}	0^{0}	0^{0}	0^{0}	0^{0}	0^{0}	0^{x}	0^{0}	0^{0}	0^{0}	0^{0}	0^{0}	13=
Italy	**5^{5}**	**10^{5}**	**10^{0}**	**10^{0}**	**15^{5}**	**20^{5}**	**20^{0}**	**25^{5}**	**28^{3}**	**31^{3}**	**36^{5}**	**36^{x}**	**41^{5}**	**44^{3}**	**49^{5}**	**49^{0}**	**1**
Yugoslavia	0^{0}	0^{0}	0^{0}	0^{0}	0^{0}	0^{0}	0^{0}	0^{0}	0^{0}	0^{0}	0^{0}	0^{0}	0^{x}	0^{0}	0^{0}	0^{0}	13=
Switzerland	0^{0}	0^{0}	0^{0}	0^{0}	0^{0}	0^{0}	0^{0}	0^{0}	0^{0}	0^{0}	0^{0}	0^{0}	0^{0}	0^{x}	0^{0}	0^{0}	13=
Belgium	0^{0}	0^{0}	0^{0}	0^{0}	0^{0}	0^{0}	0^{0}	0^{0}	0^{0}	1^{1}	2^{1}	2^{0}	2^{0}	2^{0}	2^{x}	2^{0}	10=
Spain	0^{0}	0^{0}	0^{0}	0^{0}	0^{0}	0^{0}	0^{0}	0^{0}	0^{0}	0^{0}	0^{0}	1^{1}	1^{0}	1^{0}	1^{0}	1^{x}	12

★ ★

1964 EUROVISION SONG CONTEST

Host country: Denmark ★ *Venue:* Tivoli Concert Hall, Copenhagen
Date: 21 March ★ *Presenter:* Lotta Waever
Voting structure: Each nation awarded 5, 3 and 1 point to its top 3 songs
Total entries: 16 ★ *Debut countries:* Portugal

Country	Performer	Song	Pts	Pos.
Luxembourg	Hugues Aufray	Dès Que Le Printemps Revient	14	4
Netherlands	Anneke Grönloh	Jij Bent Mijn Leven	2	10
Norway	Arne Bendiksen	Spiral	6	8
Denmark	Bjørn Tidmand	Sangen Om Dig	4	9
Finland	Lasse Mårtenson	Laiskotellen	9	7
Austria	Udo Jürgens	Warum Nur Warum?	11	6
France	Rachel	Le Chant De Mallory	14	4
United Kingdom	Matt Monro	I Love The Little Things	17	2
Germany	Nora Nova	Man Gewöhnt Sich So Schnell An Das Schöne	0	13
Monaco	Romuald	Où Sont-Elles Passées?	15	3
Portugal	Antonio Calvario	Oração	0	13
Italy	**Gigliola Cinquetti**	**Non Ho L'Eta**	**49**	**1**
Yugoslavia	Sabahudin Kurt	Zivot Je Sklopio Krug	0	13
Switzerland	Anita Traversi	I Miei Pensieri	0	13
Belgium	Robert Cogoi	Près De Ma Rivière	2	10
Spain	Nelly, Tim and Tony	Caracola	1	12

appearances for Gigliola as a performer (she came a fairly distant second to Abba in 1974, and also co-hosted the 1991 Contest with Toto Cutugno), but it was the first of three appearances for two other singers, one of whom would go on to win. Romuald, singing for Monaco that year, was to sing for Luxembourg in 1969 and for Monaco again in 1974, without ever coming higher than third, while Udo Jürgens and his piano became a familiar sight at Eurovision over the next three years, culminating in his win in 1966. His entry in 1964 was probably the biggest international hit of his three songs, even though it was the lowest-placed, at sixth. Matt Monro, Britain's entrant, liked what he heard when Udo sang, and recorded the song, in English, as 'Walk Away'. His own song, 'I Love The Little Things', never made the charts in his homeland, but 'Walk Away' climbed to number four, and also hit the American top thirty early in 1965. Monro also delved into the Udo Jürgens songbook a year later, when the Austrian's 'Du Sollst Die Welt Für Mich Sein' became 'Without You' and hit the British top forty.

'Walk Away' was not the only English language version of a Eurovision song that year. Vera Lynn, who was thirty years older than Gigliola Cinquetti and therefore plenty old enough in 1967 to love anybody, recorded an English version of the winning song under the title 'This Is My Prayer'. Sadly, it was not answered by the record-buying public. It was, indeed, a bad year for prayers, as Portugal's debut entry, 'Oração'/'Prayer' scored no points at all.

The voting system was constantly being overhauled during the early 1960s. This was the fourth consecutive year in which a different system was being used, but it was also the third consecutive year in which four different entries scored no points at all. Portugal was just one of the four non-scorers, along with Germany, Switzerland and Yugoslavia. Yugoslav-born Robert Cogoi, singing for Belgium, scarcely fared better, earning only two points, but that was one more than Nelly, Tim and Tony scored for Spain. After a disastrous year for Scandinavia in 1963, it was a terrible year for the Iberian peninsula in 1964.

Over the years, thirty-two songs have finished with no points, half of them being performed in the four years from 1962 to 1965. Seventeen nations have shared in the ignominy at least once – with Norway, of course, holding the record for having failed to trouble the scorers four times. Austria, Spain and Finland have all ended up with nothing three times.

It was a poor system that allowed one quarter of the entrants to score no points at all for their efforts, but it was going to be two more years before the system was changed again. Even then, it reverted to the system in use in 1961. It took until 1975 to create a voting system that not only came up with a definite winner but also gave encouragement to the weakest, most of the time. In the twenty-three Contests since 1975, only twelve songs have been awarded the infamous 'nul points', and only in two contests – in 1983 and 1997 – have two songs tied for last place with nothing. No song sung in English has yet scored zero, and only four sung in French, one each by Belgium (1962), Monaco (1966), Switzerland (1967) and Luxembourg (1978).

VOTING BIAS

PORTUGAL

Countries most likely to vote for Portugal:

Spain
France
Luxembourg
Turkey
Greece

Countries least likely to vote for Portugal:

Ireland
Austria
UK
Denmark
Malta

Countries for whom Portugal is most likely to vote:

Italy
Germany
Luxembourg
Belgium
Israel

Countries for whom Portugal is least likely to vote:

Ireland
Yugoslavia
Finland
Turkey
Sweden

Italy was the recipient of the first ever top mark given by Portugal in 1964. From then on a pattern was set as Portugal tended to favour the Italians over its Spanish neighbours.

★ ★

THE EUROVISION SONG CONTEST

1965

Won by Luxembourg: 'Poupée De Cire, Poupée De Son'

Written by Serge Gainsbourg

Performed by France Gall

Orchestra conducted by Alain Goraguer

The 1965 Eurovision Song Contest belonged to France Gall. The seventeen-year-old French girl sang a song written by Serge Gainsbourg, to become the first to win with a song about little toy people. For some reason, dolls, marionettes and puppets seem to be a popular subject for Eurovision, but only twice has it proved a winning theme. Serge Gainsbourg, more famous for his notorious 'Je T'Aime … Moi Non Plus' duet with Jane Birkin three years later, is not

1965	Netherlands	UK	Spain	Ireland	W. Germany	Austria	Norway	Belgium	Monaco	Sweden	France	Portugal	Italy	Denmark	Luxembourg	Finland	Yugoslavia	Switzerland	**Position**
Netherlands	0^{x}	0^{0}	0^{0}	0^{0}	0^{0}	0^{0}	5^{5}	5^{0}	5^{0}	5^{0}	5^{0}	5^{0}	5^{0}	5^{0}	5^{0}	5^{0}	5^{0}	5^{0}	11
UK	0^{0}	0^{x}	5^{5}	5^{0}	5^{0}	5^{0}	6^{1}	12^{6}	12^{0}	15^{3}	15^{0}	15^{0}	16^{1}	21^{5}	21^{0}	21^{0}	21^{0}	26^{5}	2
Spain	0^{0}	0^{0}	0^{x}	0^{0}	0^{0}	0^{0}	0^{0}	0^{0}	0^{0}	0^{0}	0^{0}	0^{0}	0^{0}	0^{0}	0^{0}	0^{0}	0^{0}	0^{0}	15=
Ireland	0^{0}	0^{0}	0^{0}	0^{x}	0^{0}	0^{0}	0^{0}	0^{0}	0^{0}	0^{0}	0^{0}	3^{3}	8^{5}	8^{0}	8^{0}	8^{0}	11^{3}	11^{0}	6
W. Germany	0^{0}	0^{0}	0^{0}	0^{0}	0^{x}	0^{0}	0^{0}	0^{0}	0^{0}	0^{0}	0^{0}	0^{0}	0^{0}	0^{0}	0^{0}	0^{0}	0^{0}	0^{0}	15=
Austria	0^{0}	3^{3}	3^{0}	8^{5}	8^{0}	8^{x}	8^{0}	8^{0}	8^{0}	8^{0}	8^{0}	13^{5}	16^{3}	16^{0}	16^{0}	16^{0}	16^{0}	16^{0}	4
Norway	0^{0}	0^{0}	0^{0}	0^{0}	0^{0}	1^{1}	1^{x}	1^{0}	1^{0}	1^{0}	1^{0}	1^{0}	1^{0}	1^{0}	1^{0}	1^{0}	1^{0}	1^{0}	13=
Belgium	0^{0}	0^{0}	0^{0}	0^{0}	0^{0}	0^{0}	0^{0}	0^{x}	0^{0}	0^{0}	0^{0}	0^{0}	0^{0}	0^{0}	0^{0}	0^{0}	0^{0}	0^{0}	15=
Monaco	0^{0}	$\mathbf{5^{5}}$	5^{0}	5^{0}	5^{0}	5^{0}	5^{0}	5^{0}	5^{x}	5^{0}	5^{0}	5^{0}	5^{0}	5^{0}	5^{0}	5^{0}	6^{1}	7^{1}	9
Sweden	0^{0}	0^{0}	0^{0}	0^{0}	0^{0}	0^{0}	0^{0}	0^{0}	0^{0}	0^{x}	0^{0}	0^{0}	0^{0}	3^{3}	3^{0}	6^{3}	6^{0}	6^{0}	10
France	1^{1}	1^{0}	4^{3}	5^{1}	8^{3}	8^{0}	8^{0}	8^{0}	13^{5}	13^{0}	13^{x}	13^{0}	13^{0}	13^{0}	16^{3}	17^{1}	22^{5}	22^{0}	3
Portugal	0^{0}	0^{0}	0^{0}	0^{0}	0^{0}	0^{0}	0^{0}	0^{0}	1^{1}	1^{0}	1^{0}	1^{x}	1^{0}	1^{0}	1^{0}	1^{0}	1^{0}	1^{0}	13=
Italy	3^{3}	4^{1}	4^{0}	4^{0}	5^{1}	5^{0}	5^{0}	8^{3}	11^{3}	11^{0}	14^{3}	14^{0}	14^{x}	14^{0}	15^{1}	15^{0}	15^{0}	15^{0}	5
Denmark	0^{0}	0^{0}	0^{0}	0^{0}	0^{0}	0^{0}	0^{0}	0^{0}	0^{0}	5^{5}	5^{0}	5^{0}	5^{0}	5^{x}	10^{5}	10^{0}	10^{0}	10^{0}	7
Luxembourg	$\mathbf{5^{5}}$	$\mathbf{5^{0}}$	$\mathbf{6^{1}}$	$\mathbf{9^{3}}$	$\mathbf{14^{5}}$	$\mathbf{19^{5}}$	$\mathbf{22^{3}}$	$\mathbf{22^{0}}$	$\mathbf{22^{0}}$	$\mathbf{23^{1}}$	$\mathbf{23^{0}}$	$\mathbf{23^{0}}$	$\mathbf{23^{0}}$	$\mathbf{24^{1}}$	$\mathbf{24^{x}}$	$\mathbf{29^{5}}$	$\mathbf{29^{0}}$	$\mathbf{32^{3}}$	**1**
Finland	0^{0}	0^{0}	0^{0}	0^{0}	0^{0}	0^{0}	0^{0}	0^{0}	0^{0}	0^{0}	0^{0}	0^{0}	0^{0}	0^{0}	0^{0}	0^{x}	0^{0}	0^{0}	15=
Yugoslavia	0^{0}	0^{0}	0^{0}	0^{0}	0^{0}	0^{0}	0^{0}	0^{0}	0^{0}	0^{0}	1^{1}	2^{1}	2^{0}	2^{0}	2^{0}	2^{0}	2^{x}	2^{0}	12
Switzerland	0^{0}	0^{0}	0^{0}	0^{0}	0^{0}	3^{3}	3^{0}	3^{0}	3^{0}	3^{0}	8^{5}	8^{0}	8^{0}	8^{0}	8^{0}	8^{0}	8^{0}	8^{x}	8

1965 EUROVISION SONG CONTEST

Host country: Italy ★ *Venue:* RAI Concert Hall, Naples
Date: 20 March ★ *Presenter:* Renata Maura
Voting structure: Each nation awarded 5, 3 and 1 point to its top 3 songs
Total entries: 18 ★ *Debut countries:* Ireland

Country	Performer	Song	Pts	Pos.
Netherlands	Conny van den Bos	'T Het Is Genoeg	5	11
United Kingdom	Kathy Kirby	I Belong	26	2
Spain	Conchita Bautista	Que Bueno, Que Bueno	0	15
Ireland	Butch Moore	I'm Walking The Streets In The Rain	11	6
Germany	Ulla Wiesner	Paradies, Wo Bist Du?	0	15
Austria	Udo Jürgens	Sag Ihr, Ich Lass Sie Grüssen	16	4
Norway	Kirsti Sparboe	Karusell	1	13
Belgium	Lize Marke	Als Het Weer Lente Is	0	15
Monaco	Marjorie Noël	Va Dire A L'Amour	7	9
Sweden	Ingvar Wixell	Absent Friend	6	10
France	Guy Mardel	N'Avoue Jamais	22	3
Portugal	Simone de Oliveira	Sol De Inverno	1	13
Italy	Bobby Solo	Se Piangi, Se Ridi	15	5
Denmark	Birgit Brüel	For Din Skyld	10	7
Luxembourg	**France Gall**	**Poupée De Cire, Poupée De Son**	**32**	**1**
Finland	Viktor Klimenko	Aurinko Laskee Lånteen	0	15
Yugoslavia	Vice Vukov	Ceznja	2	12
Switzerland	Yovanna	Non A Jamais Sans Toi	8	8

a name that you would immediately associate with the joyful innocence of Eurovision, but he was persuaded to write a song for his god-daughter France Gall, whose singing career was just beginning. The fact that neither Gainsbourg nor Gall were Luxembourgeois did not seem to matter: Gall's father Robert had written songs for the previous year's Luxembourg entrant, Hugues Aufray, so the family obviously had a strong connection with the organizers. The song was a clear leader in the voting from the very first round, and it was never overtaken. This despite the fact that the UK won six points from Belgium, rather than the apparent maximum of five, because under rules then in operation, if a jury picked only two songs as its favourites, they scored six and three. Luxembourg was still the easy winner. The UK finished second, but despite winning twenty-one points from just four juries, it could win only five more from the other thirteen.

Among the other entrants was a succession of statuesque women, and plenty of songs with bongos featuring heavily in the orchestration. There was also Ingvar Wixell, an operatic tenor

VOTING BIAS

SPAIN

Countries most likely to vote for Spain:
Greece
Turkey
Italy
Cyprus
Malta

Countries least likely to vote for Spain:
Sweden
UK
Denmark
Ireland
Norway

Countries for whom Spain is most likely to vote:
Portugal
Italy
Greece
Germany
Malta

Countries for whom Spain is least likely to vote:
Switzerland
Sweden
France
Norway
UK

Spain continues to lavish praise on Portugal, largely without reciprocation. In the thirty-one times they have appeared together, Spain has awarded Portugal sixty-five more votes than it would, on average, expect.

who sang in English for Sweden, and Viktor Klimenko, a vast Finn with an Abraham Lincoln beard, who had just finished starring in the Helsinki version of Anthony Newley's musical, *Stop the World, I Want to Get Off.* The connection between Eurovision and the musical theatre is, not surprisingly, very strong, and over the years there have been many stars of the musical stage who have had a go at Eurovision, usually with little success. France Gall herself went on to marry Michel Berger, the composer of the fabulously successful French musical, *Starmania.* It is at this point that one of the co-authors of the book must reveal his Eurovision connections. *Starmania* was translated into English as *Tycoon* by Tim Rice, featuring Céline Dion (Switzerland, 1988). Rice also tried to write an entry for Eurovision in 1969 with Andrew Lloyd Webber. It was called 'Try It And See', but it failed to make the short list for the UK entry that year. All was not wasted, however as, with new lyrics, the song became 'King Herod's Song' in *Jesus Christ Superstar.* Anne-Marie David (Luxembourg, 1973) played Mary Magdalene in the French production of that show. Tim Rice has also worked with the 1974 winners Björn Ulvaeus and Benny Andersson of Abba to create the stage musical *Chess,* whose stars included two other regular Swedish Eurovision competitors, Tommy Körberg and Björn Skifs. C. T. Wilkinson (Ireland, 1978) has appeared in many musicals, as have Michael Ball (UK, 1992) and Frances Ruffelle (UK, 1994). Malcolm Roberts (Luxembourg, 1985) appeared in Lionel Bart's *Maggie May* in London. Linda Lepomme (Belgium, 1985) has appeared as Eva Peron in *Evita* and as Eliza Doolittle in *My Fair Lady* in Antwerp. Ingrid Bjørnov and Benedicte Adrian, the two members of Dollie de Luxe (Norway, 1984), devised, wrote and starred in the musical *Which Witch,* which was hugely successful in Scandinavia but less enthusiastically received when it came to London in 1992, despite featuring Jahn Teigen (Norway, 1978, 1982 and 1983).

★ ★

THE EUROVISION SONG CONTEST

1966

Won by Austria: 'Merci Chérie'

Written by Udo Jürgens and Thomas Horbiger

Performed by Udo Jürgens

Orchestra conducted by Hans Hammerschmid

After the 1965 success of France Gall – a pretty young girl singing a bouncy little song – most of the entrants decided that what was needed to win was a pretty young girl singing a bouncy little song. So the first eight songs performed in 1966 were just that. Germany's was rather more of a ballad, Denmark's involved a daring departure into choreography, while Belgium's entry was just annoyingly jolly. Norway brought on a woman in a trouser suit carrying an

1966	W. Germany	Denmark	Belgium	Luxembourg	Yugoslavia	Norway	Finland	Portugal	Austria	Sweden	Spain	Switzerland	Monaco	Italy	France	Netherlands	Ireland	UK	Position
W. Germany	0^{x}	0^{0}	1^{1}	1^{0}	1^{0}	1^{0}	1^{0}	1^{0}	1^{0}	1^{0}	1^{0}	6^{5}	6^{0}	7^{1}	7^{0}	7^{0}	7^{0}	7^{0}	10=
Denmark	0^{0}	0^{x}	0^{0}	0^{0}	0^{0}	1^{1}	4^{3}	4^{0}	4^{0}	4^{0}	4^{0}	4^{0}	4^{0}	4^{0}	4^{0}	4^{0}	4^{0}	4^{0}	14
Belgium	**5^{5}**	**5^{0}**	**5^{x}**	5^{0}	5^{0}	5^{0}	5^{0}	8^{3}	8^{0}	9^{1}	9^{0}	9^{0}	9^{0}	9^{0}	9^{0}	14^{5}	14^{0}	14^{0}	4=
Luxembourg	0^{0}	0^{0}	0^{0}	0^{x}	0^{0}	0^{0}	0^{0}	0^{0}	1^{1}	6^{5}	6^{0}	6^{0}	6^{0}	6^{0}	7^{1}	7^{0}	7^{0}	7^{0}	10=
Yugoslavia	3^{3}	3^{0}	3^{0}	3^{0}	3^{x}	3^{0}	4^{1}	4^{0}	4^{0}	4^{0}	4^{0}	4^{0}	4^{0}	4^{0}	4^{0}	4^{0}	4^{0}	9^{5}	7=
Norway	1^{1}	1^{0}	1^{0}	1^{0}	1^{0}	1^{x}	1^{0}	1^{0}	4^{3}	7^{3}	10^{3}	10^{0}	10^{0}	15^{5}	15^{0}	15^{0}	15^{0}	15^{0}	3
Finland	0^{0}	3^{3}	3^{0}	3^{0}	3^{0}	6^{3}	6^{x}	6^{0}	6^{0}	6^{0}	6^{0}	6^{0}	6^{0}	6^{0}	6^{0}	7^{1}	7^{0}	7^{0}	10=
Portugal	0^{0}	1^{1}	1^{0}	1^{0}	1^{0}	1^{0}	1^{0}	1^{x}	1^{0}	1^{0}	6^{5}	6^{0}	6^{0}	6^{0}	6^{0}	6^{0}	6^{0}	6^{0}	13
Austria	0^{0}	0^{0}	**5^{5}**	**10^{5}**	**15^{5}**	**15^{0}**	**15^{0}**	**16^{1}**	**16^{x}**	**16^{0}**	**17^{1}**	**20^{3}**	**25^{5}**	**28^{3}**	**31^{3}**	**31^{0}**	**31^{0}**	**31^{0}**	1
Sweden	0^{0}	**5^{5}**	**5^{0}**	5^{0}	5^{0}	10^{5}	**15^{5}**	15^{0}	15^{0}	15^{x}	15^{0}	16^{1}	16^{0}	16^{0}	16^{0}	16^{0}	16^{0}	16^{0}	2
Spain	0^{0}	0^{0}	0^{0}	0^{0}	1^{1}	1^{0}	1^{0}	6^{5}	6^{0}	6^{0}	6^{x}	6^{0}	6^{0}	6^{0}	6^{0}	6^{0}	6^{0}	9^{3}	7=
Switzerland	0^{0}	0^{0}	0^{0}	1^{1}	1^{0}	1^{0}	1^{0}	1^{0}	6^{5}	6^{0}	6^{0}	6^{x}	9^{3}	9^{0}	9^{0}	9^{0}	12^{3}	12^{0}	6
Monaco	0^{0}	0^{0}	0^{0}	0^{0}	0^{0}	0^{0}	0^{0}	0^{0}	0^{0}	0^{0}	0^{0}	0^{0}	0^{x}	0^{0}	0^{0}	0^{0}	0^{0}	0^{0}	17=
Italy	0^{0}	0^{0}	0^{0}	0^{0}	0^{0}	0^{0}	0^{0}	0^{0}	0^{0}	0^{0}	0^{0}	0^{0}	0^{0}	0^{x}	0^{0}	0^{0}	0^{0}	0^{0}	17=
France	0^{0}	0^{0}	0^{0}	0^{0}	0^{0}	0^{0}	0^{0}	0^{0}	0^{0}	0^{0}	0^{0}	0^{0}	1^{1}	1^{0}	1^{x}	1^{0}	1^{0}	1^{0}	16
Netherlands	0^{0}	0^{0}	0^{0}	0^{0}	0^{0}	0^{0}	0^{0}	0^{0}	0^{0}	0^{0}	0^{0}	0^{0}	0^{0}	0^{0}	0^{0}	0^{x}	1^{1}	2^{1}	15
Ireland	0^{0}	0^{0}	3^{3}	3^{0}	6^{3}	6^{0}	6^{0}	6^{0}	6^{0}	6^{0}	6^{0}	6^{0}	6^{0}	6^{0}	11^{5}	14^{3}	14^{x}	14^{0}	4
UK	0^{0}	0^{0}	0^{0}	3^{3}	3^{0}	3^{0}	3^{0}	3^{0}	3^{0}	3^{0}	3^{0}	3^{0}	3^{0}	3^{0}	3^{0}	3^{0}	8^{5}	8^{x}	9

★ ★

1966 EUROVISION SONG CONTEST

Host country: Luxembourg ★ *Venue:* Grand Auditorium de RTL, Villa Louvigny
Date: 5 March ★ *Presenter:* Josiane Shen
Voting structure: Each nation awarded 5, 3 and 1 point to its top 3 songs
Total entries: 18 ★ *Debut countries:* None

Country	Performer	Song	Pts	Pos.
Germany	Margot Eskens	Die Zeiger Der Uhr	7	10
Denmark	Ulla Pia	Stop, Mens Legen Er Go	4	14
Belgium	Tonia	Un Peu De Poivre, Un Peu De Sel	14	4
Luxembourg	Michèle Torr	Ce Soir Je T'Attendais	7	10
Yugoslavia	Berta Ambroz	Brez Besed	9	7
Norway	Åse Kleveland	Intet Er Nytt Under Solen	15	3
Finland	Ann Christine Nyström	Play Boy	7	10
Portugal	Madalena Iglesias	Ele E Ela	6	13
Austria	**Udo Jürgens**	**Merci Chérie**	**31**	**1**
Sweden	Lill Lindfors and Svante Thuresson	Nygammal Vals	16	2
Spain	Raphael	Yo Soy Aquel	9	7
Switzerland	Madeleine Pascal	Ne Vois-tu Pas?	12	6
Monaco	Tereza	Bien Plus Fort	0	17
Italy	Domenico Modugno	Dio Come Ti Amo	0	17
France	Dominique Walter	Chez Nous	1	16
Netherlands	Milly Scott	Fernando En Philippo	2	15
Ireland	Dickie Rock	Come Back To Stay	14	4
United Kingdom	Kenneth McKellar	A Man Without Love	8	9

acoustic guitar. She went on to become Norway's Minister of Culture and to present the 1986 Contest, but she did not collect enough votes to win. Monaco and Italy collected no votes at all: Tereza for Monaco complained that her love was much stronger than the wind, while Italy's Domenico Modugno, back for another go, had come up with a song that was more sound effects than tune, and a good minute and a half too long. The Netherlands introduced the first ever black performer into the Contest, with Milly Scott singing a daft little number about two Mexicans, who were there on stage, complete with ponchos and guitars. Even the United Kingdom produced a man in a kilt, hoping no doubt that he would be mistaken for a pretty young girl singing a bouncy little song. There were songs with traces of all the hits of the day, from 'It's Not Unusual' to 'It's My Party', but most were trying to be 'Poupée De Cire, Poupée De Son, Part Two'. It was left to Udo Jürgens, competing for Austria for the third year in a row and playing his piano as moodily as ever, to break the unremitting diet of bouncy little women (except for Luxembourg's Michèle Torr, who was very tall) and walk away with the prize. Second place also went against the run of play, with the Swedish duo of Lill Lindfors and the bearded Svante Thuresson presenting a comedy number about a swineherd that involved much laughter and a flautist.

There have been many suggestions over the years that the voting is done according to international affiliations rather than the merits of the song, but there is not usually a great deal of substance to these claims. However, once or twice the voting seems to follow such strict international preference lines that you begin to wonder why they bothered to perform the songs before the voting began. Such a year was 1966.

Denmark began the fun by giving five points to Sweden and three to Finland. Then Norway, a country that has always had a cavalier attitude to the winning of Europoints, gave its five-three-one to Sweden, Finland and Denmark, keeping it in the Scandinavian family. Its five points for Sweden earned the biggest laugh of the night from the studio audience. When Finland, the next country to vote, also gave five to Sweden, the audience not only laughed, but whistled as well. Finland also gave three to Denmark, but to show its international credentials, awarded its final vote to Yugoslavia. Portugal then gave five to Spain, and Spain gave five to Portugal. France's only point came from neighbours Monaco. Austria gave five to Switzerland, Switzerland gave five to Germany, both keeping their big votes for the German-language songs. Ireland gave five to the United Kingdom, perhaps because Kenneth McKellar was Scottish. Even the Irish jury foreman announcing the vote laughed at this.

Only Austria, with votes from nine of the juries, broke out of the regional factionalism that was threatening to swamp the show. No wonder – when he was asked to perform the winning song again at the close of the show – that Udo Jürgens began with a pun on the title of his winning song, 'Merci, juries'.

VOTING BIAS

AUSTRIA

Countries most likely to vote for Austria:

Ireland
UK
Greece
Denmark
Italy

Countries least likely to vote for Austria:

Norway
Switzerland
Finland
Netherlands
Luxembourg

Countries for whom Austria is most likely to vote:

UK
Ireland
Sweden
France
Netherlands

Countries for whom Austria is least likely to vote:

Germany
Cyprus
Italy
Portugal
Belgium

Like the Swiss, the Austrians are wary of voting for their German neighbours. Instead, again like the Swiss, they vote for the United Kingdom who usually (although not in 1966) respond favourably.

THE EUROVISION SONG CONTEST

1967

Won by United Kingdom: 'Puppet On A String'
Written by Bill Martin and Phil Coulter
Performed by Sandie Shaw
Orchestra conducted by Kenny Woodman

The 1967 Eurovision Song Contest was the first staged in Austria, the last to be televised in black and white only, and the first in which fewer countries competed than in the previous year. Denmark dropped out only four years after winning and would not return until 1978, leaving only seventeen countries to compete for the prize. At least that meant one less language in which presenter Erica Vaal could greet her audience: as it was, her five-language introduction, in English, French, German, Italian and Spanish, lasted almost ten minutes.

1967	Netherlands	Luxembourg	Austria	France	Portugal	Switzerland	Sweden	Finland	W. Germany	Belgium	UK	Spain	Norway	Monaco	Yugoslavia	Italy	Ireland	**Position**
Netherlands	0^{x}	0^{0}	0^{0}	0^{0}	0^{0}	0^{0}	0^{0}	0^{0}	0^{0}	0^{0}	1^{1}	1^{0}	1^{0}	1^{0}	1^{0}	1^{0}	2^{1}	14=
Luxembourg	$\mathbf{4^{4}}$	4^{x}	4^{0}	4^{0}	4^{0}	4^{0}	4^{0}	6^{2}	6^{0}	7^{1}	9^{2}	10^{1}	10^{0}	11^{1}	12^{1}	15^{3}	17^{2}	4
Austria	0^{0}	0^{0}	0^{x}	0^{0}	1^{1}	1^{0}	1^{0}	1^{0}	1^{0}	1^{0}	1^{0}	1^{0}	1^{0}	1^{0}	2^{1}	2^{0}	2^{0}	14=
France	1^{1}	3^{2}	4^{1}	4^{x}	4^{0}	5^{1}	9^{4}	9^{0}	11^{2}	11^{0}	13^{2}	13^{0}	13^{0}	15^{2}	19^{4}	19^{0}	20^{1}	3
Portugal	0^{0}	0^{0}	0^{0}	1^{1}	1^{x}	2^{1}	2^{0}	2^{0}	2^{0}	2^{0}	2^{0}	3^{1}	3^{0}	3^{0}	3^{0}	3^{0}	3^{0}	12=
Switzerland	0^{0}	0^{0}	0^{0}	0^{0}	0^{0}	0^{x}	0^{0}	0^{0}	0^{0}	0^{0}	0^{0}	0^{0}	0^{0}	0^{0}	0^{0}	0^{0}	0^{0}	17
Sweden	0^{0}	0^{0}	0^{0}	0^{0}	1^{1}	1^{0}	1^{x}	2^{1}	2^{0}	2^{0}	2^{0}	2^{0}	4^{2}	4^{0}	5^{1}	5^{0}	7^{2}	8=
Finland	1^{1}	1^{0}	1^{0}	1^{0}	2^{1}	2^{0}	2^{0}	2^{x}	2^{0}	2^{0}	2^{0}	2^{0}	2^{0}	2^{0}	2^{0}	3^{1}	3^{0}	12=
W. Germany	0^{0}	0^{0}	0^{0}	0^{0}	1^{1}	1^{0}	2^{1}	2^{0}	2^{x}	3^{1}	4^{1}	4^{0}	5^{1}	5^{0}	5^{0}	6^{1}	7^{1}	8=
Belgium	0^{0}	0^{0}	0^{0}	0^{0}	1^{1}	1^{0}	1^{0}	4^{3}	5^{1}	5^{x}	6^{1}	6^{0}	6^{0}	6^{0}	7^{1}	7^{0}	8^{1}	7
UK	$\mathbf{2^{2}}$	$\mathbf{7^{5}}$	$\mathbf{10^{3}}$	$\mathbf{17^{7}}$	$\mathbf{18^{1}}$	$\mathbf{25^{7}}$	$\mathbf{26^{1}}$	$\mathbf{28^{2}}$	$\mathbf{31^{3}}$	$\mathbf{34^{3}}$	$\mathbf{34^{x}}$	$\mathbf{34^{0}}$	$\mathbf{41^{7}}$	$\mathbf{44^{3}}$	$\mathbf{44^{0}}$	$\mathbf{46^{2}}$	$\mathbf{47^{1}}$	**1**
Spain	1^{1}	2^{1}	3^{1}	3^{0}	5^{2}	5^{0}	5^{0}	5^{0}	5^{0}	6^{1}	6^{0}	6^{x}	6^{0}	8^{2}	9^{1}	9^{0}	9^{0}	6
Norway	1^{1}	1^{0}	1^{0}	1^{0}	1^{0}	1^{0}	2^{1}	2^{0}	2^{0}	2^{0}	2^{0}	2^{0}	2^{x}	2^{0}	2^{0}	2^{0}	2^{0}	14=
Monaco	0^{0}	0^{0}	2^{2}	3^{1}	3^{0}	3^{0}	4^{1}	4^{0}	4^{0}	4^{0}	4^{0}	9^{5}	9^{0}	9^{x}	9^{0}	10^{1}	10^{0}	5
Yugoslavia	0^{0}	1^{1}	1^{0}	2^{1}	3^{1}	3^{0}	3^{0}	3^{0}	3^{0}	4^{1}	4^{0}	6^{2}	6^{0}	6^{0}	6^{x}	7^{1}	7^{0}	8=
Italy	0^{0}	0^{0}	0^{0}	0^{0}	0^{0}	1^{1}	1^{0}	1^{0}	1^{0}	1^{0}	2^{1}	3^{1}	3^{0}	3^{0}	3^{0}	3^{x}	4^{1}	11
Ireland	0^{0}	1^{1}	4^{3}	4^{0}	5^{1}	5^{0}	7^{2}	9^{2}	13^{4}	16^{3}	18^{2}	18^{0}	18^{0}	20^{2}	21^{1}	22^{1}	22^{x}	2

1967 EUROVISION SONG CONTEST

Host country: Austria ★ *Venue:* Grosser Festsaal, Wiener Hofburg, Vienna
Date: 8 April ★ *Presenter:* Erica Vaal
Voting structure: 10 jury members from each country, each of whom awarded 1 point to their favourite song
Total entries: 17 ★ *Debut countries:* None

Country	Performer	Song	Pts	Pos.
Netherlands	Thérèse Steinmetz	Ringe Ding	2	14
Luxembourg	Vicky	L'Amour Est Bleu	17	4
Austria	Peter Horten	Warum Es 100,000 Sterne Gibt	2	14
France	Noëlle Cordier	Il Doit Faire Beau Là-bas	20	3
Portugal	Eduardo Nascimento	O Vento Mudou	3	12
Switzerland	Géraldine	Quel Coeur Vas-tu Briser?	0	17
Sweden	Östen Warnerbring	Som En Dröm	7	8
Finland	Fredi	Varjoon-Suojaan	3	12
Germany	Inge Bruck	Anouschka	7	8
Belgium	Louis Neefs	Ik Heb Zorgen	8	7
United Kingdom	**Sandie Shaw**	**Puppet On A String**	**47**	**1**
Spain	Raphael	Hablemos Del Amor	9	6
Norway	Kirsti Sparboe	Dukkemann	2	14
Monaco	Minouche Barelli	Boum Badaboum	10	5
Yugoslavia	Lado Leskovar	Vse Roze Sveta	7	8
Italy	Claudio Villa	Non Andare Piu Lontano	4	11
Ireland	Sean Dunphy	If I Could Choose	22	2

The voting system used for the past few years was now abandoned in favour of the system that had been used from 1957 to 1961, in which ten jury members from each country each awarded one point to their favourite song. There seemed to be no clear reason for it being changed, but on any scoring system, the 1967 winner would have romped home.

The winning song was 'Puppet On A String', a song Sandie Shaw has often said that she loathes. It was the first British Eurovision winner, and it gained over twice as many votes as the second-placed song, the Irish entry. If UK had gained no further points after the sixth country, Switzerland, had voted, it would still have won. It is not possible to compare exactly the winning margins in different years, but only 'Tom Pillibi' in 1960 could so far claim as easy a win. 'Puppet On A String' went on to conquer the charts all over Europe, and provide Sandie Shaw with the biggest hit of her career, as well as an obligation to sing the damned thing at every live performance – a situation that may have been a factor in her decision to drop out of music in the 1970s. The

VOTING BIAS

UNITED KINGDOM

Countries most likely to vote for the UK:
Austria
Switzerland
Luxembourg
France
Denmark

Countries least likely to vote for the UK:
Greece
Spain
Iceland
Cyprus
Italy

Countries for whom the UK is most likely to vote:
Switzerland
Germany
Belgium
Austria
Iceland

Countries for whom the UK is least likely to vote:
Italy
Spain
France
Portugal
Netherlands

Were it not for the Cod War, rowdy lager-swilling sunseekers and a certain Lord Elgin, the United Kingdom would have lifted the Eurovision trophy more times than even the Irish.

song also became a benchmark for Euro-pop for several years to come, and contests were infested with pale imitations of Bill Martin and Phil Coulter's original and very catchy tune, until Abba gave the whole competition a jolt in 1974.

Yet, as was becoming increasingly common, the song that was to prove the biggest worldwide hit of the year did not win the Contest. Seventeen-year-old Vicky Leandros, singing as just plain Vicky, and on behalf of Luxembourg rather than her native Greece, performed a song written by André Popp and Pierre Cour, the writers of the 1960 winner, 'Tom Pillibi'. The song was called 'L'Amour Est Bleu'/'Love Is Blue', and it finished a solid fourth. Ten months and two days later, in an instrumental version by the French orchestra leader Paul Mauriat, the song began a five-week stay at the top of the American charts; two weeks after that, no fewer than four different versions of the song – but not Vicky's – were in *Billboard*'s Hot 100.

Portugal tried an early example of political correctness in order to win. Its entry, 'O Vento Muduo'/'The Wind Has Changed' was sung by Eduardo Nascimento from Angola, to prove that Portugal's colonial policy was working well. The winds of change were indeed blowing through Africa, but not enough to enable Eduardo to become the first African to win Eurovision. He scored three points and finished equal twelfth.

The wind was not the only thing that kept changing. The set was a stage of revolving mirrors throwing up ever-changing images, which seemed to distract both the performers and the audience. They may well have distracted presenter Erica Vaal and the scoreboard operators as well, because the scrutineer Clifford Brown had to interrupt the voting more often than usual. Miss Vaal began her final speech congratulating the United Kingdom on its victory, even before she had allowed Ireland to vote. Not that it made any difference: the UK still won, without even breaking a sweat.

THE EUROVISION SONG CONTEST

1968

Won by Spain: 'La La La'

Written by Ramon Arcusa and Manuel de la Calva

Performed by Massiel

Orchestra conducted by Rafael Ibarbia

When Katie Boyle came on stage at the Royal Albert Hall in London to get the thirteenth Eurovision Song Contest under way, there was only one question viewers wanted to know the answer to – who would come second to the UK? The host nation's entry was 'Congratulations', written by the previous year's winning composers Bill Martin and Phil Coulter and sung by Europe's most popular singer, Cliff Richard. The song was already high in the charts all over Europe, and it was poised to top the charts in Britain, to give Cliff his ninth British

1968	Portugal	Netherlands	Belgium	Austria	Luxembourg	Switzerland	Monaco	Sweden	Finland	France	Italy	UK	Norway	Ireland	Spain	W. Germany	Yugoslavia	**Position**
Portugal	0^{x}	0^{0}	0^{0}	0^{0}	0^{0}	0^{0}	0^{0}	0^{0}	0^{0}	0^{0}	0^{0}	0^{0}	2^{2}	2^{0}	5^{3}	5^{0}	5^{0}	11=
Netherlands	0^{0}	0^{x}	0^{0}	0^{0}	0^{0}	0^{0}	0^{0}	0^{0}	0^{0}	0^{0}	1^{1}	1^{0}	1^{0}	1^{0}	1^{0}	1^{0}	1^{0}	16=
Belgium	1^{1}	1^{0}	1^{x}	1^{0}	2^{1}	2^{0}	2^{0}	2^{0}	3^{1}	4^{1}	7^{3}	8^{1}	8^{0}	8^{0}	8^{0}	8^{0}	8^{0}	7=
Austria	0^{0}	0^{0}	0^{0}	0^{x}	0^{0}	0^{0}	0^{0}	0^{0}	0^{0}	0^{0}	0^{0}	0^{0}	0^{0}	0^{0}	2^{2}	2^{0}	2^{0}	13=
Luxembourg	0^{0}	1^{1}	1^{0}	2^{1}	2^{x}	2^{0}	3^{1}	3^{0}	3^{0}	4^{1}	4^{0}	5^{1}	5^{0}	5^{0}	5^{0}	5^{0}	5^{0}	11=
Switzerland	0^{0}	0^{0}	0^{0}	0^{0}	0^{0}	0^{x}	0^{0}	0^{0}	0^{0}	0^{0}	0^{0}	0^{0}	0^{0}	0^{0}	0^{0}	0^{0}	2^{2}	13=
Monaco	0^{0}	2^{2}	2^{0}	2^{0}	3^{1}	3^{0}	3^{x}	3^{0}	6^{3}	6^{0}	6^{0}	7^{1}	7^{0}	8^{1}	8^{0}	8^{0}	8^{0}	7=
Sweden	1^{1}	2^{1}	2^{0}	2^{0}	2^{0}	2^{0}	2^{0}	2^{x}	3^{1}	3^{0}	3^{0}	5^{2}	11^{6}	15^{4}	15^{0}	15^{0}	15^{0}	5
Finland	0^{0}	0^{0}	0^{0}	0^{0}	0^{0}	0^{0}	0^{0}	0^{0}	0^{x}	0^{0}	0^{0}	0^{0}	1^{1}	1^{0}	1^{0}	1^{0}	1^{0}	16=
France	0^{0}	3^{3}	**9^{6}**	**11^{2}**	**14^{3}**	**17^{3}**	**17^{0}**	**18^{1}**	18^{0}	18^{x}	20^{2}	20^{0}	20^{0}	20^{0}	20^{0}	20^{0}	20^{0}	3
Italy	1^{1}	1^{0}	1^{0}	1^{0}	1^{0}	3^{2}	3^{0}	3^{0}	3^{0}	3^{0}	3^{x}	3^{0}	3^{0}	3^{0}	5^{2}	5^{0}	7^{2}	10
UK	1^{1}	3^{2}	5^{2}	5^{0}	6^{1}	10^{4}	15^{5}	**18^{3}**	**20^{2}**	**24^{4}**	**25^{1}**	**25^{x}**	**25^{0}**	**26^{1}**	**26^{0}**	28^{2}	28^{0}	2
Norway	0^{0}	0^{0}	0^{0}	0^{0}	1^{1}	1^{0}	1^{0}	1^{0}	1^{0}	1^{0}	1^{0}	1^{0}	1^{x}	1^{0}	2^{1}	2^{0}	2^{0}	13=
Ireland	1^{1}	2^{1}	3^{1}	7^{4}	8^{1}	8^{0}	8^{0}	12^{4}	12^{0}	12^{0}	12^{0}	12^{0}	12^{0}	12^{x}	12^{0}	12^{0}	18^{6}	4
Spain	**4^{4}**	**4^{0}**	4^{0}	6^{2}	7^{1}	7^{0}	11^{4}	11^{0}	14^{3}	18^{4}	21^{3}	21^{0}	22^{1}	23^{1}	23^{x}	**29^{6}**	**29^{0}**	**1**
W. Germany	0^{0}	0^{0}	0^{0}	0^{0}	1^{1}	2^{1}	2^{0}	4^{2}	4^{0}	4^{0}	4^{0}	9^{5}	9^{0}	9^{0}	11^{2}	11^{x}	11^{0}	6
Yugoslavia	1^{1}	1^{0}	2^{1}	3^{1}	3^{0}	3^{0}	3^{0}	3^{0}	3^{0}	3^{0}	3^{0}	3^{0}	3^{0}	6^{3}	6^{0}	8^{2}	8^{x}	7=

1968 EUROVISION SONG CONTEST

Host country: United Kingdom ★ *Venue:* Royal Albert Hall, London
Date: 6 April ★ *Presenter:* Katie Boyle
Voting structure: 10 jury members from each country, each of whom awarded 1 point to their favourite song
Total entries: 17 ★ *Debut countries:* None

Country	Performer	Song	Pts	Pos.
Portugal	Carlos Mendes	Verão	5	11
Netherlands	Ronnie Tober	Morgen	1	16
Belgium	Claude Lombard	Quand Tu Reviendras	8	7
Austria	Karel Gott	Tausend Fenster	2	13
Luxembourg	Chris Baldo and Sophie Garel	Nous Vivrons D'Amour	5	11
Switzerland	Gianni Mascolo	Guardando Il Sole	2	13
Monaco	Line and Willy	A Chacun Sa Chanson	8	7
Sweden	Claes-Göran Hederström	Det Börjar Verka Kärlek Banne Mej	15	5
Finland	Kristiina Hautala	Kun Kello Käy	1	16
France	Isabelle Aubret	La Source	20	3
Italy	Sergio Endrigo	Marianne	7	10
United Kingdom	Cliff Richard	Congratulations	28	2
Norway	Odd Børre	Stress	2	13
Ireland	Pat McGeegan	Chance Of A Lifetime	18	4
Spain	**Massiel**	**La La La**	**29**	**1**
Germany	Wencke Myhre	Ein Hoch Der Liebe	11	6
Yugoslavia	Luci Kapurso and Hamo Hajdarhodzic	Jedan Dan	8	7

number one by the end of the week. There were no other major names performing in the contest, apart from the 1962 winner Isabelle Aubret, so Cliff seemed to have a clear run.

The contest was the first to be broadcast in colour, a fact that Miss Boyle celebrated by wearing the largest diamond brooch seen east of Hollywood for many a year. She proudly announced that 'Two hundred million people could be watching tonight.' By the time the extraordinarily dreadful Portuguese entry had got things off to a conventional Eurobouncy start, the viewing figures were probably down to no more than 190 million. The curse of the early performers carried on (no winner had sung in the first six since André Claveau sang third in 1958, when there were only ten entries) and it was not until Claes-Göran Hederström sang a number for Sweden, involving the snapping of fingers and more than a little taste of Elvis Presley in 'Return To Sender' mode, that the audience began to sit up and take notice. He was singing eighth.

It was a very masculine Contest, with only five of the seventeen entries sung by solo women.

Finland's Kristiina Hautala came last equal with a big up tempo love song with Ossi Runne's baton leading the orchestra to a frenzy, but the other four came first, third, sixth and seventh, which shows that the Eurovision juries like the ladies even when they are few and far between. Three of them wore minidresses, but Belgium's Claude Lombard wore a long purple skirt and her long blonde hair in the style of Mary Travers of Peter, Paul and Mary. Isabelle Aubret's attempt to win for a second time was undertaken in a long blue evening dress. Her song was a wordy and very French song: nobody could ever accuse the French entries over the years of betraying their roots, but that does not always make for victory. Their 1968 efforts ended in honourable defeat – a third place for Isabelle six years after she won in Luxembourg. The other girls – for girls they were – wore minis in lime green (Finland), pink (Spain) and yellow (Germany).

Cliff Richard, singing twelfth out of seventeen, came on in ruffles and a blue suit to a welter of screams and great expectations. He did not let anybody down, moving around the stage with a hand-held mike and giving the song his all. The screams never stopped and the applause at the end was exceptional. It looked to be in the bag – even more so when Norway's Odd Børre followed Cliff with a song entitled 'Stress', which involved him looking at his watch and singing lyrics such as 'Ma Ma Ma Ma', 'Bra Bra Bra Bra' and 'Wem Wem Wem Wem', which made almost any other song ever submitted for Eurovision sound intelligent. Ireland presented a gentle ballad in Val Doonican mode, performed by Pat McGeegan, who gained greater fame in later years as the father of world champion boxer Barry McGuigan. It was Pat who sang 'Danny Boy' in the ring before his son's fights, but his performance in Eurovision was not quite enough to knock out all other opposition.

That was left to Maria de los Angeles Santamaria, known as Massiel, who thrust 'La La La' into the eardrums of the world. She was not even the original singer chosen to perform the song, but a late substitute for Joan Manuel Serrat, who was dropped from the competition when he insisted on singing in Catalan. This seems rather an unnecessary stand to make, as presumably 'La La La' sounds very much the same in whatever language it is sung (although the song was subsequently translated into English as 'He Gives Me Love'). This was proved by the very next entry, 'Ein Hoch Der Liebe', the lyrics for which included the Euro-friendly 'Vive l'amour, three cheers for love, viva l'amor', and the chorus of which was based entirely around those well-used syllables, 'la la la'.

Yugoslavia proved its ability to be original, even at the expense of votes, by bringing on two men in medieval doublets and what looked like waders, singing 'Jedan Dan', yet another alliterative singalong number with a martial beat that failed to win much sympathy.

The voting was bizarre. France took an early lead, but then virtually stopped gaining any points at all after the sixth jury had voted, giving the UK the chance to surge into the lead. Spain was always picking up a few points, but those who claimed the next day that tactical voting had spoilt the UK's chances had little real evidence for their views. France, which finished third, gave four votes each to Britain and Spain, while neither the UK nor Spain awarded each other any votes at all. With two rounds to go, Cliff was well ahead, but six votes for Spain from Germany (which also gave two to the UK) turned it around. This after the UK had given Germany five votes – Spain only gave them two. The final jury, from Yugoslavia, awarded six votes to Pat McGeegan, two to Italy and originally three to Switzerland. When it was pointed out that this made eleven votes for ten jurors, it reduced Switzerland's tally by one. But it still gave none to either of the two leaders.

So there it was. Massiel won by one vote, and the hot favourites were beaten.

THE EUROVISION SONG CONTEST

1969

A four-way tie between

Spain: 'Vivo Cantando'
Written by Maria José De Cerato and Aniano Alcalde, performed by Salomé
Orchestra conducted by Augusto Alguero

Netherlands: 'De Troubadour'
Written by David Hartsema and Lenny Kuhr, performed by Lenny Kuhr
Orchestra conducted by Franz de Kok

United Kingdom: 'Boom Bang-A-Bang'
Written by Alan Moorhouse and Peter Warne, performed by Lulu
Orchestra conducted by Johnny Harris

France: 'Un Jour, Un Enfant'
Written by Emile Stern and Eddy Marnay
Performed by Frida Boccara
Orchestra conducted by Franck Pourcel

The only Eurovision Song Contest that has not had a single winner was the 1969 event, which resulted in a four-way tie. As there was no mechanism for sorting out one winner in the event of the scores being level, the EBU scrutineer Clifford Brown had to shrug his shoulders and

1969	Yugoslavia	Luxembourg	Spain	Monaco	Ireland	Italy	UK	Netherlands	Sweden	Belgium	Switzerland	Norway	W. Germany	France	Portugal	Finland	**Position**
Yugoslavia	0^x	0^0	1^1	1^0	1^0	1^0	1^0	1^0	1^0	2^1	2^0	2^0	2^0	2^0	5^3	5^0	13=
Luxembourg	1^1	1^x	1^0	4^3	4^0	4^0	4^0	5^1	5^0	6^1	6^0	6^0	7^1	7^0	7^0	7^0	11
Spain	1^1	3^2	3^x	**6^3**	**7^1**	7^0	7^0	7^0	7^0	10^3	10^0	11^1	14^3	16^2	**18^2**	**18^0**	**1=**
Monaco	0^0	0^0	2^2	2^x	2^0	6^4	6^0	8^2	10^2	11^1	11^0	11^0	11^0	11^0	11^0	11^0	6
Ireland	0^0	0^0	0^0	0^0	0^x	0^0	1^1	2^1	3^1	3^0	6^3	6^0	7^1	7^0	7^0	10^3	7=
Italy	1^1	1^0	1^0	2^1	3^1	3^x	3^0	3^0	3^0	3^0	3^0	3^0	3^0	3^0	4^1	5^1	13=
UK	2^2	**6^4**	**6^0**	**6^0**	6^0	**9^3**	9^x	10^1	**15^5**	**15^0**	**15^0**	**15^0**	**16^1**	16^0	17^1	**18^1**	**1=**
Netherlands	0^0	2^2	2^0	3^1	3^0	6^3	6^0	6^x	6^0	7^1	11^4	12^1	12^0	**18^6**	**18^0**	**18^0**	**1=**
Sweden	0^0	0^0	0^0	0^0	0^0	0^0	0^0	1^1	1^x	1^0	1^0	4^3	4^0	4^0	5^1	8^3	9=
Belgium	0^0	0^0	2^2	2^0	2^0	2^0	5^3	6^1	6^0	6^x	8^2	10^2	10^0	10^0	10^0	10^0	7=
Switzerland	2^2	2^0	2^0	2^0	5^3	5^0	7^2	7^0	7^0	8^1	8^x	9^1	11^2	11^0	11^0	13^2	5
Norway	0^0	0^0	0^0	0^0	0^0	0^0	0^0	0^0	1^1	1^0	1^0	1^x	1^0	1^0	1^0	1^0	16
W. Germany	**3^3**	3^0	5^2	5^0	5^0	5^0	5^0	5^0	5^0	6^1	6^0	7^1	7^x	8^1	8^0	8^0	9=
France	0^0	1^1	1^0	3^2	**7^4**	7^0	**11^4**	**13^2**	14^1	14^0	**15^1**	**15^0**	**16^1**	16^x	**18^2**	**18^0**	**1=**
Portugal	0^0	0^0	2^2	2^0	2^0	2^0	2^0	2^0	2^0	3^1	3^0	3^0	3^0	4^1	4^x	4^0	15
Finland	0^0	1^1	2^1	2^0	3^1	3^0	3^0	4^1	4^0	4^0	4^0	5^1	6^1	6^0	6^0	6^x	12

★ ★

1969 EUROVISION SONG CONTEST

Host country: Spain ★ *Venue:* Teatro Real, Madrid
Date: 29 March ★ *Presenter:* Laurita Valenzuela
Voting structure: 10 jury members from each country, each of whom awarded 1 point to their favourite song
Total entries: 16 ★ *Debut countries:* None

Country	Performer	Song	Pts	Pos.
Yugoslavia	Ivan	Pozdrav Svijetu	5	13
Luxembourg	Romuald	Cathérine	7	11
Spain	**Salomé**	**Vivo Cantando**	**18**	**1**
Monaco	Jean-Jacques	Maman Maman	11	6
Ireland	Muriel Day and the Lindsays	The Wages Of Love	10	7
Italy	Iva Zanicchi	Due Grosse Lacrime Bianche	5	13
United Kingdom	**Lulu**	**Boom Bang-A-Bang**	**18**	**1**
Netherlands	**Lenny Kuhr**	**De Troubadour**	**18**	**1**
Sweden	Tommy Korberg	Judy Min Vaen	8	9
Belgium	Louis Neefs	Jennifer Jennings	10	7
Switzerland	Paola	Bonjour Bonjour	13	5
Norway	Kirsti Sparboe	Oj, Oj, Oj, Så Glad Jeg Skal Bli	1	16
Germany	Siw Malmqvist	Prima Ballerina	8	9
France	**Frida Boccara**	**Un Jour, Un Enfant**	**18**	**1**
Portugal	Simone de Oliveira	Desfolhada	4	15
Finland	Jarkko and Laura	Kuin Silloin Ennen	6	12

confirm that, this year, there were four winners of the Contest.

There was one less entrant than the year before because of the refusal of Austria to participate in a Contest held in Franco's Spain, but even if they had competed, it is unlikely there would have been a major change to the result, as the UK, France and Netherlands are all countries for whom Austria historically likes to vote. It had even given Spain two votes the year before, which had been enough to bring the Contest to Madrid.

It was not the scoring system itself that produced the result, although the small number of total points available at that time was always more likely to give a hung result than the higher scoring system now used. The main reason for the four-way tie was that there was no outstanding song on show. The majority of the songs (ten out of the sixteen) were sung by female soloists, while one more was by a male/female duo and another by a boy soprano, Jean-Jacques of Monaco. Several songs were in the 'Puppet On A String' Euro-pop mould, and several more dealt with themes from the mainstream of Eurovision – multilanguage (Yugoslavia, Switzerland), family values (Monaco) and the 'la la la' chorus

VOTING BIAS

NETHERLANDS

Countries most likely to vote for the Netherlands:

France
Israel
Ireland
Germany
Turkey

Countries least likely to vote for the Netherlands:

Belgium
Finland
Portugal
Denmark
UK

Countries for whom the Netherlands is most likely to vote:

France
Belgium
Israel
Switzerland
Norway

Countries for whom the Netherlands is least likely to vote:

Italy
Spain
Austria
Germany
Yugoslavia

The Dutch have a liking for the French tongue. Not only do they generally support France, they also prefer Belgian entries sung in French rather than Flemish, which is virtually the same language as Dutch.

(Netherlands, Portugal). Only France's big emotional ballad in the Piaf mould seemed different, but even that was very much part of the French tradition. Lenny Kuhr for the Netherlands wore her hair long and severe and carried an acoustic guitar, and Jarkko of Finland wore a straw boater. Otherwise, we were in a sea of stridently coloured miniskirts and trouser suits and carefully piled up hair. With no outstanding song and no outstanding performance it was not really surprising that the voting reflected the weakness of the field. Lulu's 'Boom Bang-A-Bang' has almost become shorthand for the worst of Eurovision, but the song is not as dreadful as legend would have it. It gets a simple message across effectively, which is usually the secret of a successful Eurovision song. It was chosen to represent the UK ahead of, among others, 'I've Been Loving You Too Long' written by Elton John and Bernie Taupin, who were then just beginning their writing partnership.

Spain and France both received votes from nine juries, while the UK was voted for by eight and the Netherlands by only seven. But the biggest single score was the six votes given to the Netherlands by France, and the next biggest was Sweden's five points for the UK. If we exclude the votes given by the four winning countries' juries to each other, then the UK would have won with seventeen votes, with Spain second on sixteen, but that is not a logical way of trying to find a winner. Each of the four winners received the outright top vote from two other juries, so finding a suitable mechanism for picking a single winner would have been difficult, even if the organizers had thought about it beforehand.

The worst thing about the four-way tie was the fact that the audience, both in the Royal Theatre and across Europe, had to listen to all four songs being reprised. In order to avoid such a dreadful thing happening again, the EBU put their minds to finding a better scoring system. It was 1975 before a reliable system was finally settled upon.

*◀ **1956** LYS ASSIA won for the host country under curious circumstances, but she had a victory coming. She had originated the song 'Oh Mein Papa', but Eddie Calvert heard it on his car radio, recorded it and had the international smash.*

*▲ **1959** TEDDY SCHOLTEN holds the medal she was presented for her victory. The Netherlands' triumph marked the first time a country had won the Contest twice.*

*◀ **1960** Forget about Teddy Scholten's medal, JACQUELINE BOYER has what hostess Katie Boyle called 'a silver gilt vase' to embrace. Katie returned to the Contest; Jacqueline did not.*

▲ ***1962*** *Isabelle Aubret gave France its third triumph in five years. She is shown just prior to the 1968 competition, in which she fared less well and was placed third.*

◀ ***1961*** *Luxembourg has won the Eurovision Song Contest five times, a performance wildly disproportionate to its population. This is thanks in large measure to being represented by foreign stars like the Frenchman Jean-Claude Pascal, who sang its first winning entry.*

▶ ***1963*** *Ester Ofarim (centre) for Switzerland looks as if she actually doesn't mind that Grethe and Jorgen Ingmann (right) have deprived her of victory at the very last moment. Emilio Pericoli (left) is still smiling at the thought of his 1.3 million sales of 1961's 'Al Di La'.*

▲ *1963 The internationally minded Greek star* NANA MOUSKOURI *represented Luxembourg and contributed to that year's UN compilation* All-Star Festival.

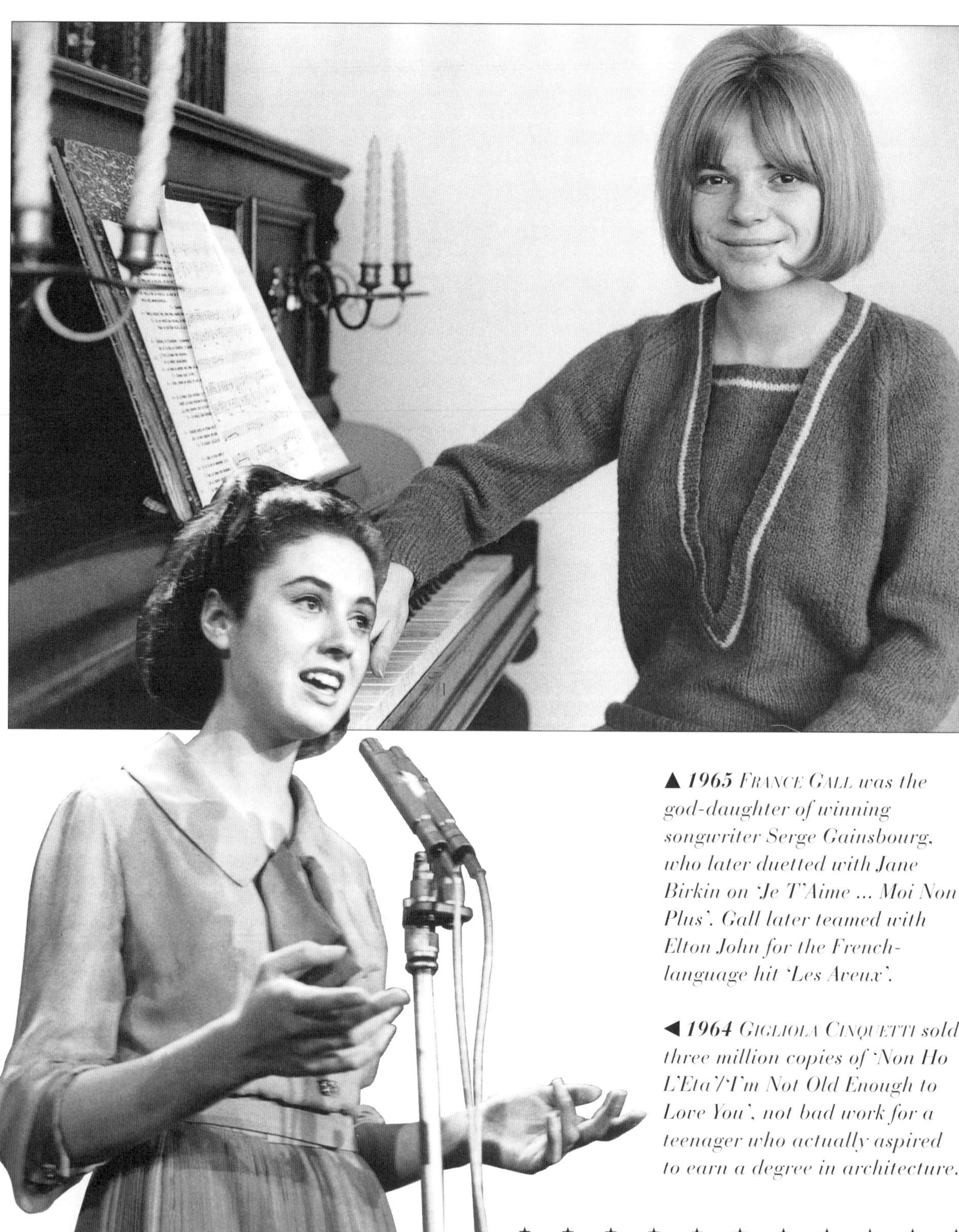

▲ *1965* *France Gall was the god-daughter of winning songwriter Serge Gainsbourg, who later duetted with Jane Birkin on 'Je T'Aime ... Moi Non Plus'. Gall later teamed with Elton John for the French-language hit 'Les Aveux'.*

◀ *1964* *Gigliola Cinquetti sold three million copies of 'Non Ho L'Eta'/'I'm Not Old Enough to Love You', not bad work for a teenager who actually aspired to earn a degree in architecture.*

▶ ***1966*** *UDO JÜRGENS came in sixth, then fourth, then first in his three successive appearances for Austria. The following year he retired from the competition. His country scored only two points and never won again.*

▼ ***1967*** *The winning song 'Puppet On A String', penned by (from left) Phil Coulter and Bill Martin, was chosen to represent Britain by viewers of a BBC television show hosted by Rolf Harris (right). Performer SANDIE SHAW gazes at the gold.*

▲ *1968* CLIFF RICHARD *sings 'Congratulations', the favourite going into the Contest and the favourite after it, outdistancing all other entries with over a million sales. It finished second on the night.*

► *1968 'La La La' means 'La La La' in any language, and a Eurovision victory for* MASSIEL *(Maria de los Angeles Santamaria), who was never ahead until the penultimate jury voted.*

▲ *1970 A young* JULIO IGLESIAS, *looking as if he had borrowed the frills from Cliff Richard's 1968 costume, gave little indication that within a decade he would be the non-English-speaking world's best-selling male vocalist.*

◀ *1969 Defending champion Spain retained the crown with 'Vivo Cantando' as sung by* SALOMÉ, *but had to share it with three other countries. When the Eurovision Song Contest ends in a tie, it does so in a big way.*

▶ *1969* LULU *shared a number one with Take That in 1993 and Eurovision title in 1969.*

▲ ***1972*** *Greece has never won the Contest, but the Greek songstress* VICKY LEANDROS *did succeed singing for Luxembourg.*

▶ ***1975*** *The 1974 winner 'Waterloo' by Abba sold over five million copies, and the 1975 victor 'Ding Dinge Dong' by* TEACH-IN *did not, and that is the way of the world.*

▼ ***1974*** ABBA *chose Eurovision as the platform on which they would break out of Sweden. They were joined after their triumph by conductor Sven-Olof Walldoff, dressed as Napoleon, and 'Waterloo' co-author Stig Anderson.*

THE EUROVISION SONG CONTEST

1970

Won by Ireland: 'All Kinds Of Everything'
Written by Derry Lindsay and Jackie Smith
Performed by Dana
Orchestra conducted by Dolf van der Linden

After the shambles of the 1969 voting, there was a lot of credibility to be won back by the organizers of Eurovision. The Netherlands, one of the four winners from the year before, agreed to act as hosts, bringing the contest back to Holland for the first time since 1958. But only twelve countries entered, the Scandinavian bloc of Norway, Sweden and Finland having decided not to enter, along with Portugal. As these four countries had gained only nineteen points between them in 1969, it was perhaps not such a great cultural blow as it was a political one. With only a dozen songs battling for supremacy, would the Contest be seen as worth carrying on?

In the event, the show was saved by the winning entry, 'All Kinds Of Everything', which gave Ireland the first of its seven wins to date, launched the career of its performer Dana and became a massive hit all across Europe. Belfast-born Dana was at the time described as 'an ordinary eighteen-year-old Irish girl with an extraordinarily pure voice', a description that (apart from the details of nationality and age) could have applied to at least three other entrants.

1970	Netherlands	Switzerland	Itlay	Yugoslavia	Belgium	France	UK	Luxembourg	Spain	Monaco	W. Germany	Ireland	**Position**
Netherlands	0^{x}	0^{0}	3^{3}	6^{3}	6^{0}	6^{0}	7^{1}	7^{0}	7^{0}	7^{0}	7^{0}	7^{0}	7
Switzerland	2^{2}	2^{x}	2^{0}	2^{0}	2^{0}	4^{2}	5^{1}	5^{0}	5^{0}	5^{0}	7^{2}	8^{1}	4$^{=}$
Italy	0^{0}	0^{0}	0^{x}	1^{1}	1^{0}	1^{0}	1^{0}	1^{0}	3^{2}	3^{0}	5^{2}	5^{0}	8$^{=}$
Yugoslavia	0^{0}	0^{0}	0^{0}	0^{x}	0^{0}	0^{0}	4^{4}	4^{0}	4^{0}	4^{0}	4^{0}	4^{0}	11
Belgium	0^{0}	0^{0}	0^{0}	0^{0}	0^{x}	3^{3}	3^{0}	4^{1}	4^{0}	4^{0}	4^{0}	5^{1}	8$^{=}$
France	0^{0}	0^{0}	1^{1}	3^{2}	3^{0}	3^{x}	3^{0}	3^{0}	3^{0}	5^{2}	5^{0}	8^{3}	4$^{=}$
UK	3^{3}	5^{2}	7^{2}	**11^{4}**	11^{0}	13^{2}	13^{x}	15^{2}	15^{0}	19^{4}	23^{4}	26^{3}	2
Luxembourg	0^{0}	0^{0}	0^{0}	0^{0}	0^{0}	0^{0}	0^{0}	0^{x}	0^{0}	0^{0}	0^{0}	0^{0}	12
Spain	0^{0}	0^{0}	3^{3}	3^{0}	3^{0}	3^{0}	3^{0}	5^{2}	5^{x}	8^{3}	8^{0}	8^{0}	4$^{=}$
Monaco	0^{0}	1^{1}	1^{0}	1^{0}	2^{1}	4^{2}	4^{0}	4^{0}	5^{1}	5^{x}	5^{0}	5^{0}	8$^{=}$
W. Germany	0^{0}	1^{1}	2^{1}	2^{0}	2^{0}	2^{0}	2^{0}	5^{3}	9^{4}	10^{1}	10^{x}	12^{2}	3
Ireland	**5^{5}**	**11^{6}**	**11^{0}**	**11^{0}**	**20^{9}**	**21^{1}**	**25^{4}**	**27^{2}**	**30^{3}**	**30^{0}**	**32^{2}**	**32^{x}**	**1**

1970 EUROVISION SONG CONTEST

Host country: Netherlands ★ *Venue:* Rai Congrescentrum, Amsterdam
Date: 21 March ★ *Presenter:* Willy Dobbe
Voting structure: 10 jury members from each country, each of whom awarded 1 point to their favourite song
Total entries: 12 ★ *Debut countries:* None

COUNTRY	PERFORMER	SONG	PTS	POS.
Netherlands	Patricia and Hearts of Soul	Waterman	7	7
Switzerland	Henri Dès	Retour	8	4
Italy	Gianni Morandi	Occhi Di Ragazza	5	8
Yugoslavia	Eva Srsen	Pridi, Dala Ti Bom Cvet	4	11
Belgium	Jean Vallée	Viens L'Oublier	5	8
France	Guy Bonnet	Marie Blanche	8	4
United Kingdom	Mary Hopkin	Knock Knock – Who's There?	26	2
Luxembourg	David Alexandre Winter	Je Suis Tombé Du Ciel	0	12
Spain	Julio Iglesias	Gwendolyne	8	4
Monaco	Dominique Dussault	Marlène	5	8
Germany	Katja Ebstein	Wunder Gibt Es Immer Wieder	12	3
Ireland	**Dana**	**All Kinds Of Everything**	**32**	**1**

Eva Srsen, representing Yugoslavia, was also eighteen, although her voice was not as reliable as Dana's, while Monaco's Dominique Dussault was just sixteen. The United Kingdom had turned to the ordinary twenty-year-old Welsh girl with an extraordinarily pure voice, Mary Hopkin, who a year before had stormed the world's charts with her first single, 'Those Were The Days'. She was to prove Dana's only serious challenger.

The men in the show included a young Julio Iglesias, performing for Spain a song he had helped to write, which gave a clear indication of the vocal style that was to captivate the whole world a few years later, but his electric-blue suit (contrasting with backing singers in pink trouser suits) did nothing for his reputation as a fashion guru. His song, 'Gwendolyne' had a few of the obligatory 'la la la's in the chorus (la la la's that two years before had won for Spain), but was not strong enough to make him a serious contender.

Mary Hopkin was the pre-Contest favourite, but Dana took a commanding lead from the start. After big points scores from the host country and from Switzerland, Ireland saw its lead eroded by solid appreciation for 'Knock Knock – Who's There' until Belgium, voting fifth, gave nine of its ten votes to Dana, the highest ever score given to one song under this voting system. After that it was all a formality. The next year, Norway, Sweden, Finland and Portugal all returned to the fold, along with Austria, which had last appeared in 1968, and Malta, which entered for the first time. The Eurovision Song Contest was back on the rails.

RUNAWAY VICTORIES

THIS TABLE LISTS THE TEN MOST OVERWHELMING VICTORIES IN THE HISTORY OF THE CONTEST.

Year	Position	Country	Song	Performer	No. of votes	% lead
1964	**1st**	**Italy**	**Non Ho L'Eta**	**Gigliola Cinquetti**	**49**	**65.3%**
	2nd	UK	I Love The Little Things	Matt Monro	17	
1967	**1st**	**UK**	**Puppet On A String**	**Sandie Shaw**	**47**	**53.2%**
	2nd	Ireland	If I Could Choose	Sean Dunphy	22	
1962	**1st**	**France**	**Un Premier Amour**	**Isabelle Aubret**	**26**	**50.0%**
	2nd	Monaco	Dis Rien	François Deguelt	13	
1966	**1st**	**Austria**	**Merci Chérie**	**Udo Jürgens**	**31**	**48.4%**
	2nd	Sweden	Nygammal Vals	Lill Lindfors and Svante Thuresson	16	
1957	**1st**	**Netherlands**	**Net Als Toen**	**Corry Brokken**	**31**	**45.2%**
	2nd	France	La Belle Amour	Paule Desjardins	17	
1982	**1st**	**Germany**	**Ein Bisschen Frieden**	**Nicole**	**161**	**37.9%**
	2nd	Israel	Hora	Avi Toledano	100	
1997	**1st**	**UK**	**Love Shine A Light**	**Katrina and the Waves**	**227**	**30.8%**
	2nd	Ireland	Mysterious Woman	Marc Roberts	157	
1996	**1st**	**Ireland**	**The Voice**	**Eimear Quinn**	**162**	**29.6%**
	2nd	Norway	I Evighet	Elisabeth Andreassen	114	
1994	**1st**	**Ireland**	**Rock 'N' Roll Kids**	**Paul Harrington with Charlie McGettigan**	**226**	**26.6%**
	2nd	Poland	To Nie Ja!	Edyta Gorniak	166	
1974	**1st**	**Sweden**	**Waterloo**	**Abba**	**24**	**25.0%**
	2nd	Italy	Si	Gigliola Cinquetti	18	

Eurovision's most successful song, 'Save Your Kisses For Me' by Brotherhood of Man, scored 164 points in 1976, but it led the second-placed song, Catherine Ferry's 'Un, Deux, Trois' (147 points), by a mere 10.4per cent. Monaco's 'Toi, La Musique Et Moi' by Mary Cristy was in third place with 93 points, 36.7per cent behind Ms Ferry.

THE EUROVISION SONG CONTEST

1971

Won by Monaco: 'Un Banc, Un Arbre, Une Rue'

Written by Jean-Pierre Bourtayre and Yves Dessca

Performed by Sèverine

Orchestra conducted by Jean-Claude Petit

The 1971 Eurovision Song Contest, held in Dublin for the first time, featured several interesting changes. It was the first Contest to be introduced in Gaelic, with a long prologue by Bernadette Ni Gallchoir – dressed all in green, of course – in the local language before she lapsed into English and French, the two official languages of the Contest. It was also the first Contest to feature Irish folk dancing, which was to become such a feature two decades later. In 1971,

1971	Austria	Malta	Monaco	Switzerland	W. Germany	Spain	France	Luxembourg	UK	Belgium	Italy	Sweden	Ireland	Netherlands	Portugal	Yugoslavia	Finland	Norway	**Position**
Austria	0^{x}	3^{3}	8^{5}	10^{2}	17^{7}	19^{2}	22^{3}	24^{2}	27^{3}	30^{3}	36^{6}	40^{4}	46^{6}	49^{3}	54^{5}	58^{4}	61^{3}	66^{5}	16
Malta	4^{4}	4^{x}	6^{2}	8^{2}	11^{3}	16^{5}	19^{3}	21^{2}	24^{3}	28^{4}	32^{4}	34^{2}	38^{4}	43^{5}	45^{2}	47^{2}	50^{3}	52^{2}	18
Monaco	4^{4}	9^{5}	9^{x}	19^{10}	29^{10}	31^{2}	39^{8}	43^{4}	51^{8}	**61^{10}**	**65^{4}**	**75^{10}**	**84^{9}**	**93^{9}**	**101^{8}**	**111^{10}**	**118^{7}**	**128^{10}**	**1**
Switzerland	5^{5}	10^{5}	14^{4}	14^{x}	20^{6}	22^{2}	28^{6}	30^{2}	36^{6}	39^{3}	46^{7}	50^{4}	55^{5}	60^{5}	66^{6}	70^{4}	74^{4}	78^{4}	12
W. Germany	6^{6}	11^{5}	18^{7}	24^{6}	24^{x}	32^{8}	40^{8}	42^{2}	48^{6}	55^{7}	61^{6}	67^{6}	72^{5}	77^{5}	84^{7}	91^{7}	96^{5}	100^{4}	3
Spain	4^{4}	12^{4}	**22^{10}**	**27^{5}**	**34^{7}**	34^{x}	44^{10}	48^{4}	55^{7}	59^{4}	64^{5}	70^{6}	79^{9}	85^{6}	92^{7}	99^{7}	108^{9}	116^{8}	2
France	3^{3}	5^{2}	13^{8}	21^{8}	26^{5}	31^{5}	31^{x}	33^{2}	38^{5}	41^{3}	45^{4}	49^{4}	55^{6}	64^{9}	69^{5}	74^{5}	77^{3}	82^{5}	10
Luxembourg	2^{2}	9^{7}	15^{6}	18^{3}	20^{2}	24^{4}	29^{5}	29^{x}	35^{6}	38^{3}	41^{3}	43^{2}	48^{5}	51^{3}	57^{6}	61^{4}	66^{5}	70^{4}	13
UK	4^{4}	12^{8}	20^{8}	26^{6}	31^{5}	33^{2}	41^{8}	45^{4}	45^{x}	53^{8}	56^{3}	61^{5}	68^{7}	73^{5}	80^{7}	86^{6}	92^{6}	98^{6}	4
Belgium	3^{3}	5^{2}	10^{5}	14^{4}	16^{2}	18^{2}	23^{5}	25^{2}	31^{6}	31^{x}	34^{3}	39^{5}	43^{4}	49^{6}	55^{6}	58^{3}	64^{6}	68^{4}	14=
Italy	4^{4}	10^{6}	19^{9}	27^{8}	33^{6}	**39^{6}**	**48^{9}**	**50^{2}**	**56^{6}**	58^{2}	58^{x}	65^{7}	71^{6}	73^{2}	76^{3}	84^{8}	86^{2}	91^{5}	5
Sweden	**7^{7}**	11^{4}	15^{4}	24^{9}	28^{4}	30^{2}	35^{5}	37^{2}	42^{5}	48^{6}	54^{6}	54^{x}	57^{3}	66^{9}	69^{3}	75^{6}	79^{4}	85^{6}	6=
Ireland	7^{7}	**13^{6}**	19^{6}	22^{3}	26^{4}	31^{5}	38^{7}	40^{2}	46^{6}	49^{3}	55^{6}	57^{2}	57^{x}	62^{5}	66^{4}	71^{5}	75^{4}	79^{4}	11
Netherlands	6^{6}	8^{2}	14^{6}	19^{5}	23^{4}	28^{5}	35^{7}	37^{2}	42^{5}	44^{2}	46^{2}	52^{6}	57^{5}	57^{x}	66^{9}	71^{5}	77^{6}	85^{8}	6=
Portugal	4^{4}	7^{3}	13^{6}	15^{2}	20^{5}	30^{10}	38^{8}	43^{5}	49^{6}	53^{4}	57^{4}	59^{2}	62^{3}	67^{5}	67^{x}	73^{6}	78^{5}	83^{5}	9
Yugoslavia	6^{6}	8^{2}	12^{4}	14^{2}	21^{7}	27^{6}	33^{6}	35^{2}	38^{3}	40^{2}	45^{5}	47^{2}	52^{5}	56^{4}	60^{4}	60^{x}	63^{3}	68^{5}	14=
Finland	4^{4}	8^{4}	12^{4}	16^{4}	20^{4}	23^{3}	27^{4}	29^{2}	39^{10}	49^{10}	51^{2}	55^{4}	61^{6}	64^{3}	72^{8}	78^{6}	78^{x}	84^{6}	8
Norway	3^{3}	6^{3}	12^{6}	16^{4}	18^{2}	20^{2}	25^{5}	27^{2}	34^{7}	40^{6}	42^{2}	44^{2}	51^{7}	53^{2}	58^{5}	62^{4}	65^{3}	65^{x}	17

★ ★

1971 EUROVISION SONG CONTEST

Host country: Ireland ★ *Venue:* Gaiety Theatre, Dublin
Date: 3 April ★ *Presenter:* Bernadette Ni Gallchoir
Voting structure: Each nation had 2 jury members, one under and one over 25, who awarded between 1 and 5 points to each song
Total entries: 18 ★ *Debut countries:* Malta

Country	Performer	Song	Pts	Pos.
Austria	Marianne Mendt	Musik	66	16
Malta	Joe Grech	Marija L-Maltija	52	18
Monaco	**Sèverine**	**Un Banc, Un Arbre, Une Rue**	**128**	**1**
Switzerland	Peter, Sue and Marc	Les Illusions De Nos Vingt Ans	78	12
Germany	Katja Ebstein	Diese Welt	100	3
Spain	Karina	En Un Mundo Nuevo	116	2
France	Serge Lama	Un Jardin Sur La Terre	82	10
Luxembourg	Monique Melsen	Pomme, Pomme, Pomme	70	13
United Kingdom	Clodagh Rodgers	Jack In The Box	98	4
Belgium	Lily Castel and Jacques Raymond	Goeie Morgen, Morgen	68	14
Italy	Massimo Ranieri	L'Amore E Un Attimo	91	5
Sweden	Family Four	Vita Vidder	85	6
Ireland	Angela Farrell	One Day Love	79	11
Netherlands	Saskia and Serge	De Tijd	85	6
Portugal	Tonicha	Menina	83	9
Yugoslavia	Krunoslav Slabinac	Tvoj Djecak Je Tuzan	68	14
Finland	Markku Aro and the Koivisto Sisters	Tie Uuteen Päivään	84	8
Norway	Hanne Krogh	Lykken Er ...	65	17

this was merely a brief display by the Shannon Castle Entertainers, who kept the screens busy while the votes were being worked out.

Another major change was to the voting system. There had been problems with the old system, which had created the four-way split decision in 1969, but they were not solved by the new methods decided upon by the Contest organizers, using a logic that can only be guessed at. The one problem that *was* overcome was that of unreliable telecommunications around Europe: the jurors were all brought to Ireland to take part in the voting, rather than having to rely on crackly telephone lines. However, everything else about the system served only to compound the problems. It was the good fortune of Eurovision that for the first two years this system was tried, there were very clear-cut winners, who would have won under any system, but when the 1973 result came so close, the cracks quickly appeared.

It was decided for 1971 that each country would have just two jurors, one over the age of

VOTING BIAS

MALTA

Countries most likely to vote for Malta:
Croatia
Turkey
Ireland
Bosnia
Spain

Countries least likely to vote for Malta:
Iceland
Finland
Israel
Cyprus
Hungary

Countries for whom Malta is most likely to vote:
Turkey
Slovakia
Spain
Luxembourg
Greece

Countries for whom Malta is least likely to vote:
France
Sweden
Norway
Portugal
UK

Malta champions the underdog more than any other nation and gives an average of just five marks to each year's winner. Either that or it votes tactically, to give its own song a better chance of winning.

twenty-five and one under. There was no stipulation about whether or not they had to be interested in music, or very much over or under twenty-five, or whether they should be male or female. The only qualification seemed to be a free weekend in their diaries early in April. Each juror was then asked to allocate a score between one and five to every song. They were not allowed to allocate no points, and although they had seventeen songs from other nations to vote for, they could not give more than a maximum of five points to any one song. The Contest organizers were in effect asking them not to rank the songs in order of preference, but to give them some kind of absolute score, like Dudley Moore rating Bo Derek as a '10'. To make matters worse, the marks were taken away for checking by the team of scrutineers as the Contest went along, so that a voter who had given an early song a five, for example, could not change their mind when a better song came along later in the programme. That vote had already been cast. Eurovision songs simply cannot stand up to that sort of scrutiny.

One effect of this system was that France, for example, gave 107 points out at an average of 6.3 per song, while Luxembourg awarded only 42 points. As the minimum they could have given was thirty-four (two points to each song other than their own nation's), the reality was that Luxembourg's judges considered only four songs to be above the lowest possible rank. For the record, these four were Monaco, Spain, UK and lastly Portugal, to whom they gave their most generous mark of the night, a whole five points.

Monaco's Sèverine had a very strong song, and she sang it powerfully. Spain and Germany came a fairly distant second and third, while almost at the rear were Lily Castel and Jacques Raymond for Belgium. They were only there as very late replacements for Nicole and Hugo, who had to drop out when Nicole developed jaundice. Nicole and Hugo did get their chance two years later when they came a resounding last.

★ ★

THE EUROVISION SONG CONTEST

1972

Won by Luxembourg: 'Après Toi'

Written by Mario Panas, Klaus Monro and Yves Dessca

Performed by Vicky Leandros

Orchestra conducted by Klaus Monro

There were no fewer than six male/female vocal duos in the 1972 Contest, but only one of them, Sandra and Andres from the Netherlands, gave Greek-born Hamburg resident Vicky Leandros a run for her, or rather Luxembourg's, money. In the entire history of the contest, only two duos have ever won, and neither of those were the stereotypical blending of male and female voices in beautiful harmony. One was a duet of two Irishmen with pianos, Paul

1972	W. Germany	France	Ireland	Spain	UK	Norway	Portugal	Switzerland	Malta	Finland	Austria	Italy	Yugoslavia	Sweden	Monaco	Belgium	Luxembourg	Netherlands	**Position**
W. Germany	0^{x}	8^{8}	14^{6}	23^{9}	28^{5}	34^{6}	40^{6}	45^{5}	49^{4}	54^{5}	59^{5}	66^{7}	71^{5}	79^{8}	87^{8}	94^{7}	101^{7}	107^{6}	3
France	5^{5}	5^{x}	10^{5}	12^{2}	21^{9}	28^{7}	30^{2}	33^{3}	38^{5}	42^{4}	44^{2}	47^{3}	52^{5}	54^{2}	60^{6}	67^{7}	75^{8}	81^{6}	11
Ireland	4^{4}	7^{3}	7^{x}	11^{4}	15^{4}	21^{6}	25^{4}	28^{3}	34^{6}	37^{3}	41^{4}	44^{3}	47^{3}	52^{5}	57^{5}	61^{4}	67^{6}	72^{5}	15
Spain	7^{7}	12^{5}	17^{5}	17^{x}	20^{3}	28^{8}	34^{6}	37^{3}	41^{4}	45^{4}	50^{5}	53^{3}	55^{2}	62^{7}	70^{8}	73^{3}	78^{5}	83^{5}	10
UK	8^{8}	**17^{9}**	23^{6}	25^{2}	25^{x}	35^{10}	39^{4}	47^{8}	49^{2}	56^{7}	63^{7}	70^{7}	79^{9}	85^{6}	94^{9}	98^{4}	106^{8}	114^{8}	2
Norway	4^{4}	7^{3}	13^{6}	18^{5}	22^{4}	22^{x}	27^{5}	29^{2}	34^{5}	41^{7}	44^{3}	46^{2}	51^{5}	55^{4}	59^{4}	63^{4}	69^{6}	73^{4}	14
Portugal	3^{3}	7^{4}	14^{7}	21^{7}	25^{4}	27^{2}	27^{x}	33^{6}	38^{5}	40^{2}	44^{4}	53^{9}	57^{4}	64^{7}	68^{4}	75^{7}	85^{10}	90^{5}	7
Switzerland	4^{4}	9^{5}	15^{6}	20^{5}	24^{4}	31^{7}	33^{2}	33^{x}	37^{4}	44^{7}	52^{8}	57^{5}	62^{5}	66^{4}	72^{6}	76^{4}	83^{7}	88^{5}	8
Malta	3^{3}	5^{2}	9^{4}	11^{2}	17^{6}	19^{2}	21^{2}	23^{2}	23^{x}	28^{5}	30^{2}	32^{2}	34^{2}	37^{3}	40^{3}	42^{2}	44^{2}	48^{4}	18
Finland	4^{4}	7^{3}	10^{3}	16^{6}	21^{5}	27^{6}	31^{4}	34^{3}	37^{3}	37^{x}	40^{3}	43^{3}	47^{4}	51^{4}	56^{5}	64^{8}	70^{6}	78^{8}	12
Austria	6^{6}	12^{6}	18^{6}	24^{6}	27^{3}	32^{5}	37^{5}	44^{7}	49^{5}	53^{4}	53^{x}	59^{6}	67^{8}	77^{10}	82^{5}	86^{4}	91^{5}	100^{9}	5
Italy	4^{4}	9^{5}	12^{3}	14^{2}	17^{3}	23^{6}	30^{7}	39^{9}	45^{6}	51^{6}	57^{6}	57^{x}	61^{4}	69^{8}	75^{6}	81^{6}	87^{6}	92^{5}	6
Yugoslavia	7^{7}	11^{4}	16^{5}	24^{8}	29^{5}	33^{4}	38^{5}	40^{2}	44^{4}	47^{3}	50^{3}	52^{2}	52^{x}	56^{4}	65^{9}	73^{8}	81^{8}	87^{6}	9
Sweden	5^{5}	8^{3}	13^{5}	16^{3}	19^{3}	24^{5}	28^{4}	30^{2}	34^{4}	39^{5}	43^{4}	46^{3}	53^{7}	53^{x}	58^{5}	65^{7}	70^{5}	75^{5}	13
Monaco	4^{4}	7^{3}	11^{4}	14^{3}	19^{5}	25^{6}	27^{2}	29^{2}	34^{5}	39^{5}	42^{3}	45^{3}	49^{4}	52^{3}	52^{x}	56^{4}	60^{4}	65^{5}	16
Belgium	2^{2}	5^{3}	9^{4}	11^{2}	16^{5}	18^{2}	21^{3}	24^{3}	29^{5}	33^{4}	35^{2}	38^{3}	40^{2}	42^{2}	46^{4}	46^{x}	52^{6}	55^{3}	17
Luxembourg	**9^{9}**	**17^{8}**	**26^{9}**	**28^{2}**	**38^{10}**	**46^{8}**	**53^{7}**	**59^{6}**	**63^{4}**	**69^{6}**	**77^{8}**	**86^{9}**	**96^{10}**	**104^{8}**	**111^{7}**	**119^{8}**	**119^{x}**	**128^{9}**	**1**
Netherlands	6^{6}	12^{6}	20^{8}	**28^{8}**	37^{9}	45^{8}	50^{5}	56^{6}	59^{3}	68^{9}	74^{6}	77^{3}	86^{9}	92^{6}	97^{5}	99^{2}	106^{7}	106^{x}	4

★ ★

1972 EUROVISION SONG CONTEST

Host country: United Kingdom ★ *Venue:* Usher Hall, Edinburgh
Date: 25 March ★ *Presenter:* Moira Shearer
Voting structure: Each nation had 2 jury members, one under and one over 25, who awarded between 1 and 5 points to each song
Total entries: 18 ★ *Debut countries:* None

Country	Performer	Song	Pts	Pos.
Germany	Mary Roos	Nur Die Liebe Lässt Uns Leben	107	3
France	Betty Mars	Comé-Comédie	81	11
Ireland	Sandie Jones	Ceol An Ghrà	72	15
Spain	Jaime Morey	Amanece	83	10
United Kingdom	New Seekers	Beg, Steal Or Borrow	114	2
Norway	Grethe Kausland and Benny Borg	Småting	73	14
Portugal	Carlos Mendes	A Festa Da Vida	90	7
Switzerland	Véronique Müller	C'est La Chanson De Mon Amour	88	8
Malta	Helen and Joseph	L-Imhabba	48	18
Finland	Päivi Paunu and Kim Floor	Muistathan	78	12
Austria	The Milestones	Falter Im Wind	100	5
Italy	Nicola di Bari	I Giorni Dell' Arcobaleno	92	6
Yugoslavia	Tereza	Muzika I Ti	87	9
Sweden	Family Four	Härliga Sommardag	75	13
Monaco	Anne-Marie Godart and Peter McLane	Comme On S'Aime	65	16
Belgium	Serge and Christine Ghisoland	A La Folie Ou Pas Du Tout	55	17
Luxembourg	**Vicky Leandros**	**Après Toi**	**128**	**1**
Netherlands	Sandra and Andres	Als Het Om De Liefde Gaat	106	4

Harrington and Charlie McGettigan, in 1994, and the other was the Danish husband and wife team of Grethe and Jørgen Ingmann, who won in 1963. Jørgen did not sing, though; he merely played his guitar while his wife sang 'Dansevise'. Yet for some reason, in 1972, six different countries thought that a husband and wife team, or a brother and sister or just two passing strangers teamed up for the night, would be the sure way to success.

Sandra and Andres stood out from the rest of the duos not just because they sang last and therefore stuck in the jurors' minds. Andres wore a suit of such shocking light emerald green that nobody could miss him, while Sandra bounced along with the chorus ('Na na na na na', etc.) in a dress made from deckchair material. This was the first of Sandra's three entries for the Netherlands: in 1976 she came back as Sandra Reemer to finish in ninth place; and in 1979, now leader of a band called Xandra, she was twelfth.

The Dutch entry was not the only one with a simple chorus. Sweden and Finland both made frequent use of the phrase 'la la la', Sweden in the second appearance of the Family Four, who were an older and folksier Abba, a couple of years ahead of their time. The Finnish song, featuring one of the many bearded men on display that night, sounded more like an Israeli entry than any of the actual Israeli entries, but as Israel did not make its debut until the following year, Finland almost got away with it. That country does not seem to have a musical style of its own. It repeatedly takes other national styles (American country and western and Jamaican reggae are just two examples) and gives them a Finnish finish. Without much success, it must be said.

The Irish entry was sung in Gaelic ('Ceol An Ghrà'/'The Music Of Love) by a lady wearing green but with a Welsh name, Sandie Jones. As the Maltese entry was also sung in the local language, Britain's 'Beg, Steal Or Borrow' by the New Seekers was the only song sung in English. There were five entries in French, including the eventual winner from Luxembourg.

The dreadful marking system continued, without much obvious advantage. The difference in marking between the younger and older juries was not significant. Luxembourg got exactly the same score as Monaco had done the year before and what is more, exactly the same split – sixty-three votes from the under-twenty-fives, and sixty-five from the older jurors. Both countries would have won, whatever age group was consulted. There were some songs that appealed more to one age group than another (Portugal came fifth among the under-twenty-fives, but fifteenth with the older jurors; Spain, Norway and Belgium all scored more heavily among the over-twenty-fives), but all in all, the voting system took both the fun and the tension out of the voting process. What had been an exciting finale to the evening became a flat and ordinary ending, which took much of the thrill out of the winning country's eventual triumph. It was Luxembourg's third victory, just one behind the record four by France.

VOTING BIAS

LUXEMBOURG

Countries most likely to vote for Luxembourg:
Ireland
Portugal
Malta
France
Italy

Countries least likely to vote for Luxembourg:
Switzerland
Turkey
Norway
Denmark
Israel

Countries for whom Luxembourg is most likely to vote:
UK
Portugal
Malta
Spain
Israel

★ ★ ★

Countries for whom Luxembourg is least likely to vote:
Cyprus
Austria
Yugoslavia
Finland
Denmark

Ten per cent of the population speak Portuguese as a first language, hence the slight bias towards Portugal. Otherwise Luxembourg's votes closely concur with the average given to each nation.

THE EUROVISION SONG CONTEST

1973

Won by Luxembourg: 'Tu Te Reconnaîtras'

Written by Claude Morgan and Vline Buggy

Performed by Anne-Marie David

Orchestra conducted by Jean Claudric

Why did Cliff Richard decide to have another go at Eurovision? Five years after his narrow defeat at the hands of Spain's Massiel, he came back for a second try, because 'I needed another hit.' Looking back on his second crack at the title, Cliff said, 'In 1968, it was odds-on that I would win. Most of the orchestra had bets on me and were very fed up that I didn't win. "Congratulations" had sold two million for me, and I wanted another million-seller. It's a great chance to present music to a huge captive audience, and even though it's full of flaws in

1973	Finland	Belgium	Portugal	W. Germany	Norway	Monaco	Spain	Switzerland	Yugoslavia	Italy	Luxembourg	Sweden	Netherlands	Ireland	UK	France	Israel	**Position**
Finland	0^{0}	9^{9}	14^{5}	20^{6}	26^{6}	31^{5}	37^{6}	43^{6}	50^{7}	52^{2}	58^{6}	65^{7}	70^{5}	75^{5}	84^{9}	88^{4}	93^{5}	6
Belgium	4^{4}	4^{x}	7^{3}	11^{4}	14^{3}	20^{6}	26^{6}	30^{4}	34^{4}	36^{2}	40^{4}	42^{2}	45^{3}	49^{4}	54^{5}	56^{2}	58^{2}	17
Portugal	4^{4}	10^{6}	10^{x}	15^{5}	20^{5}	24^{4}	32^{8}	40^{8}	46^{6}	49^{3}	53^{4}	55^{2}	60^{5}	64^{4}	69^{5}	75^{6}	80^{5}	10=
W. Germany	2^{2}	7^{5}	13^{6}	13^{x}	17^{4}	22^{5}	31^{9}	38^{7}	42^{4}	45^{3}	52^{7}	58^{6}	63^{5}	69^{6}	74^{5}	81^{7}	85^{4}	8=
Norway	8^{8}	13^{5}	18^{5}	24^{6}	24^{x}	31^{7}	37^{6}	44^{7}	50^{6}	55^{5}	62^{7}	65^{3}	68^{3}	71^{3}	74^{3}	80^{6}	89^{9}	7
Monaco	6^{6}	9^{3}	11^{2}	15^{4}	18^{3}	18^{x}	24^{6}	29^{5}	38^{9}	46^{8}	52^{6}	56^{4}	61^{5}	67^{6}	76^{9}	81^{5}	85^{4}	8=
Spain	3^{3}	11^{8}	20^{9}	**29^{9}**	33^{4}	42^{9}	42^{x}	50^{8}	59^{9}	69^{10}	77^{8}	84^{7}	94^{10}	104^{10}	108^{4}	117^{9}	125^{8}	2
Switzerland	4^{4}	7^{3}	10^{3}	14^{4}	21^{7}	26^{5}	33^{7}	33^{x}	39^{6}	43^{4}	49^{6}	52^{3}	60^{8}	67^{7}	74^{7}	76^{2}	79^{3}	12
Yugoslavia	5^{5}	8^{3}	11^{3}	15^{4}	17^{2}	22^{5}	30^{8}	36^{6}	36^{x}	38^{2}	42^{4}	44^{2}	48^{4}	53^{5}	57^{4}	61^{4}	65^{4}	15=
Italy	2^{2}	7^{5}	10^{3}	15^{5}	20^{5}	25^{5}	30^{5}	37^{7}	42^{5}	42^{x}	47^{5}	52^{5}	56^{4}	60^{4}	65^{5}	70^{5}	74^{4}	13
Luxembourg	6^{6}	12^{6}	20^{8}	27^{7}	**35^{8}**	42^{7}	**48^{6}**	**58^{10}**	**67^{9}**	**76^{9}**	76^{x}	84^{8}	93^{9}	101^{8}	**111^{10}**	**121^{10}**	**129^{8}**	**1**
Sweden	8^{8}	12^{4}	16^{4}	21^{5}	29^{8}	34^{5}	41^{7}	50^{9}	56^{6}	61^{5}	67^{6}	67^{x}	73^{6}	78^{5}	85^{7}	89^{4}	94^{5}	5
Netherlands	4^{4}	8^{4}	10^{2}	15^{5}	20^{5}	24^{4}	29^{5}	34^{5}	39^{5}	43^{4}	50^{7}	53^{3}	53^{x}	58^{5}	61^{3}	67^{6}	69^{2}	14
Ireland	3^{3}	10^{7}	12^{2}	16^{4}	22^{6}	28^{6}	35^{7}	40^{5}	45^{5}	50^{5}	56^{6}	61^{5}	67^{6}	67^{x}	72^{5}	76^{4}	80^{4}	10=
UK	**9^{9}**	**15^{6}**	**21^{6}**	28^{7}	**35^{7}**	**43^{8}**	47^{4}	55^{8}	63^{8}	68^{5}	**78^{10}**	**87^{9}**	**97^{10}**	**106^{9}**	106^{x}	114^{8}	123^{9}	3
France	4^{4}	7^{3}	9^{2}	13^{4}	17^{4}	22^{5}	27^{5}	31^{4}	38^{7}	40^{2}	43^{3}	48^{5}	53^{5}	58^{5}	63^{5}	63^{x}	65^{2}	15=
Israel	6^{6}	12^{6}	17^{5}	24^{7}	29^{5}	36^{7}	40^{4}	46^{6}	53^{7}	60^{7}	68^{8}	74^{6}	80^{6}	87^{7}	92^{5}	97^{5}	97^{x}	4

1973 EUROVISION SONG CONTEST

Host country: Luxembourg ★ *Venue:* Nouveau Théâtre
Date: 7 April ★ *Presenter:* Helga Guitton
Voting structure: Each nation had 2 jury members, one under and one over 25, who awarded between 1 and 5 points to each song
Total entries: 17 ★ *Debut countries:* Israel

Country	Performer	Song	Pts	Pos.
Finland	Marion Rung	Tom Tom Tom	93	6
Belgium	Nicole and Hugo	Baby Baby	58	17
Portugal	Fernando Tordo	Tourada	80	10
Germany	Gitte	Junger Tag	85	8
Norway	Bendik Singers	It's Just A Game	89	7
Monaco	Marie	Un Train Qui Part	85	8
Spain	Mocedades	Eres Tu	125	2
Switzerland	Patrick Juvet	Je Vais Me Marier, Marie	79	12
Yugoslavia	Zdravko Colic	Gori Vatra	65	15
Italy	Massimo Ranieri	Chi Sarà Con Te	74	13
Luxembourg	**Anne-Marie David**	**Tu Te Reconnaîtras**	**129**	**1**
Sweden	The Nova and the Dolls	You're Summer	94	5
Netherlands	Ben Cramer	De Oude Muzikant	69	14
Ireland	Maxi	Do I Dream	80	10
United Kingdom	Cliff Richard	Power To All Our Friends	123	3
France	Martine Clémenceau	Sans Toi	65	15
Israel	Ilanit	Ei Sham	97	4

terms of how I'd want it to be, it's compulsive viewing.' Cliff had long been what he calls 'a bit of a romantic' about Eurovision. Even in 1997, when he was touring Britain with his musical *Heathcliff*, they were watching the Contest on television backstage and following the course of the voting between exits and entrances. He was the biggest star ever to have appeared in the Contest, and admits that he had little in common with his fellow participants, almost all of whom were unknown before the Contest, and sank back into obscurity fairly quickly. 'If a few other stars took the risk of losing,' he says, 'the Contest might have gained credibility. It should be a showcase for the best of European pop/rock, a representation of what popular music was doing in each country, but somehow it lacks integrity.'

In 1973, the Contest had its usual run of odd stories. The husband and wife team of Nicole and Hugo finally represented Belgium, two years after having to drop out at the last minute because Nicole contracted jaundice. Not that it was much of an experience for them, because they came last of the seventeen entrants. Abba submitted Benny

VOTING BIAS

ISRAEL

Countries most likely to vote for Israel:
Switzerland
Finland
Netherlands
Portugal
Yugoslavia

Countries least likely to vote for Israel:
Greece
Turkey
Italy
Denmark
Cyprus

Countries for whom Israel is most likely to vote:
Yugoslavia
Netherlands
Finland
UK
Denmark

Countries for whom Israel is least likely to vote:
Italy
Ireland
Belgium
Malta
Germany

On the sixteen occasions that Israel and Greece have both competed, Greece has awarded Israel a total of just twenty-two points – forty-two fewer than Israel would have, on average, expected over that period.

and Björn's 'Ring Ring' as a potential Swedish entry, but were beaten in the selection process by 'You're Summer', which finished a respectable fifth, and left Abba to wait another year for glory. This was the second year in succession that the Swedish song had been about summer, while the year before that it had been about winter – the seasons are important to the Swedes. The lyricist of Portugal's entry, 'Tourada'/'Bullfight', was jailed briefly because of the song's supposedly political content, while Spain's six-member Mocedades went on to the American top ten with their second-placed 'Eres Tu', renamed 'Touch The Wind' for the English-speaking market. Yet again, the song that was to prove the biggest hit world-wide did not win the Contest.

The winner was Anne-Marie David, giving Luxembourg its second successive outright winner, the first time any country had achieved this feat. It was also a record-equalling fourth victory for the principality, and a ninth win in eighteen years for a song sung in French. The song was 'Tu Te Reconnaîtras'. As Cliff Richard remembers it, 'Anne-Marie David sang sweetly and beautifully, but it was a dull song.' In 1968, Cliff had refused to go into the green room during the voting, and instead had locked himself in the toilet and waited until somebody knocked on the door to tell him the result. 'I was not going to be photographed showing how thrilled I was to be losing.' In 1973, he was just as nervous, so David Bryce from his management team suggested he took a Valium to calm his nerves. Unfortunately, the pill he gave Cliff was so strong that he fell asleep on the way to the Nouveau Théâtre. The risk of a 'Cliff On Drugs' headline had never been greater. 'They had great trouble waking me up to perform', says Cliff, but perform he did, well enough to come in third, just two points behind Spain and six behind Luxembourg. He almost got his million-seller, too, for 'Power To All Our Friends' became a hit all over Europe, despite not winning the Grand Prix.

THE EUROVISION SONG CONTEST

1974

Won by Sweden: 'Waterloo'

Written by Stig Anderson, Benny Andersson and Björn Ulvaeus

Performed by Abba

Orchestra conducted by Sven-Olof Walldoff

The most successful, most talented and most widely remembered act ever to perform at Eurovision was Abba, and 1974 was their year. After failing to qualify in 1972 with 'Better To Have Loved' and in 1973 with 'Ring Ring' (later a hit all over the Continent), they came to Brighton with the strongest up tempo song yet heard at Eurovision, and an image that was perfect for its time. The conductor, Sven-Olof Walldoff, even dressed as Napoleon for the night. Unlike Napoleon at Waterloo, Abba triumphed, and from then on the world was at their feet. They eclipsed

1974	Finland	Luxembourg	Israel	Norway	UK	Yugoslavia	Greece	Ireland	Denmark	Portugal	Netherlands	Sweden	Spain	Monaco	Switzerland	Belgium	Italy	**Position**
Finland	0^{x}	0^{0}	2^{2}	2^{0}	3^{1}	3^{0}	3^{0}	4^{1}	4^{0}	4^{0}	4^{0}	4^{0}	4^{0}	4^{0}	4^{0}	4^{0}	4^{0}	13
UK	1^{1}	1^{0}	1^{0}	1^{0}	1^{x}	5^{4}	6^{1}	7^{1}	9^{2}	9^{0}	9^{0}	9^{0}	9^{0}	9^{0}	10^{1}	11^{1}	14^{3}	4=
Spain	0^{0}	1^{1}	1^{0}	3^{2}	3^{0}	3^{0}	3^{0}	3^{0}	4^{1}	6^{2}	7^{1}	7^{0}	7^{x}	10^{3}	10^{0}	10^{0}	10^{0}	9=
Norway	0^{0}	0^{0}	0^{0}	0^{x}	0^{0}	0^{0}	0^{0}	0^{0}	0^{0}	0^{0}	0^{0}	1^{1}	1^{0}	2^{1}	2^{0}	3^{1}	3^{0}	14=
Greece	0^{0}	0^{0}	0^{0}	0^{0}	0^{0}	0^{0}	0^{x}	0^{0}	0^{0}	1^{1}	5^{4}	7^{2}	7^{0}	7^{0}	7^{0}	7^{0}	7^{0}	11
Israel	0^{0}	0^{0}	0^{x}	0^{0}	2^{2}	2^{0}	2^{0}	3^{1}	3^{0}	5^{2}	7^{2}	8^{1}	8^{0}	8^{0}	8^{0}	8^{0}	11^{3}	7=
Yugoslavia	1^{1}	1^{0}	1^{0}	1^{0}	1^{0}	1^{x}	1^{0}	1^{0}	1^{0}	2^{1}	2^{0}	2^{0}	3^{1}	3^{0}	3^{0}	4^{1}	6^{2}	12
Sweden	**5^{5}**	**6^{1}**	**8^{2}**	**10^{2}**	**10^{0}**	**11^{1}**	**11^{0}**	**12^{1}**	**14^{2}**	**15^{1}**	**18^{3}**	**18^{x}**	**19^{1}**	**19^{0}**	**24^{5}**	**24^{0}**	**24^{0}**	**1**
Luxembourg	0^{0}	0^{x}	2^{2}	2^{0}	2^{0}	4^{2}	5^{1}	8^{3}	9^{1}	9^{0}	9^{0}	9^{0}	10^{1}	11^{1}	11^{0}	12^{1}	14^{2}	4=
Monaco	0^{0}	2^{2}	3^{1}	4^{1}	4^{0}	4^{0}	4^{0}	5^{1}	7^{2}	8^{1}	8^{0}	9^{1}	11^{2}	11^{x}	12^{1}	14^{2}	14^{0}	4=
Belgium	0^{0}	3^{3}	3^{0}	5^{2}	5^{0}	5^{0}	10^{5}	10^{0}	10^{0}	10^{0}	10^{0}	10^{0}	10^{0}	10^{0}	10^{0}	10^{x}	10^{0}	9=
Netherlands	1^{1}	1^{0}	2^{1}	3^{1}	3^{0}	6^{3}	8^{2}	9^{1}	10^{1}	11^{1}	11^{x}	14^{3}	14^{0}	14^{0}	14^{0}	15^{1}	15^{0}	3
Ireland	0^{0}	2^{2}	3^{1}	5^{2}	6^{1}	6^{0}	6^{0}	6^{x}	6^{0}	6^{0}	6^{0}	8^{2}	10^{2}	11^{1}	11^{0}	11^{0}	11^{0}	7=
W. Germany	0^{0}	0^{0}	0^{0}	0^{0}	0^{0}	0^{0}	1^{1}	1^{0}	1^{x}	1^{0}	1^{0}	1^{0}	1^{0}	1^{0}	2^{1}	3^{1}	3^{0}	14=
Switzerland	0^{0}	0^{0}	0^{0}	0^{0}	1^{1}	1^{0}	1^{0}	1^{0}	2^{1}	2^{0}	2^{0}	2^{0}	2^{0}	2^{0}	2^{x}	3^{1}	3^{0}	14=
Portugal	0^{0}	0^{0}	0^{0}	0^{0}	0^{0}	0^{0}	0^{0}	0^{0}	0^{0}	0^{x}	0^{0}	0^{0}	1^{1}	1^{0}	3^{2}	3^{0}	3^{0}	14=
Italy	2^{2}	3^{1}	4^{1}	4^{0}	9^{5}	9^{0}	9^{0}	10^{1}	10^{0}	11^{1}	11^{0}	11^{0}	13^{2}	17^{4}	17^{0}	18^{1}	18^{x}	2

★ ★

1974 EUROVISION SONG CONTEST

Host country: United Kingdom ★ *Venue:* The Dome, Brighton
Date: 6 April ★ *Presenter:* Katie Boyle
Voting structure: 10 jury members from each country, each of whom awarded 1 point to their favourite song
Total entries: 17 ★ *Debut countries:* Greece

Country	Performer	Song	Pts	Pos.
Finland	Carita	Keep Me Warm	4	13
United Kingdom	Olivia Newton-John	Long Live Love	14	4
Spain	Peret	Canta Y Se Feliz	10	9
Norway	Anne-Karine Strøm and the Bendik Singers	The First Day Of Love	3	14
Greece	Marinella Krassi	Thalassa Ke T'agori Mou	7	11
Israel	Poogy	Natati La Khaiai	11	7
Yugoslavia	Korni	Generacija '42	6	12
Sweden	**Abba**	**Waterloo**	**24**	**1**
Luxembourg	Ireen Sheer	Bye Bye, I Love You	14	4
Monaco	Romuald	Celui Qui Reste Et Celui Qui S'en Va	14	4
Belgium	Jacques Hustin	Fleur De Liberté	10	9
Netherlands	Mouth and MacNeal	I See A Star	15	3
Ireland	Tina Reynolds	Cross Your Heart	11	7
Germany	Cindy and Bert	Die Sommermelodie	3	14
Switzerland	Piera Martell	Mein Ruf Nach Dir	3	14
Portugal	Paulo de Cavalho	E Depois Do Adeus	3	14
Italy	Gigliola Cinquetti	Si	18	2

Volvo as Sweden's highest foreign currency earners in 1982, and even in 1993 – over ten years after they had disbanded – they were named Sweden's best-selling artists of the year at the World Music Awards in Monte Carlo. Many of the records that their fans bought that year would have featured 'Waterloo' as a lead track.

Abba were up against some strong opposition, and the betting beforehand had not made them favourites. There was 1964 winner Gigliola Cinquetti, British hit-maker Olivia Newton-John, as well as several Eurovision regulars like Romuald competing for the third time, and Anne-Karine Strøm and the Bendik Singers (back after their entry the previous year). But Abba still won easily, leading from start to finish in the voting. They would also have been up against a competitor from the very first Eurovision in 1956, but France withdrew at a late stage after the death of President Pompidou, so Dany Dauberson did not perform France's chosen song, 'La Vie A Vingt-Cinq Ans'. Paulo de Cavalho, for Portugal, was making his first appearance at the finals after six previous attempts. His effort came equal last, but achieved greater fame in his homeland as a symbol for the beginning of the 1974 Portuguese revolution. It was also the year of Greece's debut in the competition, and it did quite respectably. But with a very ethnic sound, all bouzoukis and Greek rhythms, and no Cyprus to vote for it yet, it was not surprising that the song never looked like winning.

1974 gave us more chart hits than any other year. In Britain, then Europe's largest singles market, not only did Abba top the charts for two weeks, but the runner-up, 'Si' by Gigliola Cinquetti, translated into English as 'Go', reached number eight in the charts the week that 'Waterloo' dropped out of the top ten. The next week, she was knocked off the number eight spot by the song that came third in Brighton, 'I See A Star' by Holland's Mouth and MacNeal. They were also seasoned world hit-makers, having reached the US top ten in 1972 with a song called 'How Do You Do'. Never before had the top three songs in Europe all been top ten hits in Britain. To add to the list of hits that year, Olivia Newton-John's British entry reached number eleven. Obviously the British record-buying public agreed almost exactly with the Eurovision juries. The importance of this British market was emphasized by the fact that six of the seventeen songs were sung in English, and a seventh, 'Bye Bye, I Love You', had an English title, even though it was actually sung in French.

The only downside of Abba's victory was the number of copycat acts they spawned in years to come. Like 'Puppet On A String' before them and 'Ne Partez Pas Sans Moi' later, 'Waterloo' defined a new style of Eurovision song, which many other countries thought would bring them success. Unfortunately for them – and for the hundreds of millions who watch Eurovision – nobody ever reached the standard set by the four super Swedes in 1974.

VOTING BIAS

GREECE

Countries most likely to vote for Greece:

Cyprus
Spain
France
Malta
Israel

Countries least likely to vote for Greece:

Germany
Ireland
Denmark
Belgium
Turkey

Countries for whom Greece is most likely to vote:

Cyprus
Spain
Finland
Austria
Portugal

Countries for whom Greece is least likely to vote:

UK
Israel
Germany
Sweden
Norway

The relationship between Greece and Cyprus is the cosiest in Eurovision. Cyprus has given Greece an astonishing 109 votes more than average and, in return, Greece has boosted Cypriot scores by 88 votes.

THE EUROVISION SONG CONTEST

1975

Won by Netherlands: 'Ding Dinge Dong'

Written by Dick Bakker, Wil Luikinga and Eddy Owens

Performed by Teach-In

Orchestra conducted by Harry van Hoof

This was the year in which the current Eurovision scoring system was introduced, so it was perhaps unfortunate that this system – which most people agree is as fair as any subjective scoring system can be – came up with one of the truly bad songs of the past twenty-five years as the winner. As in 1974, the rules allowed songs to be performed in any language, and

1975	Netherlands	Ireland	France	W. Germany	Luxembourg	Norway	Switzerland	Yugoslavia	UK	Malta	Belgium	Israel	Turkey
Netherlands	0[x]	8[8]	13[5]	21[8]	31[10]	43[12]	49[6]	57[8]	**69[12]**	**81[12]**	**84[3]**	**96[12]**	**100[4]**
Ireland	6[6]	6[x]	12[6]	12[0]	12[0]	16[4]	23[7]	24[1]	30[6]	34[4]	46[12]	46[0]	46[0]
France	8[8]	20[12]	20[x]	20[0]	20[0]	20[0]	23[3]	23[0]	31[8]	38[7]	40[2]	47[7]	48[1]
W. Germany	0[0]	0[0]	0[0]	0[x]	8[8]	8[0]	8[0]	8[0]	8[0]	11[3]	11[0]	11[0]	11[0]
Luxembourg	**12[12]**	**22[10]**	**25[3]**	25[0]	25[x]	25[0]	25[0]	32[7]	35[3]	40[5]	40[0]	46[6]	51[5]
Norway	2[2]	2[0]	2[0]	2[0]	2[0]	2[x]	2[0]	2[0]	2[0]	2[0]	2[0]	2[0]	2[0]
Switzerland	7[7]	9[2]	19[10]	25[6]	27[2]	28[1]	28[x]	28[0]	33[5]	39[6]	47[8]	47[0]	54[7]
Yugoslavia	3[3]	7[4]	7[0]	9[2]	9[0]	9[0]	9[0]	9[x]	9[0]	9[0]	14[5]	14[0]	14[0]
UK	4[4]	7[3]	19[12]	**29[10]**	**41[12]**	**48[7]**	**56[8]**	**68[12]**	68[x]	76[8]	86[10]	**96[10]**	96[0]
Malta	1[1]	1[0]	9[8]	9[0]	14[5]	16[2]	20[4]	22[2]	22[0]	22[x]	29[7]	30[1]	32[2]
Belgium	5[5]	5[0]	5[0]	12[7]	12[0]	12[0]	12[0]	15[3]	15[0]	15[0]	15[x]	15[0]	15[0]
Israel	10[10]	11[1]	12[1]	13[1]	14[1]	19[5]	21[2]	21[0]	22[1]	22[0]	23[1]	23[x]	29[6]
Turkey	0[0]	0[0]	0[0]	0[0]	0[0]	0[0]	0[0]	0[0]	0[0]	0[0]	0[0]	0[0]	0[x]
Monaco	0[0]	0[0]	0[0]	3[3]	7[4]	7[0]	7[0]	7[0]	9[2]	10[1]	10[0]	12[2]	12[0]
Finland	0[0]	5[5]	5[0]	17[12]	23[6]	33[10]	45[12]	50[5]	54[4]	54[0]	54[0]	62[8]	62[0]
Portugal	0[0]	0[0]	2[2]	2[0]	2[0]	2[0]	2[0]	2[0]	2[0]	2[0]	2[0]	2[0]	14[12]
Spain	0[0]	7[7]	7[0]	12[5]	12[0]	15[3]	20[5]	24[4]	24[0]	24[0]	28[4]	32[4]	35[3]
Sweden	0[0]	0[0]	7[7]	7[0]	14[7]	22[8]	23[1]	29[6]	36[7]	38[2]	38[0]	41[3]	49[8]
Italy	0[0]	6[6]	10[4]	14[4]	17[3]	23[6]	33[10]	43[10]	53[10]	63[10]	69[6]	74[5]	84[10]

several nations decided to perform in English, including Norway, Sweden, Finland and the Netherlands. The Norwegians gave us 'Touch My Life With Summer', which did not touch singer Ellen Nikolaysen's life with many votes; the Swedes followed up the ground-breaking 'Waterloo' with a bland song called 'Jennie, Jennie', which came eighth, making it the highest-placed song by a male soloist; and the Finns gave us a piece of country and western music called 'Old Man Fiddle', which did better than most Finnish entries. But the Dutch kicked off the show with a group so clearly modelled on Abba that it was a surprise that the Swedish quartet did not sue for plagiarism. However, Teach-In lacked one vital ingredient that Abba always had – talent.

'Ding Dinge Dong' was a bouncy enough number, but the lyrics placed it even beyond the stultifyingly daft 'Boom Bang-A-Bang', 'Tom Tom Tom' and 'La La La' branch of Eurovision philosophical thought. 'Dinge Dong every hour, when you pick a flower, even when your lover is gone gone gone, sing dinge dong.' Anybody who sings 'dinge dong' every hour, and when picking flowers, would find their lover had gone a long time ago. Yet the song romped home, the only one to receive votes from every single jury. Second came the United Kingdom, represented by The Shadows, and third were Wess and Dori Ghezzi, a husband and wife team from Italy. In fourth place was the only really fine song on show that night, Nicole Rieu's 'Et Bonjour A Toi L'Artiste', which started and ended strongly in the voting, but slumped badly in the middle. The Netherlands, which voted first, gave only four votes to the UK and none at all to Italy, which certainly helped its own cause. After that, the Dutch were slow to start picking up big votes, and it was not until the sixth jury to vote, the Norwegian jury, that they received a maximum twelve points. At this stage, they were well behind the UK entry. They did not take the lead until the UK jury gave its full twelve to the Netherlands, which was not very clever tactical voting. The British had only themselves to blame for the magnitude of their defeat. Italy showed more sense, giving the Dutch entry just one point, its lowest score of the night.

The voting went reasonably well, bearing everything in mind. Karin Falck, the hapless presenter, had difficulty with repeating the scores in both French and English, blaming the slowness of the scoreboard for her increasingly faltering translations. The link with Israel was, as was becoming traditional, studded with repeated bursts of 'Can you hear me?' At one stage, Miss Falck said in English, 'Italy seven votes. Er … how much is that in French?' Turkey's Eurovision debut meant that Greece decided not to take part,

Monaco	Finland	Portugal	Spain	Sweden	Italy	Position
110^{10}	**120^{10}**	**127^{7}**	**139^{12}**	**151^{12}**	**152^{1}**	**1**
46^{0}	47^{1}	51^{4}	54^{3}	64^{10}	68^{4}	9
55^{7}	55^{0}	67^{12}	75^{8}	83^{8}	91^{8}	4
11^{0}	11^{0}	11^{0}	15^{4}	15^{0}	15^{0}	17
51^{0}	56^{5}	64^{8}	70^{6}	74^{4}	84^{10}	5
4^{2}	4^{0}	4^{0}	4^{0}	4^{0}	11^{7}	18
59^{5}	63^{4}	65^{2}	65^{0}	65^{0}	77^{12}	6
14^{0}	14^{0}	15^{1}	15^{0}	22^{7}	22^{0}	13=
108^{12}	115^{7}	120^{5}	130^{10}	135^{5}	138^{3}	2
32^{0}	32^{0}	32^{0}	32^{0}	32^{0}	32^{0}	12
15^{0}	15^{0}	15^{0}	15^{0}	17^{2}	17^{0}	15
29^{0}	32^{3}	32^{0}	32^{0}	38^{6}	40^{2}	11
3^{3}	3^{0}	3^{0}	3^{0}	3^{0}	3^{0}	19
12^{x}	14^{2}	17^{3}	17^{0}	17^{0}	22^{5}	13=
70^{8}	70^{x}	70^{0}	71^{1}	74^{3}	74^{0}	7
14^{0}	14^{0}	14^{x}	16^{2}	16^{0}	16^{0}	16
39^{4}	47^{8}	47^{0}	47^{x}	47^{0}	53^{6}	10
55^{6}	61^{6}	67^{6}	72^{5}	72^{x}	72^{0}	8
85^{1}	97^{12}	107^{10}	114^{7}	115^{1}	115^{x}	3

★ ★

1975 EUROVISION SONG CONTEST

Host country: Sweden ★ *Venue:* St Eriks Mässan Alvsjoe, Stockholm
Date: 22 March ★ *Presenter:* Karin Falck
Voting structure: Each country awarded 12 to its top song, 10 to the second, 8 to the third and 7, 6, 5, 4, 3, 2 and 1 point for the next seven. This system still operates.
Total entries: 19 ★ *Debut countries:* Turkey

Country	Performer	Song	Pts	Pos.
Netherlands	**Teach-In**	**Ding Dinge Dong**	**152**	**1**
Ireland	The Swarbriggs	That's What Friends Are For	68	9
France	Nicole Rieu	Et Bonjour A Toi L'Artiste	91	4
Germany	Joy Fleming	Ein Lied Kann Eine Brücke Sein	15	17
Luxembourg	Géraldine	Toi	84	5
Norway	Ellen Nikolaysen	Touch My Life With Summer	11	18
Switzerland	Simone Drexel	Mikado	77	6
Yugoslavia	Blood and Ashes	Dan Ljubezni	22	13
United Kingdom	The Shadows	Let Me Be The One	138	2
Malta	Renato	Singing This Song	32	12
Belgium	Ann Christy	Gelukkig Zijn	17	15
Israel	Shlomo Artzi	At Ve'Ani	40	11
Turkey	Semiha Yanki	Seninle Bir Dakika	3	19
Monaco	Sophie	Une Chanson C'est Une Lettre	22	13
Finland	Pihasoittajat	Old Man Fiddle	74	7
Portugal	Duarte Mendes	Madrugada	16	16
Spain	Sergio and Estibaliz	Tu Volveras	53	10
Sweden	Lars Berghagen	Jennie, Jennie	72	8
Italy	Wess and Dori Ghezzi	Era	115	3

and the presence of an untried performer and an untried jury gave an added interest to the competition. Semiha Yanki, an attractive young woman wearing a patchwork quilt, was too ethnic to appeal to the bulk of the juries, with only Monaco giving her any points at all, and even then, the scoreboard seemed reluctant to show the meagre total, persisting in keeping the counter on zero.

The Turkish jury certainly put the cat among the pigeons, however. It gave its top mark to Portugal, represented by an army lieutenant called Duarte Mendes. That represented three-quarters of Portugal's entire vote on the night. Turkey was also the only country not to vote for the UK at all, but to even things out it gave only four points to 'Ding Dinge Dong', its second lowest score of the night. Teach-In went on to a certain amount of chart glory with their winning song, but then disappeared into Euro-obscurity.

THE EUROVISION SONG CONTEST

1976

Won by United Kingdom: 'Save Your Kisses For Me'
Written by Tony Hiller, Martin Lee and Lee Sheriden
Performed by Brotherhood of Man
Orchestra conducted by Alyn Ainsworth

For the first contest to be held in the Netherlands since 1970, the 1957 winner Corry Brokken put away her law books and came out of show business retirement to act as presenter. She was the only former winner involved in the Contest, although as usual there were several survivors from earlier years who had defied all reason to come back and have another go. Switzerland's Peter, Sue and Marc were back for the second of their total of four tries, while the

1976	UK	Switzerland	W. Germany	Israel	Luxembourg	Belgium	Ireland	Netherlands	Norway	Greece	Finland	Spain	Italy	Austria	Portugal	Monaco	France	Yugoslavia	**Position**
UK	0^{x}	12^{12}	20^{8}	32^{12}	40^{8}	52^{12}	55^{3}	65^{10}	77^{12}	**89^{12}**	**99^{10}**	**111^{12}**	**115^{4}**	**125^{10}**	**137^{12}**	**147^{10}**	**154^{7}**	**164^{10}**	**1**
Switzerland	**12^{12}**	12^{x}	17^{5}	21^{4}	22^{1}	29^{7}	30^{1}	36^{6}	46^{10}	48^{2}	55^{7}	59^{4}	59^{0}	67^{8}	74^{7}	78^{4}	84^{6}	91^{7}	4
W. Germany	0^{0}	2^{2}	2^{x}	2^{0}	4^{2}	5^{1}	5^{0}	5^{0}	5^{0}	5^{0}	5^{0}	7^{2}	7^{0}	7^{0}	7^{0}	7^{0}	9^{2}	12^{3}	15
Israel	6^{6}	13^{7}	16^{3}	16^{x}	23^{7}	28^{5}	32^{4}	34^{2}	41^{7}	41^{0}	49^{8}	50^{1}	60^{10}	66^{6}	68^{2}	69^{1}	69^{0}	77^{8}	6
Luxembourg	0^{0}	0^{0}	0^{0}	0^{0}	0^{x}	6^{6}	12^{6}	17^{5}	17^{0}	17^{0}	17^{0}	17^{0}	17^{0}	17^{0}	17^{0}	17^{0}	17^{0}	17^{0}	14
Belgium	7^{7}	13^{6}	13^{0}	14^{1}	14^{0}	14^{x}	14^{0}	18^{4}	24^{6}	24^{0}	36^{12}	36^{0}	44^{8}	47^{3}	55^{8}	63^{8}	68^{5}	68^{0}	8
Ireland	10^{10}	10^{0}	11^{1}	14^{3}	17^{3}	17^{0}	17^{x}	17^{0}	17^{0}	25^{8}	25^{0}	30^{5}	42^{12}	44^{2}	44^{0}	50^{6}	53^{3}	54^{1}	10
Netherlands	0^{0}	4^{4}	8^{4}	16^{8}	20^{4}	24^{4}	26^{2}	26^{x}	27^{1}	34^{7}	34^{0}	37^{3}	39^{2}	43^{4}	49^{6}	51^{2}	51^{0}	56^{5}	9
Norway	0^{0}	0^{0}	0^{0}	0^{0}	0^{0}	0^{0}	0^{0}	3^{3}	3^{x}	3^{0}	3^{0}	3^{0}	3^{0}	3^{0}	7^{4}	7^{0}	7^{0}	7^{0}	18
Greece	0^{0}	0^{0}	0^{0}	0^{0}	0^{0}	2^{2}	2^{0}	2^{0}	2^{0}	2^{x}	6^{4}	6^{0}	11^{5}	11^{0}	12^{1}	12^{0}	20^{8}	20^{0}	13
Finland	2^{2}	2^{0}	8^{6}	14^{6}	14^{0}	14^{0}	19^{5}	20^{1}	24^{4}	24^{0}	24^{x}	30^{6}	30^{0}	37^{7}	37^{0}	44^{7}	44^{0}	44^{0}	11
Spain	3^{3}	3^{0}	3^{0}	3^{0}	3^{0}	3^{0}	3^{0}	3^{0}	3^{0}	4^{1}	4^{0}	4^{x}	7^{3}	7^{0}	7^{0}	10^{3}	11^{1}	11^{0}	16
Italy	1^{1}	9^{8}	9^{0}	11^{2}	11^{0}	11^{0}	23^{12}	23^{0}	26^{3}	36^{10}	42^{6}	42^{0}	42^{x}	43^{1}	53^{10}	53^{0}	63^{10}	69^{6}	7
Austria	4^{4}	7^{3}	17^{10}	27^{10}	32^{5}	35^{3}	45^{10}	52^{7}	54^{2}	60^{6}	65^{5}	73^{8}	73^{0}	73^{x}	73^{0}	78^{5}	78^{0}	80^{2}	5
Portugal	0^{0}	0^{0}	0^{0}	0^{0}	6^{6}	6^{0}	6^{0}	6^{0}	6^{0}	10^{4}	11^{1}	11^{0}	12^{1}	12^{0}	12^{x}	12^{0}	24^{12}	24^{0}	12
Monaco	5^{5}	10^{5}	17^{7}	24^{7}	36^{12}	44^{8}	52^{8}	60^{8}	65^{5}	65^{0}	67^{2}	74^{7}	81^{7}	86^{5}	98^{3}	89^{x}	89^{0}	93^{4}	3
France	8^{8}	**18^{10}**	**30^{12}**	**35^{5}**	**45^{10}**	**55^{10}**	**62^{7}**	**74^{12}**	**82^{8}**	87^{5}	90^{3}	100^{10}	106^{6}	118^{12}	123^{5}	135^{12}	135^{x}	147^{12}	2
Yugoslavia	0^{0}	1^{1}	3^{2}	3^{0}	3^{0}	3^{0}	3^{0}	3^{0}	3^{0}	6^{3}	6^{0}	6^{0}	6^{0}	6^{0}	6^{0}	6^{0}	10^{4}	10^{x}	17

1976 EUROVISION SONG CONTEST

Host country: Netherlands ★ *Venue:* Congresgebouw, Den Haag
Date: 3 April ★ *Presenter:* Corry Brokken
Voting structure: Each country awarded 12 to its top song, 10 to the second, 8 to the third and 7, 6, 5, 4, 3, 2 and 1 point for the next seven
Total entries: 18 ★ *Debut countries:* None

Country	Performer	Song	Pts	Pos.
United Kingdom	**Brotherhood of Man**	**Save Your Kisses For Me**	**164**	**1**
Switzerland	Peter, Sue and Marc	Djambo, Djambo	91	4
Germany	Les Humphries Singers	Sing, Sang, Song	12	15
Israel	Chocolate Menta Mastik	Emor Shalom	77	6
Luxembourg	Jürgen Marcus	Chansons Pour Ceux Qui S'Aiment	17	14
Belgium	Pierre Rapsat	Judy et Cie	68	8
Ireland	Red Hurley	When	54	10
Netherlands	Sandra Reemer	The Party's Over	56	9
Norway	Anne-Karine Strøm	Mata Hari	7	18
Greece	Mariza Koch	Panaghia Mou, Panaghia Mou	20	13
Finland	Fredi and Friends	Pump-pump	44	11
Spain	Braulio	Sobran Las Palabras	11	16
Italy	Romina Power and Al Bano	Noi Lo Rivivremo Di Nuovo	69	7
Austria	Waterloo and Robinson	My Little World	80	5
Portugal	Carlos do Carmo	Uma Flor De Verde Pinho	24	12
Monaco	Mary Cristy	Toi, La Musique Et Moi	93	3
France	Catherine Ferry	Un, Deux, Trois	147	2
Yugoslavia	Ambasadori	Ne Mogu Skriti Svoju Bol	10	17

local hope Sandra Reemer had disposed of her partner Andres from 1972 for the second of her three appearances. Norway's Anne-Karine Strøm was on stage for a third time, having been part of the Bendik Singers twice before, and 110-kilo Fredi was back for Finland, nine years after his first unsuccessful effort. As for the Les Humphries Singers, representing Germany, half of them did not even manage one appearance. There were twelve members of the group, but Contest rules at the time meant that only six were allowed on stage. This was probably just as well, as 'Sing, Sang, Song' would not have been improved by the addition of six voices as much as by the subtraction of six voices. The stage itself was a hubbub of geometric shapes designed to change pattern and colour.

Brotherhood of Man became the second act in succession to win the Contest having opened the show, and only Catherine Ferry for France, who sang last but one, gave them any sort of challenge at all. 'Save Your Kisses For Me' was the pre-tournament favourite, and did not let the punters down. The voting was as clear cut as it had been for many years: seven of the sixteen countries who could have done so put France and Britain as their top two, and only Ireland and Italy failed to place either country in the top two positions. Interestingly, Ireland gave Italy the full twelve points, and Italy returned the favour. Ireland's song was written by Brendan Graham, who was to win in both 1994 and 1996, but twenty years earlier, he was still learning his Eurovision trade. Italy were represented by the husband and wife team of Romina Power and Al Bano, Romina being the Italian-born daughter of Hollywood star Tyrone Power. Their song was called, in translation, 'We'll Live It All Again', and they did, in 1985, when once again they finished seventh.

This Contest was noted for its political undertones. The writers of the Portuguese entry, 'Uma Flor De Verde Pinho'/'A Green Pine Flower' were both in politics as Socialist Party deputies in the Portuguese parliament. The Greek entry was a song in protest against the Turkish invasion of Cyprus in 1974, and Greece entered the competition only after Turkey, which had come last the year before, announced that it would not take part. The Greek entry was written and performed by Mariza Koch, who had been forced to flee her homeland in 1967 and stay in Britain for three years. The Israeli entry was performed by Chocolate Menta Mastik, a group consisting of three women who had met and begun performing in the Israeli army. One of the trio, Yardena Arazi, went on to co-host the 1979 contest in Jerusalem.

The voting was not without its cock-ups. At the end of the contest, Yugoslavia was placed last, with six points, until it was noticed some time later that France had awarded it four points, but had failed to mention the fact on the night. So some time later the four points were added back in, lifting the Yugoslav entry from eighteenth to seventeenth, and awarding Norway the wooden spoon, not for the first time in its history.

VOTING BIAS

ITALY

Countries most likely to vote for Italy:

Portugal
Spain
Finland
Switzerland
Yugoslavia

Countries least likely to vote for Italy:

Denmark
UK
Netherlands
Sweden
Israel

Countries for whom Italy is most likely to vote:

Spain
Austria
Switzerland
Monaco
Luxembourg

Countries for whom Italy is least likely to vote:

Sweden
Israel
UK
Finland
Yugoslavia

When the Swiss opt for an Italian song, the Italians are appreciative and vote accordingly. Otherwise they show a strong bias towards Spanish and Austrian entries.

★ ★

THE EUROVISION SONG CONTEST

1977

Won by France: 'L'Oiseau Et L'Enfant'
Written by Jean-Paul Cara and Joe Gracy
Performed by Marie Myriam
Orchestra conducted by Raymond Donnez

The 1977 Eurovision Song Contest, from the Wembley Conference Centre, resulted in the first outright victory for France since Isabelle Aubret had sung 'Un Premier Amour' in 1962, but it was the fifth French-language song to win since then, not including Udo Jürgens' 1966 victory with a German-language song with a French title. 'L'Oiseau Et L'Enfant', sung by Congolese-born Marie Myriam, also marked a return to the slower tempo of Eurovision winners of the past, after a

1977	Ireland	Monaco	Netherlands	Austria	Norway	W. Germany	Luxembourg	Portugal	UK	Greece	Israel	Switzerland	Sweden	Spain	Italy	Finland	Belgium	France	**Position**
Ireland	0^{x}	8^{8}	9^{1}	14^{5}	26^{12}	31^{5}	39^{8}	40^{1}	52^{12}	62^{10}	74^{12}	82^{8}	94^{12}	98^{4}	106^{8}	106^{0}	109^{3}	119^{10}	3
Monaco	5^{5}	5^{x}	5^{0}	13^{8}	14^{1}	20^{6}	21^{1}	27^{6}	34^{7}	46^{12}	48^{2}	54^{6}	64^{10}	72^{8}	84^{12}	89^{5}	91^{2}	96^{5}	4
Netherlands	3^{3}	6^{3}	6^{x}	6^{0}	6^{0}	6^{0}	6^{0}	6^{0}	7^{1}	8^{1}	9^{1}	16^{7}	16^{0}	17^{1}	17^{0}	17^{0}	27^{10}	35^{8}	12
Austria	0^{0}	5^{5}	5^{0}	5^{x}	7^{2}	7^{0}	7^{0}	7^{0}	7^{0}	10^{3}	10^{0}	10^{0}	10^{0}	10^{0}	10^{0}	11^{1}	11^{0}	11^{0}	17
Norway	0^{0}	0^{0}	0^{0}	0^{0}	0^{x}	0^{0}	3^{3}	5^{2}	7^{2}	7^{0}	7^{0}	7^{0}	8^{1}	8^{0}	13^{5}	13^{0}	18^{5}	18^{0}	14=
W. Germany	1^{1}	2^{1}	5^{3}	7^{2}	7^{0}	7^{x}	9^{2}	17^{8}	25^{8}	33^{8}	38^{5}	38^{0}	43^{5}	48^{5}	54^{6}	54^{0}	54^{0}	55^{1}	8
Luxembourg	2^{2}	2^{0}	2^{0}	2^{0}	2^{0}	2^{0}	2^{x}	2^{0}	2^{0}	2^{0}	2^{0}	2^{0}	2^{0}	9^{7}	9^{0}	17^{8}	17^{0}	17^{0}	16
Portugal	0^{0}	2^{2}	4^{2}	4^{0}	4^{0}	5^{1}	5^{0}	5^{x}	5^{0}	5^{0}	5^{0}	9^{4}	9^{0}	9^{0}	12^{3}	12^{0}	12^{0}	18^{6}	14=
UK	0^{0}	12^{12}	19^{7}	**31^{12}**	**38^{7}**	**48^{10}**	**60^{12}**	**72^{12}**	**72^{x}**	**72^{0}**	80^{8}	80^{0}	88^{8}	91^{3}	93^{2}	97^{4}	109^{12}	121^{12}	2
Greece	0^{0}	10^{10}	20^{10}	24^{4}	28^{4}	32^{4}	38^{6}	48^{10}	53^{5}	53^{x}	56^{3}	57^{1}	64^{7}	76^{12}	77^{1}	83^{6}	89^{6}	92^{3}	5
Israel	7^{7}	14^{7}	19^{5}	22^{3}	27^{5}	27^{0}	27^{0}	27^{0}	27^{0}	27^{0}	27^{x}	37^{10}	40^{3}	46^{6}	46^{0}	46^{0}	47^{1}	49^{2}	11
Switzerland	6^{6}	6^{0}	6^{0}	16^{10}	26^{10}	26^{0}	31^{5}	35^{4}	39^{4}	45^{6}	49^{4}	49^{x}	49^{0}	49^{0}	53^{4}	63^{10}	71^{8}	71^{0}	6
Sweden	0^{0}	0^{0}	0^{0}	0^{0}	0^{0}	2^{2}	2^{0}	2^{0}	2^{0}	2^{0}	2^{0}	2^{0}	2^{x}	2^{0}	2^{0}	2^{0}	2^{0}	2^{0}	18
Spain	0^{0}	0^{0}	6^{6}	7^{1}	7^{0}	14^{7}	21^{7}	21^{0}	24^{3}	28^{4}	28^{0}	31^{3}	31^{0}	31^{x}	38^{7}	45^{7}	52^{7}	52^{0}	9
Italy	8^{8}	14^{6}	14^{0}	14^{0}	14^{0}	17^{3}	17^{0}	20^{3}	20^{0}	20^{0}	20^{0}	22^{2}	22^{0}	24^{2}	24^{x}	26^{2}	26^{0}	33^{7}	13
Finland	**12^{12}**	12^{0}	16^{4}	22^{6}	30^{8}	30^{0}	30^{0}	30^{0}	30^{0}	32^{2}	39^{7}	44^{5}	46^{2}	46^{0}	46^{0}	46^{x}	46^{0}	50^{4}	10
Belgium	4^{4}	4^{0}	16^{12}	16^{0}	22^{6}	30^{8}	34^{4}	41^{7}	51^{10}	56^{5}	62^{6}	62^{0}	66^{4}	66^{0}	66^{0}	69^{3}	69^{x}	69^{0}	7
France	10^{10}	**14^{4}**	**22^{8}**	29^{7}	32^{3}	44^{12}	54^{10}	59^{5}	65^{6}	**72^{7}**	**82^{10}**	94^{12}	**100^{6}**	110^{10}	120^{10}	132^{12}	**136^{4}**	136^{x}	**1**

★ ★

1977 EUROVISION SONG CONTEST

Host country: United Kingdom ★ *Venue:* Wembley Conference Centre, London
Date: 7 May ★ *Presenter:* Angela Rippon
Voting structure: Each country awarded 12 to its top song, 10 to the second, 8 to the third and 7, 6, 5, 4, 3, 2 and 1 point for the next seven
Total entries: 18 ★ *Debut countries:* None

Country	Performer	Song	Pts	Pos
Ireland	The Swarbriggs Plus Two	It's Nice To Be In Love Again	119	3
Monaco	Michèle Torr	Une Petite Française	96	4
Netherlands	Heddy Lester	De Mallemolen	35	12
Austria	Schmetterlinge	Boom Boom Boomerang	11	17
Norway	Anita Skorgan	Casanova	18	14
Germany	Silver Convention	Telegram	55	8
Luxembourg	Anne-Marie B	Frère Jacques	17	16
Portugal	Os Amigos	Portugal No Coração	18	14
United Kingdom	Lynsey de Paul and Mike Moran	Rock Bottom	121	2
Greece	Pascalis, Marianna, Robert and Bessy	Mathema Solfege	92	5
Israel	Ilanit	Ha'ava Hi Shir Lishnayim	49	11
Switzerland	Pepe Lienhard Band	Swiss Lady	71	6
Sweden	Forbes	Beatles	2	18
Spain	Micky	Enseñame A Cantar	52	9
Italy	Mia Martini	Libera	33	13
Finland	Monica Aspelund	Lapponia	50	10
Belgium	Dream Express	A Million In One, Two, Three	69	7
France	**Marie Myriam**	**L'Oiseau Et L'Enfant**	**136**	**1**

three-year period in which bouncy up tempo numbers had ruled the roost. Songs that followed the example of recent years, like Austria's 'Boom Boom Boomerang' – or, Sweden's 'Beatles', or most obviously Belgium's pre-tournament favourite, 'A Million In One Two Three' – all came unstuck, although Britain's effort, 'Rock Bottom', performed by Lynsey de Paul and Mike Moran, struck a blow for perkiness by taking the runner-up position. Maybe the juries voted for eccentricity rather than musical accomplishment, because the British entry was conducted by musical director Ronnie Hazlehurst wielding an umbrella instead of a baton.

France had been a 16–1 outsider before the contest, behind much more well-backed entries like the UK (9–2), Germany (5–1), Ireland (6–1) and the Netherlands (9–1), but all the betting proves is that it is more difficult to pick the winner of Eurovision than of the Grand National or the World Cup. There is less form to go on, even when previous runners return for another

VOTING BIAS

FRANCE

Countries most likely to vote for France:
Switzerland
Netherlands
Monaco
Austria
Ireland

Countries least likely to vote for France:
Spain
Turkey
UK
Malta
Denmark

Countries for whom France is most likely to vote:
Portugal
Netherlands
UK
Greece
Belgium

Countries for whom France is least likely to vote:
Ireland
Sweden
Norway
Iceland
Malta

Contrary to popular opinion, the French do vote for the UK; in five of the last ten years they have given Britain either 10 or 12 points. It's the British who generally snub the French.

try. Portugal's Os Amigos included Paulo de Cavalho, who had been equal last as a soloist three years earlier in Brighton. Perhaps that is why Portugal was the outsider again this year. Dream Express from Belgium may have been made favourites in part because they included the Maesen sisters, Patricia, Stella and Bianca, who had competed for the Netherlands as Patricia and Hearts of Soul in 1970. But, as in 1970, they came seventh. Stella Maesen went on to compete a third time, simply as Stella, for Belgium in 1982. That time she came fourth.

The voting, announced by Angela Rippon and overseen by Clifford Brown in his eleventh year as EBU scrutineer, became seriously muddled. It began when Greece gave four points to two different countries, Spain and Austria, without anybody noticing, and continued when Israel forgot to announce the recipient of its four points. This was noticed and corrected at once, and by the time France came to give the final vote of the evening, it had already won the competition. That was just as well, because its own voting was a shambles. It got its scores for Portugal and Italy the wrong way round, it gave three points to two different countries, Greece and Israel, and then compounded the errors by giving one point each to two different countries, Belgium and Austria. Nobody noticed, so the result at the end of the evening showed nine of the eighteen countries with scores that were later proved to be incorrect. The totals were subsequently adjusted, with Austria losing two points and the Netherlands, Germany, the UK, Israel, Italy, Finland and Belgium all losing one point. Portugal was the only gainer, going up one point. None of these little adjustments made any difference to the positions, and France won easily, despite gaining only three top marks, compared with Britain's six and Ireland's four. France's first full marks' vote came from Germany, voting sixth, by which time Britain had established its traditional early lead, which, just as traditionally, eventually disappeared.

★ ★

THE EUROVISION SONG CONTEST

1978

Won by Israel: 'A-Ba-Ni-Bi'
Written by Nurit Hirsh and Ehud Manor
Performed by Izhar Cohen and Alphabeta
Orchestra conducted by Nurit Hirsh

1978 EUROVISION SONG CONTEST

Host country: France ★ *Venue:* Palais des Congrès, Paris
Date: 22 April ★ *Presenters:* Denise Fabré and Léon Zitrone
Voting structure: Each country awarded 12 to its top song, 10 to the second, 8 to the third and 7, 6, 5, 4, 3, 2 and 1 point for the next seven ★ *Total entries:* 20 ★ *Debut countries:* None

Country	Performer	Song	Pts	Pos.
Ireland	C. T. Wilkinson	Born To Sing	86	5
Norway	Jahn Teigen	Mil Etter Mil	0	20
Italy	Ricchi e Poveri	Questo Amore	53	12
Finland	Seija Simola	Anna Rakkaudelle Tilaisuus	2	18
Portugal	Gemini	Dai-Li-Dou	5	17
France	Joël Prévost	Il Y Aura Toujours Des Violons	119	3
Spain	José Velez	Bailemos Un Vals	65	9
United Kingdom	Co-Co	The Bad Old Days	61	11
Switzerland	Carole Vinci	Vivre	65	9
Belgium	Jean Vallée	L'Amour Ça Fait Chanter La Vie	125	2
Netherlands	Harmony	'T Is OK	37	13
Turkey	Nazar	Sevince	2	18
Germany	Ireen Sheer	Feuer	84	6
Monaco	Carine and Olivier Toussaint	Les Jardins De Monaco	107	4
Greece	Tania Tsanaklidou	Charlie Chaplin	66	8
Denmark	Mabel	Boom-Boom	13	16
Luxembourg	Baccara	Parlez-Vous Français	73	7
Israel	**Izhar Cohen and Alphabeta**	**A-Ba-Ni-Bi**	**157**	**1**
Austria	Springtime	Mrs Caroline Robinson	14	15
Sweden	Björn Skifs	Det Blir Alltid Värre Framat Natten	26	14

For the first time, a country outside Europe won the Eurovision Song Contest. Rivka Michaeli, then Head of Entertainment on Israeli Radio, described the song as 'not the best of Israeli music. We think of it more as a children's song. There is a children's language here where "B" goes after every word, so you get "A-Ba-Ni-Bi". We never believed it would win, but Izhar was so vivid and the other countries were so terrible.'

The other nineteen 'terrible' countries at the Palais des Congrès in Paris included Ireland, represented by Colm Wilkinson (later a major musical theatre star), performing a song he wrote, which was produced for him by Tim Rice, called 'Born To Sing'. Clive James, reviewing the Contest for *The Sunday Times*, said that the show 'began with an Irishman called C. T. Wilkinson, who proclaimed "I Was Born To Sing". How wrong can you be?' That was followed by Norway's Jahn Teigen scoring no points at all with 'Mil Etter Mil' and two low-scoring efforts from Finland and Portugal. Teigen's failure was the first 'nul points' for eight years and the first under the latest, and so far last, scoring system. Perversely it gave a massive boost to his singing career in Norway, which continued beyond his subsequent failures to repeat his ultimate lows in the contests of 1982 and 1983. The only strong challengers to Israel

1978	Ireland	Norway	Italy	Finland	Portugal	France	Spain	UK	Switzerland	Belgium	Netherlands	Turkey	W. Germany	Monaco
Ireland	0^{x}	12^{12}	12^{0}	15^{3}	15^{0}	20^{5}	20^{0}	20^{0}	27^{7}	37^{10}	37^{0}	47^{10}	52^{5}	52^{0}
Norway	0^{0}	0^{x}	0^{0}	0^{0}	0^{0}	0^{0}	0^{0}	0^{0}	0^{0}	0^{0}	0^{0}	0^{0}	0^{0}	0^{0}
Italy	10^{10}	16^{6}	16^{x}	16^{0}	17^{1}	21^{4}	29^{8}	35^{6}	36^{1}	37^{1}	37^{0}	38^{1}	40^{2}	48^{8}
Finland	0^{0}	2^{2}	2^{0}	2^{x}	2^{0}	2^{0}	2^{0}	2^{0}	2^{0}	2^{0}	2^{0}	2^{0}	2^{0}	2^{0}
Portugal	0^{0}	0^{0}	4^{4}	4^{0}	4^{x}	4^{0}	5^{1}	5^{0}	5^{0}	5^{0}	5^{0}	5^{0}	5^{0}	5^{0}
France	6^{6}	9^{3}	19^{10}	21^{2}	23^{2}	23^{x}	28^{5}	36^{8}	42^{6}	50^{8}	56^{6}	60^{4}	70^{10}	75^{5}
Spain	0^{0}	0^{0}	0^{0}	7^{7}	7^{0}	7^{0}	7^{x}	7^{0}	15^{8}	17^{2}	21^{4}	28^{7}	28^{0}	32^{4}
UK	3^{3}	3^{0}	3^{0}	3^{0}	9^{6}	11^{2}	14^{3}	14^{x}	16^{2}	20^{4}	22^{2}	28^{6}	36^{8}	43^{7}
Switzerland	0^{0}	5^{5}	6^{1}	7^{1}	7^{0}	14^{7}	18^{4}	20^{2}	20^{x}	27^{7}	35^{8}	35^{0}	41^{6}	43^{2}
Belgium	**12^{12}**	**19^{7}**	**25^{6}**	31^{6}	35^{4}	47^{12}	49^{2}	61^{12}	71^{10}	71^{x}	76^{5}	76^{0}	79^{3}	91^{12}
Netherlands	0^{0}	0^{0}	5^{5}	5^{0}	5^{0}	5^{0}	5^{0}	8^{3}	8^{0}	8^{0}	8^{x}	8^{0}	12^{4}	13^{1}
Turkey	0^{0}	1^{1}	1^{0}	1^{0}	1^{0}	1^{0}	1^{0}	2^{1}	2^{0}	2^{0}	2^{0}	2^{x}	2^{0}	2^{0}
W. Germany	1^{1}	1^{0}	4^{3}	16^{12}	23^{7}	23^{0}	33^{10}	33^{0}	36^{3}	41^{5}	48^{7}	56^{8}	56^{x}	66^{10}
Monaco	4^{0}	8^{4}	15^{7}	23^{8}	28^{5}	29^{1}	29^{0}	39^{10}	44^{5}	50^{6}	60^{10}	65^{5}	72^{7}	72^{x}
Greece	7^{7}	7^{0}	9^{2}	14^{5}	22^{8}	32^{10}	39^{7}	39^{0}	43^{4}	43^{0}	43^{0}	43^{0}	43^{0}	43^{0}
Denmark	0^{0}	0^{x}	0^{0}	0^{0}	0^{0}	6^{6}	6^{0}	6^{0}	6^{0}	6^{0}	7^{1}	7^{0}	7^{0}	7^{0}
Luxembourg	2^{2}	2^{0}	14^{12}	14^{0}	26^{12}	26^{0}	38^{12}	45^{7}	45^{0}	48^{3}	51^{3}	53^{2}	53^{0}	59^{6}
Israel	8^{8}	16^{8}	24^{8}	**34^{10}**	**44^{10}**	**52^{8}**	**58^{6}**	**63^{5}**	**75^{12}**	**87^{12}**	**99^{12}**	**111^{12}**	**123^{12}**	**126^{3}**
Austria	0^{0}	0^{x}	0^{0}	0^{0}	3^{3}	3^{0}	3^{0}	3^{0}	3^{0}	3^{0}	3^{0}	6^{3}	7^{1}	7^{0}
Sweden	5^{5}	15^{10}	15^{0}	19^{4}	19^{0}	22^{3}	22^{0}	26^{4}	26^{0}	26^{0}	26^{0}	26^{0}	26^{0}	26^{0}

★ ★

were three French-language songs, from Belgium, France and Monaco. The Spanish duo Maria Mendiola and Mayte Mateus – better known as Baccara and fresh from an international number one with 'Yes Sir, I Can Boogie' – could only come seventh on behalf of Luxembourg, singing 'Parlez-Vous Français'. That song was so like 'Yes Sir, I Can Boogie' that the writers of the former would have been sued for breach of copyright by the writers of the latter had they not been the same people. Eurovision regulars like Ireen Sheer, and Jean Vallée, both making their second appearances, could not overcome the simplicity of Izhar Cohen's song, nor could Björn Skifs, in the first of his two Contests for Sweden. Israel finished thirty-four points clear of Belgium, and the Contest was decided by the time the Israeli jury, eighteenth of the twenty countries voted. Only Sweden, the last country to vote, gave no points to Israel, although it was not until the ninth round of voting that a maximum score was awarded. In the twenty-three Contests since the introduction of the current scoring system in 1975, no other eventual winner has had to wait as long as nine rounds before being given a maximum: indeed only the Netherlands in 1975 and France in 1977 have even had to wait as long as six rounds. As a general rule, the ultimate winning song will receive at least one maximum vote within the first four rounds. Any song that has not done so will almost certainly not win.

Greece	Denmark	Luxembourg	Israel	Austria	Sweden	**Position**
62^{10}	62^{0}	72^{10}	72^{0}	78^{6}	86^{8}	5
0^{0}	0^{0}	0^{0}	0^{0}	0^{0}	0^{0}	20
50^{2}	50^{0}	53^{3}	53^{0}	53^{0}	53^{0}	12
2^{0}	2^{0}	2^{0}	2^{0}	2^{0}	2^{0}	18=
5^{0}	5^{0}	5^{0}	5^{0}	5^{0}	5^{0}	17
83^{8}	91^{8}	92^{1}	97^{5}	109^{12}	119^{10}	3
38^{6}	50^{12}	52^{2}	58^{6}	65^{7}	65^{0}	9=
46^{3}	46^{0}	51^{5}	53^{2}	58^{5}	61^{3}	11
43^{0}	46^{3}	54^{8}	55^{1}	65^{10}	65^{0}	9=
103^{12}	103^{0}	110^{7}	117^{7}	121^{4}	125^{4}	2
13^{0}	18^{5}	24^{6}	36^{12}	36^{0}	37^{1}	13
2^{0}	2^{0}	2^{0}	2^{0}	2^{0}	2^{0}	18=
73^{7}	74^{1}	74^{0}	77^{3}	77^{0}	84^{7}	6
76^{4}	86^{10}	86^{0}	94^{8}	95^{1}	107^{12}	4
43^{x}	47^{4}	51^{4}	61^{10}	64^{3}	66^{2}	8
7^{0}	7^{x}	7^{0}	11^{4}	13^{2}	13^{0}	16
60^{1}	67^{7}	67^{x}	67^{0}	67^{0}	73^{6}	7
131^{5}	**137^{6}**	**149^{12}**	**149^{x}**	**157^{8}**	**157^{0}**	**1**
7^{0}	9^{2}	9^{0}	9^{0}	9^{x}	14^{5}	15
26^{0}	26^{0}	26^{0}	26^{0}	26^{0}	26^{x}	14

Izhar Cohen looked a little like a dark Freddie Mercury, with the same slightly protruding teeth and flamboyant personality. 'Winning Eurovision was easy,' he was quoted as saying. 'The hard part was winning the Israeli contest and figuring out how to present the song. What we were to wear, how we were to act, that was hard.' At the time, the contest to choose the song to represent Israel at Eurovision was indeed a tough one. 'The Elton Johns of Israel are not in this festival, but unlike in England, almost all the twelve artists (in the Israeli heats) are actually stars here.'

Izhar was a star. He began performing when he was in the Israeli army, having been conscripted as were all young Israelis of his generation. 'I was eighteen when I joined the army. Within two months I had a hit record. Where else could you get radio and television exposure, plus all the training and facilities you need in such a short time? The army was a perfect place to start.' In this, he was not alone among Israel's Eurovision stars. Poogy, the group that had represented Israel in the 1974 Contest won by Abba, also got its feet on the first rungs of the ladder while its members were on military service as had Chocolate Menta Mastik who performed in 1976.

★ ★

THE EUROVISION SONG CONTEST

1979

Won by Israel: 'Hallelujah'

Written by Kobi Ashrat and Shimrit Orr

Performed by Gali Atari and Milk and Honey

Orchestra conducted by Kobi Ashrat

For the first, and so far only, Eurovision Song Contest held outside Europe, the setting was Israel's Hollywood Bowl-style Binyaney Ha'ouma Centre, which became for one evening the Euro-pop centre of the universe. The stage was equipped with what looked like a large metal gyroscope, which revolved according to the whim of the stage manager, and the significance of

1979	Portugal	Italy	Denmark	Ireland	Finland	Monaco	Greece	Switzerland	W. Germany	Israel	France	Belgium	Luxembourg
Portugal	0^{x}	6^{6}	6^{0}	6^{0}	8^{2}	13^{5}	13^{0}	17^{4}	21^{4}	21^{0}	31^{10}	36^{5}	39^{3}
Italy	8^{8}	8^{x}	8^{0}	8^{0}	16^{8}	16^{0}	16^{0}	16^{0}	16^{0}	16^{0}	16^{0}	16^{0}	16^{0}
Denmark	0^{0}	0^{0}	0^{x}	2^{2}	2^{0}	5^{3}	17^{12}	18^{1}	28^{10}	40^{12}	46^{6}	53^{7}	57^{4}
Ireland	5^{5}	10^{5}	15^{5}	15^{x}	21^{6}	21^{0}	31^{10}	37^{6}	43^{6}	46^{3}	46^{0}	56^{10}	63^{7}
Finland	0^{0}	7^{7}	7^{0}	7^{0}	7^{x}	7^{0}	14^{7}	22^{8}	27^{5}	27^{0}	32^{5}	32^{0}	38^{6}
Monaco	1^{1}	3^{2}	7^{4}	7^{0}	7^{0}	7^{x}	7^{0}	7^{0}	7^{0}	7^{0}	10^{3}	10^{0}	10^{0}
Greece	10^{10}	10^{0}	11^{1}	15^{4}	15^{0}	22^{7}	22^{x}	29^{7}	31^{2}	41^{10}	45^{4}	46^{1}	51^{5}
Switzerland	0^{0}	0^{0}	7^{7}	8^{1}	18^{10}	20^{2}	22^{2}	22^{x}	29^{7}	33^{4}	40^{7}	40^{0}	40^{0}
W. Germany	2^{2}	3^{1}	15^{12}	20^{5}	23^{3}	35^{12}	35^{0}	35^{0}	35^{x}	41^{6}	53^{12}	57^{4}	58^{1}
Israel	**12^{12}**	12^{0}	18^{6}	**30^{12}**	**42^{12}**	**50^{8}**	**54^{4}**	**59^{5}**	**59^{0}**	**59^{x}**	60^{1}	62^{2}	70^{8}
France	6^{6}	**16^{6}**	16^{0}	16^{0}	17^{1}	27^{10}	35^{8}	45^{10}	45^{0}	50^{5}	50^{x}	56^{6}	68^{12}
Belgium	0^{0}	0^{0}	2^{2}	2^{0}	2^{0}	2^{0}	2^{0}	2^{0}	3^{1}	3^{0}	3^{0}	3^{x}	3^{0}
Luxembourg	7^{7}	7^{0}	7^{0}	10^{3}	14^{4}	18^{4}	23^{5}	26^{3}	26^{0}	26^{0}	28^{2}	28^{0}	28^{x}
Netherlands	0^{0}	0^{0}	8^{8}	18^{10}	23^{5}	23^{0}	26^{3}	26^{0}	29^{3}	36^{7}	36^{0}	39^{3}	39^{0}
Sweden	0^{0}	0^{0}	0^{0}	6^{6}	6^{0}	6^{0}	7^{1}	7^{0}	7^{0}	8^{1}	8^{0}	8^{0}	8^{0}
Norway	3^{3}	6^{3}	6^{0}	14^{8}	14^{0}	20^{6}	20^{0}	20^{0}	20^{0}	22^{2}	22^{0}	30^{8}	32^{2}
UK	4^{4}	12^{8}	**22^{10}**	29^{7}	36^{7}	37^{1}	37^{0}	39^{2}	47^{8}	47^{0}	47^{0}	47^{0}	47^{0}
Austria	0^{0}	4^{4}	4^{0}	4^{0}	4^{0}	4^{0}	4^{0}	4^{0}	4^{0}	4^{0}	4^{0}	4^{0}	4^{0}
Spain	0^{0}	12^{12}	15^{3}	15^{0}	15^{0}	15^{0}	21^{6}	33^{12}	45^{12}	53^{8}	**61^{8}**	**73^{12}**	**83^{10}**

which was never really explained. Still, it did not appear to put off too many of the performers.

It was not, it must be confessed, a vintage year. Portugal's entry, a jolly number about a balloon, set the tone for blandness, which none of the next few songs did much to dispel. The only distinguishing characteristic of the show at this stage was the bizarre entr'acte mime performances, which were supposed to sum up the character of the country about to perform, but which were little more than entirely politically incorrect stereotypes designed more to insult than to inspire. However, as the history of Europe has been about loathing thy neighbour, it seems that nobody complained; in fact, everybody rather enjoyed seeing the Portuguese portrayed as port-swigging fishermen, the Brits as bearskin-wearing guards, the Swiss as clock-makers and the Belgians as ... what was it? Oh well, nobody ever remembers the Belgians. What we do remember about the Belgian entry is that it was performed in Flemish (if 'hey nana nanananana' is Flemish, of course) by Micha Marah who went on to become manager to Sandra Kim, Belgium's thirteen-year-old French-speaking winner of 1986.

Denmark's entry was called 'Disco Tango', a combination of two musical styles, neither of which is particularly Danish, while Laurent Vaguener of Monaco mentioned that well-known Monegasque musical style, rock'n'roll, in line one of his 'Notre Vie, C'est La Musique'/'Our Life Is Music'. It took Greece to break the boredom, with a remarkable tribute to the fifth-century BC Athenian philosopher Socrates. Elpida belted out her paean of praise to 'Socrates Superstar' to receive a great reaction from the audience, but a lesser one from the voting juries. To ensure that Eurovision 1979 was not going to go down as the dullest on record, the Swiss entry included a trio of musicians (Pfuri, Gorps and Kniri) playing everything from dustbin lids to garden rakes and shears, not forgetting some beautiful moments with the garden hose. 'If the judges are looking for a curiosity,' said BBC commentator John Dunn with admirable understatement, 'they could do it again.' The judges weren't. That might also explain why Germany's tribute to the thirteenth-century Mongol emperor 'Dschingis Khan', done in the style of Boney M meets the Village People, failed to win, although it did receive four first-place votes and ended up fourth.

In third place at the end of the voting was France's Anne-Marie David, who had won the contest for Luxembourg in 1973. The obscure but unique distinction she thus earned for herself is that of being the only previous winner to perform again for a different country. Nine winners in all

Netherlands	Sweden	Norway	UK	Austria	Spain	**Position**
42^{3}	45^{3}	51^{6}	51^{0}	58^{7}	64^{6}	9
16^{0}	16^{0}	19^{3}	19^{0}	19^{0}	27^{8}	15
65^{8}	66^{1}	66^{0}	69^{3}	72^{3}	76^{4}	6
63^{0}	71^{8}	76^{5}	80^{4}	80^{0}	80^{0}	5
38^{0}	38^{0}	38^{0}	38^{0}	38^{0}	38^{0}	14
10^{0}	10^{0}	10^{0}	10^{0}	10^{0}	12^{2}	16
58^{7}	60^{2}	60^{0}	60^{0}	62^{2}	69^{7}	8
40^{0}	40^{0}	48^{8}	48^{0}	60^{12}	60^{0}	10
60^{2}	66^{6}	66^{0}	74^{8}	74^{0}	86^{12}	4
71^{1}	83^{12}	95^{12}	**107^{12}**	115^{8}	**125^{10}**	**1**
80^{12}	85^{5}	92^{7}	98^{6}	103^{5}	106^{3}	3
3^{0}	3^{0}	3^{0}	5^{2}	5^{0}	5^{0}	18=
32^{4}	32^{0}	34^{2}	44^{10}	44^{0}	44^{0}	13
39^{x}	43^{4}	47^{4}	47^{0}	51^{4}	51^{0}	12
8^{0}	8^{x}	8^{0}	8^{0}	8^{0}	8^{0}	17
28^{6}	48^{10}	48^{x}	55^{7}	56^{1}	57^{1}	11
52^{5}	52^{0}	62^{10}	62^{x}	68^{6}	73^{5}	7
4^{0}	4^{0}	4^{0}	5^{1}	5^{x}	5^{0}	18=
93^{10}	**100^{7}**	**101^{1}**	106^{5}	**116^{10}**	116^{x}	2

★ ★

1979 EUROVISION SONG CONTEST

Host country: Israel ★ *Venue:* Binyaney Ha'ouma Centre, Jerusalem
Date: 31 March ★ *Presenters:* Daniel Pe'er and Yardena Arazi
Voting structure: Each country awarded 12 to its top song, 10 to the second, 8 to the third and 7, 6, 5, 4, 3, 2 and 1 point for the next seven
Total entries: 19 ★ *Debut countries:* None

Country	Performer	Song	Pts	Pos.
Portugal	Manuela Bravo	Sobe, Sobe Balão Sobe	64	9
Italy	Matia Bazar	Raggio Di Luna	27	15
Denmark	Tommy Seebach	Disco Tango	76	6
Ireland	Cathal Dunne	Happy Man	80	5
Finland	Katri Helena	Katson Sineen Taivaan	38	14
Monaco	Laurent Vaguener	Notre Vie, C'est La Musique	12	16
Greece	Elpida	Socrates	69	8
Switzerland	Peter, Sue and Marc, and Pfuri, Gorps and Kniri	Trödler und Co	60	10
Germany	Dschingis Khan	Dschingis Khan	86	4
Israel	**Milk and Honey featuring Gali Atari**	**Hallelujah**	**125**	**1**
France	Anne-Marie David	Je Suis L'Enfant Soleil	106	3
Belgium	Micha Marah	Hey Nana	5	18
Luxembourg	Jeane Manson	J'ai Déjà Vu Ça Dans Tes Yeux	44	13
Netherlands	Xandra	Colorado	51	12
Sweden	Ted Gärdestad	Satellit	8	17
Norway	Anita Skorgan	Oliver	57	11
United Kingdom	Black Lace	Mary Ann	73	7
Austria	Christine Simon	Heute In Jerusalem	5	18
Spain	Betty Missiego	Su Canciõn	116	2

have come back again for another try, and two others have won at their second or third try, but only Anne-Marie did it under a different flag.

However, the only serious challenger to Israel's simple peace message was Spain's Betty Missiego who had all the advantages – she sang last and had four little children on stage with her, singing 'la la la' in the background. They even held up little signs saying 'Thanks' in English, French, Spanish and Hebrew. But it was not quite enough to beat Gali Atari and her three friends in gold braces, who gave Israel their second successive Eurovision victory. Despite this Euro-domination, Israel decided against entering the competition the next year, because the date coincided with its Holocaust Remembrance Day. So, after becoming only the second nation to retain its title, it became the only winner to not defend it.

★ ★

THE EUROVISION SONG CONTEST 1980

Won by Ireland: 'What's Another Year?'
Written by Shay Healy
Performed by Johnny Logan
Orchestra conducted by Noel Kelehan

1980 EUROVISION SONG CONTEST

Host country: Netherlands ★ *Venue:* Congresgebouw, Den Haag
Date: 9 April ★ *Presenter:* Marlous Fluitsma
Voting structure: Each country awarded 12 to its top song, 10 to the second, 8 to the third and 7, 6, 5, 4, 3, 2 and 1 point for the next seven
Total entries: 19 ★ *Debut countries:* Morocco

Country	Performer	Song	Pts	Pos.
Austria	Blue Danube	Du Bist Musik	64	8
Turkey	Ajda Pekkan	Petr'oil	23	15
Greece	Anna Vissi	Autostop	30	13
Luxembourg	Sophie and Magaly	Le Papa Pingouin	56	9
Morocco	Samira Ben Said	Bitakat Hob	7	18
Italy	Alan Sorrenti	Non So Che Darei	87	6
Denmark	Bamses Venner	Tænker Altid På Dig	25	14
Sweden	Tomas Ledin	Just Nu	47	10
Switzerland	Paola	Cinéma	104	4
Finland	Vesa-Matti Loiri	Huilumies	6	19
Norway	Sverre Kjelsberg and Mattis Haetta	Samiid Aednan	15	16
Germany	Katja Ebstein	Theater	128	2
United Kingdom	Prima Donna	Love Enough For Two	106	3
Portugal	José Cid	Um Grande, Grande Amor	71	7
Netherlands	Maggie McNeal	Amsterdam	93	5
France	Profil	Hé, Hé, M'sieurs Dames	45	11
Ireland	**Johnny Logan**	**What's Another Year?**	**143**	**1**
Spain	Trigio Limpio	Quedate Esta Noche	38	12
Belgium	Telex	Eurovision	14	17

★ ★

The beginning of the Irish domination of the Eurovision Song Contest was Johnny Logan's 1980 ballad, 'What's Another Year?' Given a clear run because the winner in the previous two years, Israel, declined to take part, the Irish gave Eurovision its first solo male vocalist winner since 1966. Johnny Logan, born Sean Sherrard and at the time an Australian citizen (he took Irish nationality before his second win in 1987), won fairly easily from Katja Ebstein, singing again for Germany after a gap of nine years. Having come third in consecutive years in 1970 and 1971, she improved by one place, but still had to admit defeat to the Irish.

Many acts have seen their careers given a kick-start or even a huge boost by Eurovision, but few have done as well as Johnny Logan. Obviously Abba (1974) are the biggest stars to have emerged directly from the Contest, but as Cliff Richard said to Olivia Newton-John before she had decided whether or not to accept the invitation to sing for Britain in 1974, 'Do it, because you are going to sell a lot of records, win or lose.' It can be a wonderful springboard for a career, but, if worked wrongly, it can also be the kiss of death. In Britain and across most of Europe, Eurovision participation is hardly a sign of musical credibility, but street cred is not the only thing on which to build a career. For every Gali Atari who does little after a Eurovision success, there is a

1980	Austria	Turkey	Greece	Luxembourg	Morocco	Italy	Denmark	Sweden	Switzerland	Finland	Norway	W. Germany	UK
Austria	0^{x}	0^{0}	1^{1}	`1^{0}	4^{3}	8^{4}	13^{5}	14^{1}	18^{4}	23^{5}	29^{6}	33^{4}	39^{6}
Turkey	3^{3}	3^{x}	3^{0}	3^{0}	15^{12}	23^{8}	23^{0}	23^{0}	23^{0}	23^{0}	23^{0}	23^{0}	23^{0}
Greece	5^{5}	5^{0}	5^{x}	6^{1}	6^{0}	8^{2}	10^{2}	10^{0}	10^{0}	10^{0}	14^{4}	14^{0}	17^{3}
Luxembourg	1^{1}	2^{1}	2^{0}	2^{x}	2^{0}	2^{0}	6^{4}	12^{6}	12^{0}	15^{3}	22^{7}	22^{0}	30^{8}
Morocco	0^{0}	0^{0}	0^{0}	0^{0}	0^{x}	7^{7}	7^{0}	7^{0}	7^{0}	7^{0}	7^{0}	7^{0}	7^{0}
Italy	2^{2}	8^{6}	10^{2}	10^{0}	10^{0}	10^{x}	13^{3}	23^{10}	31^{8}	37^{6}	39^{2}	46^{7}	50^{4}
Denmark	0^{0}	0^{0}	4^{4}	4^{0}	6^{2}	6^{0}	6^{x}	6^{0}	12^{6}	19^{7}	20^{1}	25^{5}	25^{0}
Sweden	0^{0}	8^{8}	18^{10}	28^{10}	34^{6}	39^{5}	39^{0}	39^{x}	44^{5}	44^{0}	44^{0}	46^{2}	46^{0}
Switzerland	6^{6}	8^{2}	8^{0}	13^{5}	20^{7}	23^{3}	31^{8}	33^{2}	33^{x}	45^{12}	55^{10}	65^{10}	72^{7}
Finland	0^{0}	0^{0}	0^{0}	0^{0}	0^{0}	0^{0}	0^{0}	0^{0}	0^{0}	0^{x}	5^{5}	5^{0}	5^{0}
Norway	0^{0}	0^{0}	0^{0}	0^{0}	4^{4}	4^{0}	4^{0}	4^{0}	4^{0}	4^{0}	4^{x}	10^{6}	10^{0}
W. Germany	8^{8}	18^{10}	18^{0}	21^{3}	31^{10}	**43^{12}**	**50^{7}**	**55^{5}**	**62^{7}**	64^{2}	64^{0}	64^{x}	74^{10}
UK	7^{7}	12^{5}	12^{0}	20^{8}	28^{8}	28^{0}	38^{10}	50^{12}	60^{10}	64^{4}	64^{0}	67^{3}	67^{x}
Portugal	0^{0}	4^{4}	9^{5}	13^{4}	13^{0}	23^{10}	29^{6}	37^{8}	39^{2}	40^{1}	48^{8}	49^{1}	49^{0}
Netherlands	**12^{12}**	**24^{12}**	**30^{6}**	**42^{12}**	**42^{0}**	42^{0}	42^{0}	45^{3}	48^{3}	58^{10}	58^{0}	66^{8}	68^{2}
France	0^{0}	3^{3}	10^{7}	12^{2}	13^{1}	13^{0}	14^{1}	18^{4}	19^{1}	19^{0}	22^{3}	22^{0}	27^{5}
Ireland	10^{10}	10^{0}	22^{12}	29^{7}	29^{0}	30^{1}	42^{12}	49^{7}	61^{12}	**69^{8}**	**81^{12}**	**93^{12}**	**105^{12}**
Spain	4^{4}	11^{7}	19^{8}	25^{6}	30^{5}	36^{6}	36^{0}	36^{0}	36^{0}	36^{0}	36^{0}	36^{0}	36^{0}
Belgium	0^{0}	0^{0}	3^{3}	3^{0}	3^{0}	3^{0}	3^{0}	3^{0}	3^{0}	3^{0}	3^{0}	3^{0}	4^{1}

Johnny Logan, a Buck's Fizz, an Abba or a Céline Dion. Without Eurovision, there would probably have been far fewer acts like Julio Iglesias, Olivia Newton-John, France Gall and Vicky Leandros. Even established international stars like Cliff Richard, Sandie Shaw, Siw Malmkvist and Françoise Hardy have benefited from Eurovision appearances, while beginners like Nana Mouskouri, Ofra Haza and Ester Ofarim have used Eurovision as a way of getting their voices and singing styles in front of huge audiences, without having to compromise their entire careers for one night of Euro-pop. However, it could be argued that Telex, performing last for Belgium only a few months after their Europe-wide hit version of 'Rock Around The Clock', did indeed compromise their image for Eurovision. They never hit it big outside Belgium again.

Portugal	Netherlands	France	Ireland	Spain	Belgium	**Position**
42^{3}	45^{3}	49^{4}	59^{10}	63^{4}	64^{1}	8
23^{0}	23^{0}	23^{0}	23^{0}	23^{0}	23^{0}	15
18^{1}	26^{8}	26^{0}	30^{4}	30^{0}	30^{0}	13
30^{0}	30^{0}	37^{7}	45^{8}	48^{3}	56^{8}	9
7^{0}	7^{0}	7^{0}	7^{0}	7^{0}	7^{0}	18
62^{12}	63^{1}	65^{2}	67^{2}	77^{10}	87^{10}	6
25^{0}	25^{0}	25^{0}	25^{0}	25^{0}	25^{0}	14
46^{0}	46^{0}	46^{0}	46^{0}	47^{1}	47^{0}	10
78^{6}	88^{10}	88^{0}	100^{12}	102^{2}	104^{2}	4
5^{0}	5^{0}	6^{1}	6^{0}	6^{0}	6^{0}	19
10^{0}	12^{2}	15^{3}	15^{0}	15^{0}	15^{0}	16
82^{8}	94^{12}	104^{10}	109^{5}	121^{12}	128^{7}	2
74^{7}	81^{7}	86^{5}	92^{6}	100^{8}	106^{6}	3
49^{x}	54^{5}	60^{6}	67^{7}	67^{0}	71^{4}	7
72^{4}	72^{x}	84^{12}	85^{1}	90^{5}	93^{3}	5
27^{0}	31^{4}	31^{x}	34^{3}	40^{6}	45^{5}	11
110^{5}	**116**^{6}	**124**^{8}	**124**^{x}	**131**^{7}	**143**^{12}	**1**
38^{2}	38^{0}	38^{0}	38^{0}	38^{x}	38^{0}	12
14^{10}	14^{0}	14^{0}	14^{0}	14^{0}	14^{x}	17

Anna Vissi, singing for Greece, had the disadvantage of performing immediately after the Turkish entry. This was only the second time that Turkey and Greece had agreed to sing in the same Contest, and it was inevitable, perhaps, that it turned out also to be the second time in which Turkey and Greece failed to give each other any votes. When Anna Vissi returned in 1982, singing for Cyprus, she had a stronger song and even without the presence (and thus the twelve points) of Greece, she still managed to come fifth.

The subject matter of the songs was getting blander rather than more interesting as writers and performers searched for the formula for Europe-wide musical appeal. The only song ever called 'Eurovision' had to battle with Germany's 'Theater' and Switzerland's 'Cinéma'. Austria announced that 'Du Bist Musik'/'You Are Music', the French song said hallo, the Danish song said thank you and the Greek song just said stop.

The Irish entry for 1980 was conducted by Noel Kelehan, by far the most successful conductor in Eurovision history. There have been many famous names holding the baton at the Contest, some of them far more distinguished than the performers they were helping, but only Kelehan has conducted as many as five winning songs (1980, 1987, 1992, 1993 and 1996). Franck Pourcel, Dolf van der Linden, Raymond Lefevre and Alyn Ainsworth are among the distinguished conductors who have appeared many times at Eurovision, but nobody has had quite the success over so many years that Noel Kelehan has enjoyed.

In 1980, the only official African entrant took part in Eurovision. In the absence of Israel, Morocco was allowed in. Samira Ben Said sang well and ethnically, but failed to impress the juries. 'Bitakat Hob' finished ahead of Finland, but behind everybody else, and Israel returned the next year. The Moroccans never tried again.

★ ★

THE EUROVISION SONG CONTEST

1981

Won by United Kingdom: 'Making Your Mind Up'
Written by Andy Hill and John Danter
Performed by Buck's Fizz
Orchestra conducted by John Coleman

The twenty-sixth contest, held for the second time in Dublin, was broadcast live to twenty-nine countries, giving an audience rather generously estimated by the RTE producers as 'over 500 million'. These half a billion lucky people were first of all treated to a travelogue of

1981	Austria	Turkey	W. Germany	Luxembourg	Israel	Denmark	Yugoslavia	Finland	France	Spain	Netherlands	Ireland	Norway	UK
Austria	0^{x}	6^{6}	6^{0}	6^{0}	6^{0}	7^{1}	7^{0}	7^{0}	12^{5}	18^{6}	18^{0}	18^{0}	18^{0}	18^{0}
Turkey	0^{0}	0^{x}	0^{0}	1^{1}	1^{0}	1^{0}	4^{3}	9^{5}	9^{0}	9^{0}	9^{0}	9^{0}	9^{0}	9^{0}
W. Germany	5^{5}	**17^{12}**	17^{x}	20^{3}	28^{8}	36^{8}	38^{2}	45^{7}	53^{8}	65^{12}	68^{3}	74^{6}	78^{4}	85^{7}
Luxembourg	10^{10}	10^{0}	15^{5}	15^{x}	18^{3}	18^{0}	18^{0}	22^{4}	25^{3}	26^{1}	26^{0}	26^{0}	26^{0}	26^{0}
Israel	8^{8}	8^{0}	8^{0}	12^{4}	12^{x}	12^{0}	12^{0}	18^{6}	18^{0}	18^{0}	25^{7}	32^{7}	40^{8}	44^{4}
Denmark	0^{0}	1^{1}	2^{1}	9^{7}	9^{0}	9^{x}	9^{0}	9^{0}	13^{4}	16^{3}	18^{2}	18^{0}	18^{0}	23^{5}
Yugoslavia	0^{0}	4^{4}	4^{0}	4^{0}	4^{0}	4^{0}	4^{x}	12^{8}	12^{0}	12^{0}	12^{0}	14^{2}	15^{1}	15^{0}
Finland	0^{0}	0^{0}	0^{0}	0^{0}	2^{2}	2^{0}	2^{0}	2^{x}	3^{1}	5^{2}	10^{5}	15^{5}	15^{0}	15^{0}
France	**12^{12}**	12^{0}	**24^{12}**	**36^{12}**	**43^{7}**	45^{2}	49^{4}	**59^{10}**	59^{0}	59^{0}	65^{6}	69^{4}	74^{5}	75^{1}
Spain	0^{0}	10^{10}	10^{0}	10^{0}	16^{6}	16^{0}	16^{0}	16^{0}	16^{0}	16^{x}	20^{4}	23^{3}	33^{10}	33^{0}
Netherlands	3^{3}	8^{5}	11^{3}	11^{0}	15^{4}	22^{7}	22^{0}	22^{0}	24^{2}	31^{7}	31^{x}	31^{0}	31^{0}	37^{6}
Ireland	7^{7}	10^{3}	16^{6}	26^{10}	36^{10}	**48^{12}**	**53^{5}**	53^{0}	59^{6}	64^{5}	74^{10}	74^{x}	74^{0}	74^{0}
Norway	0^{0}	0^{0}	0^{0}	0^{0}	0^{0}	0^{0}	0^{0}	0^{0}	0^{0}	0^{0}	0^{0}	0^{0}	0^{x}	0^{0}
UK	4^{4}	12^{8}	16^{4}	21^{5}	33^{12}	43^{10}	53^{10}	56^{3}	**63^{7}**	**71^{8}**	**83^{12}**	**93^{10}**	**96^{3}**	96^{x}
Portugal	0^{0}	0^{0}	8^{8}	8^{0}	8^{0}	8^{0}	8^{0}	8^{0}	8^{0}	8^{0}	8^{0}	8^{0}	8^{0}	8^{0}
Belgium	1^{1}	8^{7}	8^{0}	8^{0}	9^{1}	15^{6}	23^{8}	25^{2}	25^{0}	25^{0}	25^{0}	25^{0}	25^{0}	28^{3}
Greece	6^{6}	6^{0}	8^{2}	14^{6}	14^{0}	14^{0}	15^{1}	15^{0}	15^{0}	25^{10}	25^{0}	26^{1}	28^{2}	36^{8}
Cyprus	0^{0}	0^{0}	0^{0}	0^{0}	5^{5}	8^{3}	14^{6}	140	14^{0}	14^{0}	22^{8}	30^{8}	37^{7}	47^{10}
Switzerland	2^{2}	4^{2}	11^{7}	19^{8}	19^{0}	23^{4}	35^{12}	47^{12}	57^{10}	61^{4}	62^{1}	74^{12}	86^{12}	**98^{12}**
Sweden	0^{0}	0^{0}	10^{10}	12^{2}	12^{0}	17^{5}	24^{7}	25^{1}	37^{12}	37^{0}	37^{0}	37^{0}	43^{6}	45^{2}

Ireland: the use of straightforward tourist promotional materials in Eurovision has become more brazen and more sophisticated as the years have passed. We had views of old castles, of the streets of Dublin, of horse racing, Gaelic football, showjumping, silver working and a hundred impressions of Ireland ancient and modern. What percentage of the half a billion decided there and then to holiday in Ireland that year is not known, but the free publicity that Eurovision gives the host nation each year is always eagerly used to the utmost in an attempt to attract the tourist mark, franc, pound, lira, drachma, krone and the rest.

We are used to the colour green when thinking of Ireland, but in 1981 everybody was determined to ensure that that particular old cliché would be forgotten. The overwhelming impression left after the show was over was of the colour yellow: it seems that every costume designer had decided to use yellow, from bright lemon to deep ochre and every shade *en route*. The RTE presenter, Doireann Ní Bhríain, set the tone with her long yellow gown.

Austria's Marty Brem opened the show with a song called 'Wenn Du Da Bist'/'Whenever You Are There'. For some reason that was not clear from the lyrical or musical content, he needed four dancing girls to help him out, one wearing what looked like an American footballer's helmet. Another one did the splits, perhaps just to show that she could.

Turkey's Modern Folk Trio and Aysegül were all in bright yellow suits. They looked like a Turkish version of Gladys Knight and the Pips, but did not have such strong material. The song was about a carousel, yet another variant on the circus and funfair theme. Lena Valaitis, representing Germany, was preceded on stage by a man with a harmonica and flat hat, but at least Lena herself was wearing black. The song she sang was called 'Johnny Blue'. Without any reference to the colour yellow, Lena eventually finished second. She was followed by Jean-Claude Pascal, who was establishing a Eurovision record by returning twenty years after his previous appearance. In 1961 he had won the competition for Luxembourg, but by 1981 his Charles Aznavour style was too old-fashioned to appeal to the juries: he finished eleventh. Jean Gabilou, the Tahitian representing France, was supported by five back-up vocalists, all in yellow, and Bacchelli, the Italian representing Spain, had two girls in yellow among those adding close harmonies in the background. Linda Williams, the Dutch entrant, was wearing yellow, as were Peter and Marc for Switzerland. The third member of their trio, Sue, was in blue.

Portugal	Belgium	Greece	Cyprus	Switzerland	Sweden	**Position**
18^{0}	18^{0}	18^{0}	18^{0}	18^{0}	20^{2}	17
9^{0}	9^{0}	9^{0}	9^{0}	9^{0}	9^{0}	18=
97^{12}	107^{10}	112^{5}	**120^{8}**	120^{0}	132^{12}	2
30^{4}	30^{0}	30^{0}	30^{0}	36^{6}	41^{5}	11=
49^{5}	49^{0}	49^{0}	49^{0}	53^{4}	56^{3}	7
25^{2}	37^{12}	37^{0}	37^{0}	37^{0}	41^{4}	11=
15^{0}	20^{5}	22^{2}	25^{3}	35^{10}	35^{0}	15
16^{1}	16^{0}	16^{0}	16^{0}	21^{5}	27^{6}	16
85^{10}	88^{3}	96^{8}	103^{7}	115^{12}	125^{10}	3
36^{3}	36^{0}	36^{0}	36^{0}	38^{2}	38^{0}	14
44^{7}	46^{2}	49^{3}	51^{2}	51^{0}	51^{0}	9
74^{0}	75^{1}	85^{10}	97^{12}	98^{1}	105^{7}	5
0^{0}	0^{0}	0^{0}	0^{0}	0^{0}	0^{0}	20
102^{6}	**110^{8}**	**116^{6}**	**120^{4}**	**128^{8}**	**136^{8}**	**1**
8^{x}	8^{0}	9^{1}	9^{0}	9^{0}	9^{0}	18=
28^{0}	28^{x}	35^{7}	40^{5}	40^{0}	40^{0}	13
36^{0}	42^{6}	42^{x}	48^{6}	55^{7}	55^{0}	8
47^{0}	54^{7}	66^{12}	66^{x}	69^{3}	69^{0}	6
106^{8}	106^{0}	110^{4}	**120^{10}**	120^{x}	121^{1}	4
45^{0}	49^{4}	49^{0}	50^{1}	50^{0}	50^{x}	10

★ ★

1981 EUROVISION SONG CONTEST

Host country: Ireland ★ *Venue:* Royal Dublin Society, Dublin
Date: 4 April ★ *Presenter:* Doireann Ní Bhríain
Voting structure: Each country awarded 12 to its top song, 10 to the second, 8 to the third and 7, 6, 5, 4, 3, 2 and 1 point for the next seven
Total entries: 20 ★ *Debut countries:* Cyprus

Country	Performer	Song	Pts	Pos.
Austria	Marty Brem	Wenn Du Da Bist	20	17
Turkey	Modern Folk Trio and Aysegül	Dönme Dolap	9	18
Germany	Lena Valaitis	Johnny Blue	132	2
Luxembourg	Jean-Claude Pascal	C'est Peut-être Pas l'Amérique	41	11
Israel	Habibi	Layla	56	7
Denmark	Debbie Cameron and Tommy Seebach	Krøller Eller Ej	41	11
Yugoslavia	Seid Memic-Vajta	Leila	35	15
Finland	Riki Sorsa	Reggae OK	27	16
France	Jean Gabilou	Humanahum	125	3
Spain	Bacchelli	Y Solo Tu	38	14
Netherlands	Linda Williams	Het Is Een Wonder	51	9
Ireland	Sheeba	Horoscopes	105	5
Norway	Finn Kalvik	Aldri I Livet	0	20
United Kingdom	**Buck's Fizz**	**Making Your Mind Up**	**136**	**1**
Portugal	Carlos Paião	Play-back	9	18
Belgium	Emly Starr	Samson	40	13
Greece	Yiannis Dimitras	Feggari Kalokerino	55	8
Cyprus	Island	Monika	69	6
Switzerland	Peter, Sue and Marc	Io Senza Te	121	4
Sweden	Björn Skifs	Fångad I En Dröm	50	10

The most-remembered costumes were probably the Flash Gordon cast-offs worn by Sheeba, described as 'three attractive Irish girls', wearing pale blue-green body stockings with bits of plastic sticking out like coat hangers in all directions. Those costumes were definitely more memorable, if no better, than the song. One member of Sheeba, Maxi, had sung for Ireland as a soloist eight years before, but then she had worn something more sensible. Finn Kalvik, Norway's record-breaking third 'nul points' man, sat on a stool plucking a guitar and, to take up the sports clothing theme started by the Austrian dancing girls, was wearing what looked like the complete Everton strip – scarf and all.

The Finnish entry was 1981's contribution to the absurdities of Eurovision. Riki Sorsa, a slightly chubby version of Rod Stewart, wore a

★ ★

yellow and electric pink top, with harlequin check trousers. The song, co-written with Englishman Jim Pembroke, was a tribute to that typically Finnish music style, 'Reggae OK', and it was certainly the only reggae song ever written with an accordion instrumental break.

But Buck's Fizz won. Mike Nolan, Bobby G, Cheryl Baker (née Rita Crudgington) and Jay Aston shook their tail feathers to the most up tempo number of the night, and set themselves up for a career as successful as any British Eurovision winner before or since. They followed Eurovision precendent by singing fairly late in the show (fourteenth out of twenty) and by having somebody in the group who had done Eurovision before (Cheryl Baker had been part of Co-Co three years earlier).

After Buck's Fizz had finished, the rest of the contest was notable only for the eighteen-year-old Sophie, wearing yellow, playing piano for Yiannis Dimitras of Greece, and for the first entry by Cyprus (five people in blue, which made a change).

The voting was very close, and there were the usual snarl-ups. EBU scrutineer Frank Naef had to interrupt the very first voting jury, from Austria, because they started by giving five points for Germany: 'You should start with the ascending order. I can't understand why you start with five.' There were problems with the scoreboard all night – it kept bouncing the Turkish score back to zero. 'Can I have your votes, please, Yugoslavia', provoked the curt reply, 'I don't have it', but in the end all was settled.

With two rounds to go, the voting was a three-way tie between Germany, the UK and Switzerland, which had yet to vote. When it gave eight points to the UK, but none to Germany, the contest was all but over. Despite a maximum for Germany from the final jury in Sweden, Buck's Fizz won by four points. When they reprised the song at the end of the broadcast, they established new standards for singing off-key, but none of the British fans seemed to mind. The song went to number one in the UK.

VOTING BIAS

CYPRUS

Countries most likely to vote for Cyprus:
Greece
Yugoslavia
Denmark
Finland
Iceland

Countries least likely to vote for Cyprus:
Turkey
Austria
Luxembourg
Sweden
Bosnia

Countries for whom Cyprus is most likely to vote:
Greece
Yugoslavia
Spain
France
Italy

Countries for whom Cyprus is least likely to vote:
UK
Turkey
Sweden
Israel
Iceland

Cyprus has never once voted for Turkey, but as Turkey does not receive a tremendous number of votes anyway, the Cypriot bias against it is not as pronounced as against the United Kingdom.

THE EUROVISION SONG CONTEST

1982

Won by Germany: 'Ein Bisschen Frieden'
Written by Ralph Siegel and Bernd Meinunger
Performed by Nicole
Orchestra conducted by Norbert Daum

The philosophy of Eurovision seems to be 'if at first you don't succeed, try, try again'. But in 1982 the two extremes of this idea were displayed to all those who were at Harrogate. (Where? The same question occurred to the BBC, which began proceedings with an animated map of Europe, from all parts of which came the same question, 'Where's Harrogate?' in a multitude of languages. Most Europeans still do not know the answer.)

1982	Potugal	Luxembourg	Norway	UK	Turkey	Finland	Switzerland	Cyprus	Sweden	Austria	Belgium	Spain	Denmark	Yugoslavia	Israel	Netherlands	Ireland	Germany	**Position**
Portugal	0^{x}	7^{7}	7^{0}	11^{4}	16^{5}	18^{2}	19^{1}	19^{0}	25^{6}	25^{0}	25^{0}	25^{0}	25^{0}	25^{0}	26^{1}	30^{4}	32^{2}	32^{0}	13
Luxembourg	6^{6}	6^{x}	13^{7}	19^{6}	22^{3}	29^{7}	29^{0}	29^{0}	29^{0}	31^{2}	39^{8}	44^{5}	48^{4}	48^{0}	53^{5}	60^{7}	70^{10}	78^{8}	6
Norway	0^{0}	6^{6}	6^{x}	6^{0}	6^{0}	6^{0}	6^{0}	10^{4}	14^{4}	20^{6}	22^{2}	24^{2}	24^{0}	24^{0}	24^{0}	24^{0}	30^{6}	40^{10}	12
UK	4^{4}	16^{12}	22^{6}	22^{x}	32^{10}	36^{4}	41^{5}	44^{3}	44^{0}	56^{12}	56^{0}	57^{1}	59^{2}	65^{6}	67^{2}	68^{1}	75^{7}	76^{1}	7
Turkey	0^{0}	8^{8}	11^{3}	11^{0}	11^{x}	12^{1}	15^{3}	15^{0}	15^{0}	18^{3}	18^{0}	18^{0}	18^{0}	18^{0}	18^{0}	20^{2}	20^{0}	20^{0}	15
Finland	0^{0}	0^{0}	0^{0}	0^{0}	0^{0}	0^{x}	0^{0}	0^{0}	0^{0}	0^{0}	0^{0}	0^{0}	0^{0}	0^{0}	0^{0}	0^{0}	0^{0}	0^{0}	18
Switzerland	2^{2}	4^{2}	8^{4}	20^{12}	22^{2}	22^{0}	22^{x}	28^{6}	30^{2}	40^{10}	52^{12}	52^{0}	59^{7}	69^{10}	79^{10}	89^{10}	97^{8}	97^{0}	3
Cyprus	5^{5}	9^{4}	21^{12}	24^{3}	24^{0}	32^{8}	40^{8}	40^{x}	40^{0}	45^{5}	48^{3}	55^{7}	55^{0}	60^{5}	67^{7}	79^{12}	79^{0}	85^{6}	5
Sweden	7^{7}	10^{3}	18^{8}	23^{5}	23^{0}	26^{3}	30^{4}	30^{0}	30^{x}	38^{8}	43^{5}	47^{4}	55^{8}	57^{2}	57^{0}	62^{5}	65^{3}	67^{2}	8
Austria	0^{0}	0^{0}	0^{0}	10^{10}	17^{7}	17^{0}	17^{0}	24^{7}	24^{0}	24^{x}	30^{6}	38^{8}	44^{6}	48^{4}	52^{4}	52^{0}	57^{5}	57^{0}	9
Belgium	8^{8}	13^{5}	18^{5}	20^{2}	26^{6}	31^{5}	33^{2}	41^{8}	48^{7}	52^{4}	52^{x}	62^{10}	72^{10}	79^{7}	85^{6}	88^{3}	92^{4}	96^{4}	4
Spain	0^{0}	1^{1}	1^{0}	1^{0}	9^{8}	15^{6}	22^{7}	32^{10}	32^{0}	32^{0}	36^{4}	36^{x}	36^{0}	37^{1}	45^{8}	45^{0}	45^{0}	52^{7}	10
Denmark	3^{3}	3^{0}	3^{0}	3^{0}	3^{0}	3^{0}	3^{0}	3^{0}	4^{1}	4^{0}	4^{0}	4^{0}	4^{x}	4^{0}	4^{0}	4^{0}	5^{1}	5^{0}	17
Yugoslavia	0^{0}	0^{0}	0^{0}	0^{0}	4^{4}	4^{0}	4^{0}	5^{1}	17^{12}	17^{0}	18^{1}	18^{0}	21^{3}	21^{x}	21^{0}	21^{0}	21^{0}	21^{0}	14
Israel	10^{10}	20^{10}	21^{1}	22^{1}	22^{0}	34^{12}	44^{10}	46^{2}	56^{10}	63^{7}	70^{7}	76^{6}	77^{1}	80^{3}	80^{x}	88^{8}	88^{0}	100^{12}	2
Netherlands	0^{0}	0^{0}	0^{0}	0^{0}	0^{0}	0^{0}	0^{0}	0^{0}	3^{3}	3^{0}	3^{0}	3^{0}	3^{0}	3^{0}	3^{0}	3^{x}	3^{0}	8^{5}	16
Ireland	1^{1}	1^{0}	3^{2}	10^{7}	11^{1}	11^{0}	17^{6}	22^{5}	27^{5}	27^{0}	27^{0}	30^{3}	35^{5}	43^{8}	46^{3}	46^{0}	46^{x}	49^{3}	11
Germany	12^{12}	12^{0}	22^{10}	30^{8}	42^{12}	52^{10}	64^{12}	76^{12}	84^{8}	85^{1}	95^{10}	107^{12}	119^{12}	131^{12}	143^{12}	149^{6}	161^{12}	161^{x}	1

★ ★

1982 EUROVISION SONG CONTEST

Host country: United Kingdom ★ *Venue:* Conference Centre, Harrogate
Date: 24 April ★ *Presenter:* Jan Leeming
Voting structure: Each country awarded 12 to its top song, 10 to the second, 8 to the third and 7, 6, 5, 4, 3, 2 and 1 point for the next seven
Total entries: 18 ★ *Debut countries:* None

COUNTRY	PERFORMER	SONG	PTS	POS.
Portugal	Doce	Bem Bom	32	13
Luxembourg	Svetlana	Cours Après Le Temps	78	6
Norway	Jahn Teigen and Anita Skorgan	Adieu	40	12
United Kingdom	Bardo	One Step Further	76	7
Turkey	Neco	Hani	20	15
Finland	Kojo	Nuku Pommiin	0	18
Switzerland	Arlette Zola	Amour On T'Aime	97	3
Cyprus	Anna Vissi	Mono I Agapi	85	5
Sweden	Chips	Dag Efter Dag	67	8
Austria	Mess	Sonntag	57	9
Belgium	Stella	Si Tu Aimes Ma Musique	96	4
Spain	Lucia	El	52	10
Denmark	Brixx	Video Video	5	17
Yugoslavia	Aska	Halo Halo	21	14
Israel	Avi Toledano	Hora	100	2
Netherlands	Bill van Dijke	Jij En Ik	8	16
Ireland	The Duskeys	Here Today, Gone Tomorrow	49	11
Germany	**Nicole**	**Ein Bisschen Frieden**	**161**	**1**

The French had obviously not heard of the idea of trying again, because after coming third the year before, with a song called 'Humanahum', declared that the Contest was 'a monument to drivel' and refused to take part. Maybe they just couldn't find Harrogate, because they were back again in 1983. Ralph Siegel, on the other hand, is a more persistent type. Having written Germany's entry in 1979, the unusual 'Dschingis Khan', which came fourth, he tried again in 1980. His song, 'Theater' came second behind Ireland's 'What's Another Year?', so Ralph tried another year. In 1981, his song 'Johnny Blue' was narrowly beaten by another English-language entry – Buck's Fizz with 'Making Your Mind Up' – so he made his mind up to win in 1982. He pulled out all the stops, combining a long-haired, seventeen-year-old, high-school girl, Nicole Hohloch, with a guitar and a stool and lyrics about peace and love. He was also lucky enough to have his song chosen to be performed last, so it was fresh in the juries' minds. Given all these advantages and the

VOTING BIAS

GERMANY

Countries most likely to vote for Germany:

Spain
Denmark
Portugal
UK
Belgium

Countries least likely to vote for Germany:

Greece
Switzerland
Norway
Austria
Finland

Countries for whom Germany is most likely to vote:

Sweden
Netherlands
Norway
Turkey
Monaco

Countries for whom Germany is least likely to vote:

Greece
Yugoslavia
Italy
Cyprus
Austria

Spain favours the southern European countries, but has made an exception for Germany. Similarly, Germany prefers the north, but, because of its significant Turkish population, is biased towards Turkey.

feebleness of much of the opposition, it was fairly astonishing that the other entries gained any votes at all. Germany gained nine first-place votes and three second place votes out of a possible seventeen, and only Luxembourg failed to vote for it at all.

The most noticeable thing about the other entries was that they were all performed by acts with short names. Twelve of the performers had one-word names, and five of those names had only four letters in them. Printer's ink must have been in short supply in Harrogate that year. The song titles ranged from the two letters of the Spanish 'El', through Israel's second-placed 'Hora' and Turkey's 'Hani?' to Ireland's 'Here Today, Gone Tomorrow', the longest title at just twenty-one letters. 'Hora' was a version of the classic Israeli dance, unashamedly based on Izhar Cohen's winning song of four years before, a song whose choreography was as important as its music and its lyrics.

The longest act name was a familiar one: Jahn Teigen and Anita Skorgan, the husband and wife team who put Norway on the Eurovision map by doing so badly as soloists in 1978 and 1979. In 1982, they came twelfth.

With 'A Little Peace' winning so easily, it was perhaps surprising that another song on the same theme should do so badly. The Finnish entry, performed by a man in a red suit called Kojo, was called 'Nuku Pommiin', which roughly translates as 'Don't You Drop That Neutron Bomb On Me'. The music was by Englishman Jim Pembroke, who had been involved with Finland's 'Reggae OK' the year before. Kojo sang it with feeling, smacking his head with his hand every time he got to the chorus. Unfortunately he never hit himself hard enough to prevent him finishing the song.

The Dutch entry, 'Jij En Ik' (seven letters in three words) was written by Dick Bakker, who had won in 1975 with 'Ding Dinge Dong'. This time his song came sixteenth. If at first you succeed, don't try again.

★ ★

THE EUROVISION SONG CONTEST

1983

Won by Luxembourg: 'Si La Vie Est Cadeau'

Written by Jean-Pierre Millers and Alain Garcia

Performed by Corinne Hermès

Orchestra conducted by Michel Bernholc

1983 EUROVISION SONG CONTEST

Host country: West Germany ★ *Venue:* Rudi Sedlmayer Halle, Munich

Date: 23 April ★ *Presenter:* Marlene Charell

Voting structure: Each country awarded 12 to its top song, 10 to the second, 8 to the third and 7, 6, 5, 4, 3, 2 and 1 point for the next seven ★ *Total entries:* 20 ★ *Debut countries:* None

Country	Performer	Song	Pts	Pos.
France	Guy Bonnet	Vivre	56	8
Norway	Jahn Teigen	Do Re Mi	53	9
United Kingdom	Sweet Dreams	I'm Never Giving Up	79	6
Sweden	Carola Häggkvist	Främling	126	3
Italy	Riccardo Fogli	Per Lucia	41	11
Turkey	Cetin Alp and Short Wave	Opera	0	19
Spain	Remedios Amaya	Quién Maneja Mi Barca	0	19
Switzerland	Mariella Farré	Io Cosi Non Ci Sto	28	15
Finland	Ami Aspelund	Fantasiaa	41	11
Greece	Christie	Mou Les	32	14
Netherlands	Bernadette	Sing Me A Song	66	7
Yugoslavia	Daniel	Dzuli	125	4
Cyprus	Stavros and Constantina	I Agapi Ahoma Zi	26	16
Germany	Hoffmann and Hoffmann	Rücksicht	94	5
Denmark	Gry Johansen	Kloden Drejer	16	17
Israel	Ofra Haza	Hi	136	2
Portugal	Armando Gama	Esta Balada Que Te Dou	33	13
Austria	Westend	Hurricane	53	9
Belgium	Pas de deux	Rendez-vous	13	18
Luxembourg	**Corinne Hermès**	**Si La Vie Est Cadeau**	**142**	**1**

In 1983, we saw how cruelly truly national music is treated, and how cruelly originality – or at least, difference – is rewarded. Luxembourg won the contest after some of the most disparate and slow voting so far recorded, with a competent ballad delivered with gusto by Corinne Hermès, but it was not a ground-breaking effort. The voting was disparate in that eight different countries received top marks at least once, and no country received votes from everyone else. Sweden had done until the final round, when leaders Luxembourg (which had already secured its victory by earning eight points from Belgium), decided against giving any points to its main rivals. The voting was also very slow, because presenter Marlene Charell was asked to show off her linguistic skills by announcing each vote in three languages (German, English and French), instead of the usual two. Every so often, her brain got bogged down by the sheer repetitiveness of it all.

The Spanish entry in 1983, like many of its entries before and since, was very obviously Spanish. 'Quién Maneja Mi Barca' means 'Who Is Sailing My Boat?' and it was sung by a leading Flamenco singer, Remedios Amaya. Like Sandie Shaw before her, she sang in bare feet, but there the similarity ended. While Sandie's winning song in 1967 had redefined the direction of Euro-pop

1983	France	Norway	UK	Sweden	Italy	Turkey	Spain	Switzerland	Finland	Greece	Netherlands	Yugoslavia	Cyprus	W. Germany
France	0^{x}	3^{3}	3^{0}	3^{0}	13^{10}	13^{0}	13^{0}	23^{10}	29^{6}	36^{7}	38^{2}	41^{3}	45^{4}	49^{4}
Norway	0^{0}	0^{x}	5^{5}	8^{3}	8^{0}	14^{6}	14^{0}	14^{0}	14^{0}	14^{0}	22^{8}	22^{0}	22^{0}	23^{1}
UK	5^{5}	10^{5}	10^{x}	22^{12}	24^{2}	29^{5}	29^{0}	37^{8}	37^{0}	42^{5}	47^{5}	47^{0}	53^{6}	56^{3}
Sweden	6^{6}	18^{12}	26^{8}	26^{x}	34^{8}	41^{7}	43^{2}	48^{5}	58^{10}	68^{10}	71^{3}	72^{1}	79^{7}	91^{12}
Italy	7^{7}	7^{0}	7^{0}	9^{2}	9^{x}	13^{4}	16^{3}	16^{0}	17^{1}	19^{2}	19^{0}	27^{8}	28^{1}	28^{0}
Turkey	0^{0}	0^{0}	0^{0}	0^{0}	0^{0}	0^{x}	0^{0}	0^{0}	0^{0}	0^{0}	0^{0}	0^{0}	0^{0}	0^{0}
Spain	0^{0}	0^{0}	0^{0}	0^{0}	0^{0}	0^{0}	0^{x}	0^{0}	0^{0}	0^{0}	0^{0}	0^{0}	0^{0}	0^{0}
Switzerland	0^{0}	1^{1}	1^{0}	1^{0}	8^{7}	8^{0}	9^{1}	9^{x}	9^{0}	9^{0}	9^{0}	16^{7}	16^{0}	16^{0}
Finland	1^{1}	3^{2}	9^{6}	9^{0}	9^{0}	12^{3}	12^{0}	16^{4}	16^{x}	24^{8}	24^{0}	24^{0}	24^{0}	31^{7}
Greece	3^{3}	3^{0}	3^{0}	3^{0}	3^{0}	3^{0}	15^{12}	15^{0}	20^{5}	20^{x}	20^{0}	20^{0}	32^{12}	32^{0}
Netherlands	2^{2}	9^{7}	10^{1}	16^{6}	20^{4}	22^{2}	22^{0}	34^{12}	37^{3}	37^{0}	37^{x}	42^{5}	47^{5}	49^{2}
Yugoslavia	0^{0}	8^{8}	20^{12}	20^{0}	21^{1}	33^{12}	43^{10}	43^{0}	55^{12}	61^{6}	68^{7}	68^{x}	76^{8}	82^{6}
Cyprus	0^{0}	4^{4}	4^{0}	4^{0}	4^{0}	4^{0}	4^{0}	5^{1}	5^{0}	5^{0}	5^{0}	11^{6}	11^{x}	16^{5}
W. Germany	10^{10}	**20^{10}**	**27^{7}**	**35^{8}**	**41^{6}**	41^{0}	41^{0}	43^{2}	47^{4}	48^{1}	58^{10}	58^{0}	58^{0}	58^{x}
Denmark	0^{0}	0^{0}	2^{2}	9^{7}	9^{0}	10^{1}	14^{4}	14^{0}	14^{0}	14^{0}	14^{0}	14^{0}	16^{2}	16^{0}
Israel	8^{8}	14^{6}	24^{10}	29^{5}	32^{3}	32^{0}	38^{6}	45^{7}	52^{7}	55^{3}	67^{12}	77^{10}	77^{0}	87^{10}
Portugal	4^{4}	4^{0}	4^{0}	5^{1}	5^{0}	5^{0}	10^{5}	16^{6}	18^{2}	18^{0}	24^{6}	26^{2}	26^{0}	26^{0}
Austria	0^{0}	0^{0}	3^{3}	7^{4}	12^{5}	22^{10}	22^{0}	22^{0}	22^{0}	26^{4}	30^{4}	34^{4}	37^{3}	37^{0}
Belgium	0^{0}	0^{0}	4^{4}	4^{0}	4^{0}	4^{0}	12^{8}	12^{0}	12^{0}	12^{0}	12^{0}	12^{0}	12^{0}	12^{0}
Luxembourg	**12^{12}**	12^{0}	12^{0}	22^{10}	34^{12}	**42^{8}**	**49^{7}**	**52^{3}**	**60^{8}**	**72^{12}**	**73^{1}**	**85^{12}**	**95^{10}**	**103^{8}**

for several years, inspiring many imitators but few worthy successors, Amaya's boat was never going to turn into a bandwagon. Being true to your national culture does not seem to work in Eurovision. Apart from Israel's occasional success (and this year it came second, with a song that was not obviously Israeli in nature), the ethnic songs of Turkey, Spain, Portugal and Greece – not to mention the Celts singing for France, Gaelic songs for Ireland or Kenneth McKellar in a kilt for the United Kingdom – have never won too many votes. Yet they ought to be more interesting than 'Brazil', 'Disco Tango' or Finland's daft 'Reggae OK', which are nothing to do with the local culture.

Denmark	Israel	Portugal	Austria	Belgium	Luxembourg	**Position**
49^{0}	50^{1}	53^{3}	53^{0}	53^{0}	56^{3}	8
31^{8}	35^{4}	41^{6}	44^{3}	51^{7}	53^{2}	9=
61^{5}	61^{0}	63^{2}	73^{10}	73^{0}	79^{6}	6
101^{10}	109^{8}	113^{4}	121^{8}	126^{5}	126^{0}	3
28^{0}	34^{6}	41^{7}	41^{0}	41^{0}	41^{0}	11=
0^{0}	0^{0}	0^{0}	0^{0}	0^{0}	0^{0}	19=
0^{0}	0^{0}	0^{0}	0^{0}	0^{0}	0^{0}	19=
16^{0}	16^{0}	16^{0}	22^{6}	23^{1}	28^{5}	15
31^{0}	38^{7}	38^{0}	40^{2}	40^{0}	41^{1}	11=
32^{0}	32^{0}	32^{0}	32^{0}	32^{0}	32^{0}	14
53^{4}	56^{3}	56^{0}	60^{4}	62^{2}	66^{4}	7
94^{12}	104^{10}	104^{0}	105^{1}	117^{12}	125^{8}	4
17^{1}	22^{5}	22^{0}	22^{0}	26^{4}	26^{0}	16
61^{3}	61^{0}	69^{8}	76^{7}	82^{6}	94^{12}	5
16^{x}	16^{0}	16^{0}	16^{0}	16^{0}	16^{0}	17
94^{7}	94^{x}	104^{10}	116^{12}	126^{10}	136^{10}	2
26^{0}	26^{0}	26^{x}	26^{0}	26^{0}	33^{7}	13
43^{6}	45^{2}	50^{5}	50^{x}	53^{3}	53^{0}	9=
12^{0}	12^{0}	13^{1}	13^{0}	13^{x}	13^{0}	18
105^{2}	**117^{12}**	**129^{12}**	**134^{5}**	**142^{8}**	**142^{x}**	**1**

The Turks tied with Spain for last place with 'nul points'. The song was very odd, to say the least. It was called 'Opera', and the lyrics were 'Opera, opera, opera, opera, Figaro, Fidelio, opera' – or words to that effect. It featured Cetin Alp, a worried-looking Turk with glasses, singing in a semi-operatic sort of baritone, while his backing singers, called Short Wave (which is about all the applause they got at the end), were dressed as opera characters and gave a dramatic feel to it all. It certainly did not deserve to win, but it merited more than the complete brush-off it received. Similarly, Belgium tried something that was described as 'proto-punk' and involved two girls in judo outfits singing 'Rendez-vous' several times over a furious drumbeat. Both songs were far more original than, for example, the Netherlands' 'Sing Me A Song' (sixty-six points) or the host country Germany's 'Rücksicht', which came fourth with ninety-four points. Norway's Jahn Teigen, back again with Anita Skorgan singing uncredited backing vocals, almost redefined unoriginality by singing a song with the chorus, 'Do Re Mi Fa So La Ti Do'. He gained fifty-three votes. Still, nobody ever won Eurovision by being different, as the Greeks learnt again when their tactic of bringing a man on stage to play the triangle was rewarded with a mere thirty-two votes, twelve of which came, as ever, from Cyprus.

There were lots of pianos on stage during the Contest, plenty of acoustic guitars and many performers so relaxed that they had to sit down as they sang. Corinne Hermès was not deflected from her course by these tactics. She gave her dramatic ballad all she could, and it was enough.

It is a useless statistic that the 461st and 462nd songs performed at Eurovision were both winners. The 461st was the last song of 1983, and the 462nd was the first of 1984. Both positions have been proven to be advantageous. However, never before or since have consecutive performances both won the Eurovision Song Contest.

THE EUROVISION SONG CONTEST

1984

Won by Sweden: 'Diggi-Loo Diggi-Ley'

Written by Torgny Söderström and Britt Lindeborg

Performed by the Herreys

Orchestra conducted by Curt-Eric Holmqvist

When Terry Wogan was asked to choose the worst song he had ever witnessed at Eurovision, he replied instantaneously. 'Diggi-Loo, Diggi-Ley' by the Herreys – 'Three boys in gold boots' – was his immediate choice. 'And they won', he added. Not everyone would agree with Mr Wogan's choice (many preferring 'Ding Dinge Dong' by Teach-In, or 'Opera' by Turkey's Cetin

1984	Sweden	Luxembourg	France	Spain	Norway	UK	Cyprus	Belgium	Ireland	Denmark	Netherlands	Yugoslavia	Austria
Sweden	0^{x}	6^{6}	12^{6}	16^{4}	26^{10}	33^{7}	45^{12}	52^{7}	64^{12}	**76^{12}**	**86^{10}**	**90^{4}**	**102^{12}**
Luxembourg	0^{0}	0^{x}	0^{0}	7^{7}	7^{0}	7^{0}	14^{7}	14^{0}	19^{5}	24^{5}	24^{0}	32^{8}	32^{0}
France	2^{2}	2^{0}	2^{x}	2^{0}	4^{2}	10^{6}	13^{3}	23^{10}	23^{0}	23^{0}	35^{12}	35^{0}	43^{8}
Spain	10^{10}	**18^{8}**	**28^{10}**	**28^{x}**	**34^{6}**	38^{4}	44^{6}	47^{3}	54^{7}	61^{7}	63^{2}	65^{2}	71^{6}
Norway	8^{8}	15^{7}	15^{0}	15^{0}	15^{x}	15^{0}	15^{0}	16^{1}	19^{3}	19^{0}	19^{0}	19^{0}	19^{0}
UK	3^{3}	4^{1}	4^{0}	7^{3}	15^{8}	15^{x}	17^{2}	19^{2}	27^{8}	28^{1}	32^{4}	33^{1}	35^{2}
Cyprus	4^{4}	4^{0}	5^{1}	5^{0}	5^{0}	5^{0}	5^{x}	5^{0}	9^{4}	19^{10}	19^{0}	31^{12}	31^{0}
Belgium	0^{0}	12^{12}	24^{12}	26^{2}	29^{3}	29^{0}	29^{0}	29^{x}	29^{0}	29^{0}	37^{8}	37^{0}	40^{3}
Ireland	**12^{12}**	17^{5}	20^{3}	30^{10}	**34^{4}**	42^{8}	**52^{10}**	**64^{12}**	64^{x}	67^{3}	74^{7}	74^{0}	84^{10}
Denmark	5^{5}	8^{3}	16^{8}	22^{6}	**34^{12}**	**46^{12}**	51^{5}	59^{8}	**69^{10}**	69^{x}	72^{3}	78^{6}	82^{4}
Netherlands	0^{0}	2^{2}	9^{7}	17^{8}	17^{0}	18^{1}	18^{0}	18^{0}	24^{6}	24^{0}	24^{x}	29^{5}	29^{0}
Yugoslavia	0^{0}	0^{0}	2^{2}	2^{0}	2^{0}	5^{3}	13^{8}	13^{0}	13^{0}	13^{0}	13^{0}	13^{x}	13^{0}
Austria	0^{0}	0^{0}	0^{0}	0^{0}	0^{0}	0^{0}	0^{0}	0^{0}	1^{1}	5^{4}	5^{0}	5^{0}	5^{x}
W. Germany	0^{0}	0^{0}	4^{4}	4^{0}	11^{7}	13^{2}	13^{0}	19^{6}	19^{0}	21^{2}	26^{5}	26^{0}	27^{1}
Turkey	6^{6}	6^{0}	6^{0}	6^{0}	6^{0}	11^{5}	11^{0}	15^{4}	17^{2}	17^{0}	18^{1}	28^{10}	28^{0}
Finland	7^{7}	7^{0}	12^{5}	13^{1}	18^{5}	18^{0}	22^{4}	22^{0}	22^{0}	28^{6}	28^{0}	31^{3}	36^{5}
Switzerland	1^{1}	1^{0}	1^{0}	1^{0}	1^{0}	1^{11}	12^{1}	17^{5}	17^{0}	25^{8}	25^{0}	25^{0}	25^{0}
Italy	0^{0}	10^{10}	10^{0}	22^{12}	23^{1}	23^{0}	23^{0}	23^{0}	23^{0}	23^{0}	23^{0}	23^{0}	30^{7}
Portugal	0^{0}	4^{4}	4^{0}	9^{5}	9^{0}	9^{0}	9^{0}	9^{0}	9^{0}	9^{0}	15^{6}	22^{7}	22^{0}

Alp in 1983), but all would agree that there have been many better winners than 1984's bouncy but entirely forgettable piece of Euro-pop. It opened the show, it had a nonsense title, an infectious – some might say lethally so – chorus, an exasperating cheeriness and a high-energy beat. In retrospect, it was no surprise it won. For the rest of the evening, the result was a foregone conclusion. The Herreys were three brothers, Per, Richard and Lewis, who were then living in the United States. They not only wore those gold boots that so caught Terry Wogan's eye, they also wore white trousers and shirts in bold single colours with the collar up in the style of the age. They each used hand mikes and they danced as though choreography was about to go out of style. Unfortunately, it did not do so before they ended their song.

W. Germany	Turkey	Finland	Switzerland	Italy	Portugal	**Position**
114^{12}	**117^{3}**	**125^{8}**	**135^{10}**	**141^{6}**	**145^{4}**	**1**
32^{0}	36^{4}	36^{0}	36^{0}	39^{3}	39^{0}	10
43^{0}	43^{0}	43^{0}	47^{4}	54^{7}	61^{7}	8
71^{0}	83^{12}	83^{0}	86^{3}	94^{8}	106^{12}	3
21^{2}	21^{0}	27^{6}	29^{2}	29^{0}	29^{0}	17
42^{7}	43^{1}	47^{4}	47^{0}	57^{10}	63^{6}	7
31^{0}	31^{0}	31^{0}	31^{0}	31^{0}	31^{0}	15
44^{4}	49^{5}	59^{10}	59^{0}	60^{1}	70^{10}	5=
94^{10}	104^{10}	111^{7}	123^{12}	135^{12}	137^{2}	2
87^{5}	89^{2}	94^{5}	95^{1}	100^{5}	101^{1}	4
29^{0}	29^{0}	29^{0}	34^{5}	34^{0}	34^{0}	13=
16^{3}	24^{8}	26^{2}	26^{0}	26^{0}	26^{0}	18
5^{0}	5^{0}	5^{0}	5^{0}	5^{0}	5^{0}	19
27^{x}	27^{0}	27^{0}	27^{0}	29^{2}	34^{5}	13=
28^{0}	28^{x}	31^{3}	37^{6}	37^{0}	37^{0}	12
37^{1}	43^{6}	43^{x}	43^{0}	43^{0}	46^{3}	9
25^{0}	25^{0}	26^{1}	26^{x}	30^{4}	30^{0}	16
36^{6}	43^{7}	55^{12}	62^{7}	62^{x}	70^{8}	5=
30^{8}	30^{0}	30^{0}	38^{8}	38^{0}	38^{x}	11

The presenter that evening, Desirée Nosbusch, was also a resident of the United States. She was only nineteen at the time, probably the youngest presenter in the history of Eurovision, but she claimed to speak five languages. Speaking in tongues was not always the prime requirement for the Eurovision presenter. For the first few years, there was little attempt to speak in more than one language at most. Some did speak a smattering of languages other than their own, but they barely needed to do much more than count to twelve in them. All they had to be was female. Between 1956 (Lohengrin Filipello) and 1977 (Angela Rippon), the host for the night was always a hostess. During this twenty-two-year period, we were guided through the shows by eighteen different presenters, including the only ones to do the job more than once – France's Jacqueline Joubert (1959 and 1961) and Britain's Katie Boyle, who hosted the show four times (1960, 1963, 1968 and 1974). In 1976, Corry Brokken became the first past performer to host the show, a novelty that twenty-one years later is still shared with only five others: Yardena Arazi, Lill Lindfors, Åse Kleveland, Gigliola Cinquetti and Toto Cutugno. Miss Arazi is unique in that she performed with Chocolate Menta Mastik in 1976, then co-hosted the 1979 show, before returning as a solo performer for Israel in 1988. Nobody else has performed at Eurovision after having been a presenter.

The first man to co-host the Contest was Léon Zitrone in Paris in 1978, and the only man to host the show on his own was the man who took his name from the character played by Paul Henreid in the classic film, *Casablanca*, Viktor Laszlo of Belgium in 1987. Only eleven Contests out of the first forty-two included a male presenter, and even when major local pop stars like Norway's Morten Harket of A-Ha (1996) and Ireland's Ronan

★ ★

1984 EUROVISION SONG CONTEST

Host country: Luxembourg ★ *Venue:* Théâtre Municipal
Date: 5 May ★ *Presenter:* Desirée Nosbusch
Voting structure: Each country awarded 12 to its top song, 10 to the second, 8 to the third and 7, 6, 5, 4, 3, 2 and 1 point for the next seven
Total entries: 19 ★ *Debut countries:* None

Country	Performer	Song	Pts	Pos.
Sweden	**Herreys**	**Diggi-Loo Diggi-Ley**	**145**	**1**
Luxembourg	Sophie Carle	100% D'Amour	39	10
France	Annick Thoumazeau	Autant D'Amoureux Que D'Etoiles	61	8
Spain	Bravo	Lady Lady	106	3
Norway	Dollie de Luxe	Lenge Leve Livet	29	17
United Kingdom	Belle and the Devotions	Love Games	63	7
Cyprus	Andy Paul	Anna Maria Lena	31	15
Belgium	Jacques Zégers	Avanti La Vie	70	5
Ireland	Linda Martin	Terminal Three	137	2
Denmark	Hot Eyes	Det' Lige Det	101	4
Netherlands	Maribelle	Ik Hou Van Jou	34	13
Yugoslavia	Vlado and Isolda	Ciao Amore	26	18
Austria	Anita	Einfach Weg	5	19
Germany	Mary Roos	Aufrecht Geh'n	34	13
Turkey	Bes Yil Önce, On Yil Sonra	Halay	37	12
Finland	Kirka	Hengaillaan	46	9
Switzerland	Rainy Day	Welche Farbe Hat Der Sonnenschein	30	16
Italy	Alice and Franco Battiato	I Treni Di Tozeur	70	5
Portugal	Maria Guinot	Silencio E Tanta Gente	38	11

Keating of Boyzone (1997) were brought in, it is the female presenter who seems to take the lead and feature more strongly in our memories of the night. Who could forget Marlene Charell dancing in the Song Contest Ballet of 1983, or Anaid Plijkan (1957) reading earnestly in untranslated German all the details of the songs, the composers, the conductors and the performers? Who can forget Desirée Nosbusch in this contest dealing with an intervention by EBU scrutineer Frank Naef by saying, 'Frank can interrupt. He can do almost anything with me'.

All presenters have trouble with the voting system and the phone lines from around the Continent – that is part of the fun of the evening – but it always seems to be the male presenters who get more worried by it. The women just enjoy the night for what it is, a night of trivial musical enjoyment, where the winner is incidental rather than the whole point of the Contest.

★ ★

THE EUROVISION SONG CONTEST

1985

Won by Norway: 'La Det Swinge'
Written by Rolf Livland
Performed by the Bobbysocks
Orchestra conducted by Terje Fjaern

1985 EUROVISION SONG CONTEST

Host country: Sweden ★ *Venue:* Scandinavium, Gothenburg
Date: 4 May ★ *Presenter:* Lill Lindfors
Voting structure: Each country awarded 12 to its top song, 10 to the second, 8 to the third and 7, 6, 5, 4, 3, 2 and 1 point for the next seven ★ *Total entries:* 19 ★ *Debut countries:* None

Country	Performer	Song	Pts	Pos.
Ireland	Maria Christian	Wait Until The Weekend Comes	91	6
Finland	Sonja Lumme	Eläköön Elämä	58	9
Cyprus	Lia Vissi	To Katalava Arga	15	16
Denmark	Hot Eyes	Sku' Du Spør Fra No'en	41	11
Spain	Paloma san Basilio	La Fiesta Terminó	36	14
France	Roger Bens	Femme Dans Ses Rêves Aussi	56	10
Turkey	MFÖ	Didai Didai Dai	36	14
Belgium	Linda Lepomme	Laat Me Nu Gaan	7	19
Portugal	Adelaide	Penso Em Ti, Eu Sei	9	18
Germany	Wind	Für Alle	105	2
Israel	Izhar Cohen and Alphabeta	Olé Olé	93	5
Italy	Romina Power and Al Bano	Magic, Oh Magic	78	7
Norway	**Bobbysocks**	**La Det Swinge**	**123**	**1**
United Kingdom	Vikki	Love Is	100	4
Switzerland	Mariella Farré and Pino Gasparini	Piano Piano	39	12
Sweden	Kikki Danielsson	Bra Vibrationer	103	3
Austria	Gary Lux	Kinder Dieser Welt	60	8
Luxembourg	Ireen Sheer, Margo, Franck Olivier, Chris and Malcolm Roberts, Diane Solomon	Children, Kinder, Enfants	37	13
Greece	Takis Biniaris	Miazoume	15	16

Twenty-five years after they first entered the Eurovision Song Contest, and only four years after they scored a second 'nul points' in four attempts, the impossible happened: Norway *won* the Eurovision Song Contest. True to its past reputation, it won with a song generally regarded as one of the weakest winners of all, and with a score of only 123 points, two fewer than the winning score achieved by Milk and Honey featuring Gali Atari for Israel in 1979 and still the lowest recorded since the introduction of the new voting system in 1975. The score represented just 56.9 per cent of the maximum, a record that lasted until 1989, when Yugoslavia's only winner, 'Rock Me' by Riva, crept past the winning post with only 54.4 per cent of the available votes. In 1995, Norway's second winner, 'Nocturne' by Secret Garden, took only 56.1 per cent of the maximum, so even though Bobbysocks won by eighteen points from Germany, two of the three narrowest victors of the past twenty-three years have been Norwegian.

The 1985 contest, from Gothenburg, was notable for sex and old friends. Among the old friends, Denmark's Hot Eyes were back for the second year in a row, but this time, with a weaker song than the year before, they did not ever look like winning. Anna Vissi's elder sister Lia sang for Cyprus, but did worse than her sister had done either for Greece in 1980 or Cyprus in 1982. The

1985	Ireland	Finland	Cyprus	Denmark	Spain	France	Turkey	Belgium	Portugal	W. Germany	Israel	Italy	Norway
Ireland	0^{x}	1^{1}	8^{7}	11^{3}	15^{4}	18^{3}	23^{5}	31^{8}	39^{8}	43^{4}	51^{8}	63^{12}	66^{3}
Finland	6^{6}	6^{x}	12^{6}	12^{0}	18^{6}	18^{0}	21^{3}	21^{0}	21^{0}	21^{0}	22^{1}	29^{7}	29^{0}
Cyprus	1^{1}	1^{0}	1^{x}	1^{0}	1^{0}	1^{0}	1^{0}	1^{0}	1^{0}	1^{0}	1^{0}	4^{3}	4^{0}
Denmark	0^{0}	0^{0}	3^{3}	3^{x}	3^{0}	13^{10}	13^{0}	16^{3}	17^{1}	23^{6}	23^{0}	25^{2}	31^{6}
Spain	2^{2}	10^{8}	11^{1}	11^{0}	11^{x}	11^{0}	23^{12}	23^{0}	25^{0}	25^{0}	25^{0}	25^{0}	25^{0}
France	0^{0}	5^{5}	9^{4}	9^{0}	9^{0}	9^{x}	10^{1}	10^{0}	13^{3}	13^{0}	16^{3}	26^{10}	26^{0}
Turkey	7^{7}	9^{2}	9^{0}	9^{0}	12^{3}	12^{0}	12^{x}	13^{1}	13^{0}	15^{2}	15^{0}	15^{0}	16^{1}
Belgium	0^{0}	0^{0}	0^{0}	0^{0}	0^{0}	0^{0}	7^{7}	7^{x}	7^{0}	7^{0}	7^{0}	7^{0}	7^{0}
Portugal	0^{0}	0^{0}	0^{0}	0^{0}	0^{0}	0^{0}	2^{2}	2^{0}	2^{x}	2^{0}	2^{0}	2^{0}	2^{0}
W. Germany	4^{4}	14^{10}	**26^{12}**	**36^{10}**	**46^{10}**	**54^{8}**	**54^{0}**	**64^{10}**	**71^{7}**	**71^{x}**	**78^{7}**	**78^{0}**	**86^{8}**
Israel	8^{8}	8^{0}	13^{5}	17^{4}	25^{8}	37^{12}	37^{0}	37^{0}	42^{5}	49^{7}	49^{x}	54^{5}	64^{10}
Italy	0^{0}	6^{6}	16^{10}	17^{1}	29^{12}	34^{5}	42^{8}	44^{2}	56^{12}	56^{0}	60^{4}	60^{x}	60^{0}
Norway	**12^{12}**	16^{4}	16^{0}	28^{12}	29^{1}	31^{1}	31^{0}	43^{12}	43^{0}	55^{12}	67^{12}	73^{6}	73^{x}
UK	5^{5}	12^{7}	12^{0}	17^{5}	22^{5}	28^{6}	38^{10}	44^{6}	50^{6}	55^{5}	57^{2}	65^{8}	72^{7}
Switzerland	0^{0}	3^{3}	5^{2}	11^{6}	11^{0}	11^{0}	17^{6}	22^{5}	26^{4}	27^{1}	27^{0}	27^{0}	32^{5}
Sweden	10^{10}	**22^{12}**	22^{0}	30^{8}	32^{2}	39^{7}	43^{4}	50^{7}	50^{0}	58^{8}	64^{6}	68^{4}	80^{12}
Austria	3^{3}	3^{0}	3^{0}	10^{7}	10^{0}	11^{1}	11^{0}	15^{4}	15^{0}	25^{10}	35^{10}	35^{0}	37^{2}
Luxembourg	0^{0}	0^{0}	0^{0}	2^{2}	2^{0}	6^{4}	6^{0}	6^{0}	16^{10}	19^{3}	24^{5}	25^{1}	29^{4}
Greece	0^{0}	0^{0}	8^{8}	8^{0}	15^{7}	15^{0}	15^{0}	15^{0}	15^{0}	15^{0}	15^{0}	15^{0}	15^{0}

sisters were not invited back again. The 1978 Contest's winners, Izhar Cohen and Alphabeta, were back for another go, but they too fell short of their first attempt. (That 1978 Contest had been broadcast to many Arab states, but while the Israeli entry was being sung, the local stations switched to advertisements or the news. When the voting patterns showed that Israel was likely to win, the broadcasts were abruptly stopped. The good citizens of Jordan, Egypt and elsewhere are probably still in ignorance about the result.) Romina Power and Al Bano came back for Italy after a nine-year gap, and achieved precisely what they had done in 1976 – seventh place. Ireen Sheer, after singing as a soloist for both Luxembourg (1974) and Germany (1978), brought several of her friends along on Luxembourg's behalf, but fared worse than ever before. Mariella Farré was Switzerland's choice for a second time, but even with Pino Gasparini to help her this time, she failed to worry the favourites. Three other acts were having such fun on their first appearance that they would come back for more: Turkey's Mazhar Fuat Özkan, Wind from Germany and Gary Lux for Austria. Wind came second this year, and again two years later – the best record of any act that has never actually won Eurovision. And Hannah Krøg of the winners, Bobbysocks, returned as part of Just 4 Fun in 1991. One old friend missing was any entrant from the Netherlands, because the date coincided with Liberation Day celebrations.

UK	Switzerland	Sweden	Austria	Luxembourg	Greece	**Position**
69^{3}	74^{5}	81^{7}	91^{10}	91^{0}	91^{0}	6
36^{7}	38^{2}	48^{10}	48^{0}	48^{0}	58^{10}	9
4^{0}	7^{3}	7^{0}	7^{0}	7^{0}	15^{8}	16=
31^{0}	31^{0}	36^{5}	41^{5}	41^{0}	41^{0}	11
29^{4}	29^{0}	29^{0}	29^{0}	30^{1}	36^{6}	14=
28^{2}	32^{4}	38^{6}	41^{3}	44^{3}	56^{12}	10
24^{8}	36^{12}	36^{0}	36^{0}	36^{0}	36^{0}	14=
7^{0}	7^{0}	7^{0}	7^{0}	7^{0}	7^{0}	19
2^{0}	2^{0}	2^{0}	2^{0}	2^{0}	9^{7}	18
87^{1}	87^{0}	95^{8}	95^{0}	105^{10}	105^{0}	2
69^{5}	76^{7}	78^{2}	85^{7}	91^{6}	93^{2}	5
60^{0}	60^{0}	60^{0}	66^{6}	78^{12}	78^{0}	7
85^{12}	91^{6}	**103^{12}**	**115^{12}**	**122^{7}**	**123^{1}**	**1**
72^{0}	82^{10}	86^{4}	88^{2}	96^{8}	100^{4}	4
32^{0}	32^{0}	33^{1}	34^{1}	36^{2}	39^{3}	12
86^{6}	**94^{8}**	94^{0}	98^{4}	103^{5}	103^{0}	3
47^{10}	48^{1}	51^{3}	51^{0}	55^{4}	60^{5}	8
29^{0}	29^{0}	29^{0}	37^{8}	37^{0}	37^{0}	13
15^{0}	15^{0}	15^{0}	15^{0}	15^{0}	15^{0}	16=

The song titles were not so much old friends as just plain repetitive. We had 'Didai Didai Dai', 'Olé Olé', 'Magic, Oh Magic', 'Piano Piano' and two different songs about children. The highest place any of them attained was fifth place, by Israel's 'Olé Olé'. On the other hand, the lowest place they filled was fourteenth, which by Turkey's standards up to that time was quite a high placing.

The sex came from the host country, Sweden. Not content with an entry called 'Bra Vibrationer', which Anglophone viewers were keen to translate incorrectly (it really means 'Good Vibrations'), the Swedes shamelessly exploited the legs of the presenter, Lill Lindfors, who had sung for Sweden in 1966. Wearing a skirt for the first half of the show, she contrived to catch it on a nail on the set back stage as she came back on for the voting, so that she had to complete the show wearing very little below the waist. She remained entirely decent, and those viewers who thought it was a rehearsed part of the show, designed to show off Miss Lindfors' legs, would have been none the wiser. It had not been in the original script, though. That would have been far too racy for Eurovision.

★ ★

THE EUROVISION SONG CONTEST

1986

Won by Belgium: 'J'Aime La Vie'

Written by Marino Atria, Jean-Paul Furnemont and Angelo Crisci

Performed by Sandra Kim

Orchestra conducted by Jo Carlier

For the first time, the Eurovision Song Contest moved to Norway and the venue chosen was the Grieghallen in Bergen, the most northerly venue for Eurovision yet. To celebrate, Iceland made its debut. The presenter was Norway's Minister of Culture and a former entrant, Åse

1986	Luxembourg	Yugoslavia	France	Norway	UK	Iceland	Netherlands	Turkey	Spain	Switzerland	Israel	Ireland	Belgium	W. Germany
Luxembourg	0^{x}	5^{5}	13^{8}	25^{12}	33^{8}	34^{1}	42^{8}	42^{0}	42^{0}	44^{2}	48^{4}	55^{7}	65^{10}	77^{12}
Yugoslavia	2^{2}	2^{x}	2^{0}	2^{0}	9^{7}	14^{5}	21^{7}	24^{3}	27^{3}	27^{0}	28^{1}	31^{3}	35^{4}	35^{0}
France	0^{0}	0^{0}	0^{x}	3^{3}	3^{0}	3^{0}	3^{0}	3^{0}	3^{0}	10^{7}	10^{0}	10^{0}	10^{0}	10^{0}
Norway	0^{0}	0^{0}	4^{4}	4^{x}	4^{0}	8^{4}	10^{2}	10^{0}	10^{0}	16^{6}	16^{0}	22^{6}	27^{5}	33^{6}
UK	4^{4}	4^{0}	14^{10}	20^{6}	20^{x}	20^{0}	20^{0}	26^{6}	28^{2}	32^{4}	34^{2}	34^{0}	34^{0}	39^{5}
Iceland	0^{0}	0^{0}	0^{0}	0^{0}	0^{0}	0^{x}	5^{5}	7^{2}	13^{6}	13^{0}	13^{0}	13^{0}	13^{0}	13^{0}
Netherlands	1^{1}	3^{2}	3^{0}	3^{0}	3^{0}	3^{0}	3^{x}	10^{7}	11^{1}	11^{0}	19^{8}	19^{0}	19^{0}	29^{10}
Turkey	6^{6}	18^{12}	18^{0}	18^{0}	20^{2}	20^{0}	26^{6}	26^{x}	26^{0}	34^{8}	37^{3}	37^{0}	43^{6}	51^{8}
Spain	7^{7}	11^{4}	17^{6}	17^{0}	18^{1}	20^{2}	20^{0}	28^{8}	28^{x}	29^{1}	29^{0}	34^{5}	37^{3}	37^{0}
Switzerland	**12^{12}**	18^{6}	25^{7}	30^{5}	35^{5}	38^{3}	50^{12}	60^{10}	64^{4}	64^{x}	76^{12}	86^{10}	98^{12}	98^{0}
Israel	0^{0}	0^{0}	1^{1}	2^{1}	2^{0}	2^{0}	2^{0}	2^{0}	2^{0}	7^{5}	7^{x}	7^{0}	7^{0}	7^{0}
Ireland	3^{3}	11^{8}	14^{3}	16^{2}	16^{0}	24^{8}	24^{0}	29^{5}	41^{12}	41^{0}	47^{6}	47^{x}	49^{2}	49^{0}
Belgium	10^{10}	**20^{10}**	**32^{12}**	**40^{8}**	**50^{10}**	**60^{10}**	**70^{10}**	**82^{12}**	**92^{10}**	**102^{10}**	**107^{5}**	**119^{12}**	**119^{x}**	**120^{1}**
W. Germany	8^{8}	9^{1}	9^{0}	9^{0}	21^{12}	21^{0}	21^{0}	21^{0}	21^{0}	21^{0}	21^{0}	29^{8}	36^{7}	36^{x}
Cyprus	0^{0}	3^{0}	3^{0}	3^{0}	3^{0}	3^{0}	3^{0}	3^{0}	3^{0}	3^{0}	3^{0}	4^{1}	4^{0}	4^{0}
Austria	0^{0}	0^{0}	0^{0}	0^{0}	0^{0}	0^{0}	0^{0}	0^{0}	0^{0}	0^{0}	0^{0}	2^{2}	3^{1}	5^{2}
Sweden	5^{5}	12^{7}	14^{2}	21^{7}	24^{3}	36^{12}	39^{3}	39^{0}	46^{7}	58^{12}	58^{0}	58^{0}	58^{0}	62^{4}
Denmark	0^{0}	0^{0}	5^{5}	15^{10}	21^{6}	28^{7}	32^{4}	32^{0}	37^{5}	40^{3}	50^{10}	54^{4}	54^{0}	61^{7}
Finland	0^{0}	0^{0}	0^{0}	0^{0}	0^{0}	6^{6}	7^{1}	8^{1}	8^{0}	8^{0}	8^{0}	8^{0}	16^{8}	19^{3}
Portugal	0^{0}	0^{0}	0^{0}	4^{4}	8^{4}	8^{0}	7^{0}	12^{4}	20^{8}	20^{0}	27^{7}	27^{0}	27^{0}	27^{0}

Kleveland, who had come third in 1966.

If Norway's twenty-five-year wait for victory seemed a long one, Belgium's thirty-year vigil must have been an eternity for the powers that be in Europe's headquarters, Brussels. Belgium, one of the original seven entrants in 1956, had adopted the politically correct plan of alternating its entries each year between the French language and Flemish, but over the previous thirty contests, the French-language songs had done conspicuously better than the Flemish ones. Belgium had come second in 1978, fourth in 1966 and 1982, and fifth in 1984, all with French songs, but the best effort by a Flemish song had been sixth out of eleven in 1959 and seventh three times, in 1967, 1969 and 1977. Flemish songs had come last three times, compared with only one last place for Belgium's French entries, and 1986 was the year for a French song.

In fact, it was the year for three French songs, because not only did thirteen-year-old Sandra Kim win for Belgium, but Daniela Simons came second for Switzerland with 'Pas Pour Moi', and Luxembourg's Sherisse Laurence completed the hat-trick for Francophone women by coming third with 'L'Amour De Ma Vie' – incidentally, the 500th song performed in a Eurovision final. Luxembourg had sung last but one the year before, so the 498th and 500th songs were both by the same country. Twice in the history of the contest, a nation has gone one better than this and sung consecutive entries, by being last to perform one year and first the next. Luxembourg sang the 106th and 107th entries in 1963 and 1964, and Yugoslavia sang the 192nd and 193rd entries in 1968 and 1969.

This was the second time that the top three songs had been in French, after 1962, when France itself had won. In 1986, France let the side down by coming seventeenth with 'Europiennes'. The only other time that one language has so dominated the results was in 1992, when Ireland, the United Kingdom and Malta took the top three places, all singing in English.

In 1986, the UK was represented by Ryder, a band fronted by Maynard Williams, singer son of comic actor Bill Maynard (who had performed in one of the elimination heats for Eurovision in 1957). A few years earlier, Maynard Williams had recorded an album produced and largely written by Tim Rice and Andrew Lloyd Webber, containing five of their songs that nobody else has ever recorded. They did not write 'Runner In The Night', which gave the UK its third seventh place in the five years since Buck's Fizz had won. Worse was to come for British entries before Katrina and the Waves would reclaim the title for the UK in 1997.

Cyprus	Austria	Sweden	Denmark	Finland	Portugal	**Position**
85^{8}	95^{10}	105^{10}	107^{2}	111^{4}	117^{6}	3
47^{12}	48^{1}	49^{1}	49^{0}	49^{0}	49^{0}	11
10^{0}	10^{0}	13^{3}	13^{0}	13^{0}	13^{0}	17
39^{6}	39^{0}	39^{0}	44^{5}	44^{0}	44^{0}	12
41^{2}	44^{3}	52^{8}	60^{8}	70^{10}	72^{2}	7
17^{4}	17^{0}	19^{2}	19^{0}	19^{0}	19^{0}	16
30^{1}	30^{0}	30^{0}	30^{0}	33^{3}	40^{7}	13
51^{0}	53^{2}	53^{0}	53^{0}	53^{0}	53^{0}	9
37^{0}	44^{7}	44^{0}	47^{3}	48^{1}	51^{3}	10
103^{5}	107^{4}	119^{12}	123^{4}	130^{7}	140^{10}	2
7^{0}	7^{0}	7^{0}	7^{0}	7^{0}	7^{0}	19
49^{0}	61^{12}	68^{7}	80^{12}	88^{8}	96^{8}	4
130^{10}	**136^{6}**	**142^{6}**	**152^{10}**	**164^{12}**	**176^{12}**	**1**
36^{0}	44^{8}	49^{5}	56^{7}	58^{2}	62^{4}	8
4^{x}	4^{0}	4^{0}	4^{0}	4^{0}	4^{0}	20
5^{0}	5^{x}	5^{0}	5^{0}	11^{6}	12^{1}	18
62^{0}	67^{5}	67^{x}	73^{6}	78^{5}	78^{0}	5
68^{7}	68^{0}	72^{4}	72^{x}	72^{0}	77^{5}	6
22^{3}	22^{0}	22^{0}	22^{0}	22^{x}	22^{0}	15
27^{0}	27^{0}	27^{0}	28^{1}	28^{0}	28^{x}	14

1986 EUROVISION SONG CONTEST

Host country: Norway ★ *Venue:* Greighallen, Bergen
Date: 3 May ★ *Presenter:* Åse Kleveland
Voting structure: Each country awarded 12 to its top song, 10 to the second, 8 to the third and 7, 6, 5, 4, 3, 2 and 1 point for the next seven
Total entries: 20 ★ *Debut countries:* Iceland

Country	Performer	Song	Pts	Pos.
Luxembourg	Sherisse Laurence	L'Amour De Ma Vie	117	3
Yugoslavia	Doris Dragovic	Zeljo Moja	49	11
France	Cocktail Chic	Europiennes	13	17
Norway	Ketil Stokkan	Romeo	44	12
United Kingdom	Ryder	Runner In The Night	72	7
Iceland	ICY	Gledibankinn	19	16
Netherlands	Frizzle Sizzle	Alles Heeft Ritme	40	13
Turkey	Klips and Onlar	Halley	53	9
Spain	Cadillac	Valentino	51	10
Switzerland	Daniela Simons	Pas Pour Moi	140	2
Israel	Moti Giladi and Sarai Tzuriel	Yavoh Yom	7	19
Ireland	Luv Bug	You Can Count On Me	96	4
Belgium	**Sandra Kim**	**J'Aime La Vie**	**176**	**1**
Germany	Ingrid Peters	Über Die Brücke Geh'n	62	8
Cyprus	Elpida	Tora Zo	4	20
Austria	Timna Brauer	Die Zeit Ist Einsam	12	18
Sweden	Lasse Holm and Monica Törnell	E' De' Det Här Du Kallar Kärlek?	78	5
Denmark	Trax	Du Er Fuld Af Løgn	77	6
Finland	Kari	Paiva Kahden Ihmisen	22	15
Portugal	Dora	Não Sejas Mau P'ra Mim	28	14

Sandra Kim, born Sandra Caldarone on 15 October 1972, was only 13 years and 200 days old when she won Eurovision, succeeding Gigliola Cinquetti (16 years old in 1964) as the youngest winner, a title she still holds. Her triumph, with an upbeat song with a simple chorus and a strong synthesized organ instrumental break, was very clear cut. Only the next three songs scored even half as many votes as Mlle Kim. Lowest of all came Cyprus, represented by Elpida, who had sung for Greece in 1979. Her song, 'Tora Zo', is often cited as one of the worst ever to be heard in Eurovision, and rumour has it that even Elpida threatened not to sing it. There was anxiety in the Cyprus camp as to whether or not she would go on stage, almost up to the time that the band struck up. She did perform, but she might just as well not have bothered as they came last with only four points.

EUROVISION NATIONS LEAGUE TABLE

Pos.	Country	Entries	Wins	2nd	3rd	4th	5th
1	United Kingdom	40	5	14	2	6	-
2	France	40	5	4	7	5	1
3	Ireland	32	7	4	1	3	3
4	Germany	41	1	4	4	3	1
5	Switzerland	41	2	3	3	5	2
6	Italy	36	2	1	4	2	4
7	Luxembourg	37	5	-	2	4	2
8	Sweden	37	3	1	4	2	3
9	Spain	37	2	4	1	2	1
10	Netherlands	39	4	-	1	1	1
11	Monaco	21	1	1	3	3	2
12	Belgium	40	1	1	-	2	2
13	Israel	20	2	2	1	1	1
14	Denmark	28	1	-	3	1	4
15	Norway	37	2	1	1	1	2
16	Austria	36	1	-	-	1	4
17	Yugoslavia	27	1	-	-	3	-
18	Finland	34	-	-	-	-	-
19	Cyprus	16	-	-	-	-	2
20	Malta	10	-	-	1	-	1
21	Greece	20	-	-	-	-	2
22	Portugal	33	-	-	-	-	-
23	Croatia	5	-	-	-	1	-
24	Iceland	12	-	-	-	1	-
25	Poland	4	-	1	-	-	-
26	Turkey	19	-	-	1	-	-
27	Estonia	3	-	-	-	-	1
28	Hungary	3	-	-	-	1	-
29	Slovenia	4	-	-	-	-	-
30	Russia	3	-	-	-	-	-
31	Bosnia-Herzegovina	5	-	-	-	-	-
32	Slovakia	2	-	-	-	-	-
33	Morocco	1	-	-	-	-	-
34	Romania	1	-	-	-	-	-
35	Lithuania	1	-	-	-	-	-

★ ★

THE EUROVISION SONG CONTEST

1987

Won by Ireland: 'Hold Me Now'

Written by Johnny Logan

Performed by Johnny Logan

Orchestra conducted by Noel Kelehan

When Johnny Logan won Eurovision for the second time, he established a new record, which he went on to extend in 1992. He became the first – and so far only – person to win

1987	Norway	Israel	Austria	Iceland	Belgium	Sweden	Italy	Portugal	Spain	Turkey	Greece	Netherlands	Luxembourg	UK	France
Norway	0^{x}	0^{0}	4^{4}	4^{0}	11^{7}	21^{10}	28^{7}	28^{0}	31^{3}	31^{0}	31^{0}	35^{4}	35^{0}	35^{0}	39^{4}
Israel	2^{2}	2^{x}	3^{1}	8^{5}	14^{6}	18^{4}	18^{0}	28^{10}	28^{0}	28^{0}	28^{0}	31^{3}	31^{0}	35^{4}	45^{10}
Austria	0^{0}	0^{0}	0^{x}	0^{0}	0^{0}	0^{0}	1^{1}	1^{0}	1^{0}	1^{0}	8^{7}	8^{0}	8^{0}	8^{0}	8^{0}
Iceland	4^{4}	4^{0}	4^{0}	4^{x}	8^{4}	8^{0}	8^{0}	8^{0}	12^{4}	12^{0}	18^{6}	18^{0}	18^{0}	18^{0}	18^{0}
Belgium	5^{5}	7^{2}	10^{3}	10^{0}	10^{x}	10^{0}	16^{6}	16^{0}	23^{7}	27^{4}	27^{0}	27^{0}	32^{5}	40^{8}	40^{0}
Sweden	0^{0}	12^{12}	12^{0}	20^{8}	21^{1}	21^{x}	24^{3}	31^{7}	31^{0}	33^{2}	33^{0}	33^{0}	33^{0}	33^{0}	36^{3}
Italy	0^{0}	3^{3}	9^{6}	12^{3}	17^{5}	18^{1}	18^{x}	30^{12}	42^{12}	50^{8}	50^{0}	50^{0}	54^{4}	55^{1}	55^{0}
Portugal	0^{0}	0^{0}	0^{0}	0^{0}	0^{0}	0^{0}	0^{0}	0^{x}	8^{8}	8^{0}	13^{5}	13^{0}	13^{0}	13^{0}	13^{0}
Spain	0^{0}	0^{0}	0^{0}	0^{0}	0^{0}	0^{0}	0^{0}	0^{0}	0^{x}	0^{0}	10^{10}	10^{0}	10^{0}	10^{0}	10^{0}
Turkey	0^{0}	0^{0}	0^{0}	0^{0}	0^{0}	0^{0}	0^{0}	0^{0}	0^{0}	0^{x}	0^{0}	0^{0}	0^{0}	0^{0}	0^{0}
Greece	0^{0}	0^{0}	0^{0}	1^{1}	3^{2}	9^{6}	17^{8}	17^{0}	17^{0}	17^{0}	17^{x}	22^{5}	29^{7}	34^{5}	41^{7}
Netherlands	0^{0}	5^{5}	7^{2}	7^{0}	7^{0}	7^{0}	17^{10}	17^{0}	22^{5}	29^{7}	32^{3}	32^{x}	40^{8}	43^{3}	55^{12}
Luxembourg	0^{0}	0^{0}	0^{0}	0^{0}	0^{0}	0^{0}	0^{0}	2^{2}	2^{0}	2^{0}	2^{0}	2^{0}	2^{x}	4^{2}	4^{0}
UK	0^{0}	10^{10}	15^{5}	15^{0}	18^{3}	23^{5}	23^{0}	26^{3}	26^{0}	29^{3}	29^{0}	29^{0}	30^{1}	30^{x}	30^{0}
France	1^{1}	1^{0}	1^{0}	5^{4}	5^{0}	5^{0}	10^{5}	10^{0}	10^{0}	10^{0}	14^{4}	15^{1}	27^{12}	27^{0}	27^{x}
W. Germany	3^{3}	11^{8}	21^{10}	33^{12}	43^{10}	**50^{7}**	54^{4}	59^{5}	60^{1}	66^{6}	66^{0}	76^{10}	82^{6}	92^{10}	98^{6}
Cyprus	6^{6}	6^{0}	6^{0}	12^{6}	12^{0}	14^{2}	14^{0}	14^{0}	14^{0}	14^{0}	26^{12}	28^{2}	28^{0}	34^{6}	39^{5}
Finland	10^{10}	10^{0}	10^{0}	10^{0}	10^{0}	13^{3}	13^{0}	17^{4}	19^{2}	19^{0}	20^{1}	28^{8}	30^{2}	30^{0}	30^{0}
Denmark	7^{7}	13^{6}	20^{7}	27^{7}	27^{0}	35^{8}	37^{2}	38^{1}	38^{0}	39^{1}	47^{8}	53^{6}	53^{0}	60^{7}	68^{8}
Ireland	8^{8}	12^{4}	24^{12}	24^{0}	36^{12}	48^{12}	**60^{12}**	**68^{8}**	**78^{10}**	**88^{10}**	**88^{0}**	**100^{12}**	**110^{10}**	**122^{12}**	**123^{1}**
Yugoslavia	**12^{12}**	**19^{7}**	**27^{8}**	**37^{10}**	**45^{8}**	45^{0}	45^{0}	51^{6}	57^{6}	69^{12}	71^{2}	71^{0}	71^{0}	71^{0}	73^{2}
Switzerland	0^{0}	1^{1}	1^{0}	3^{2}	3^{0}	3^{0}	3^{0}	3^{0}	3^{0}	8^{5}	8^{0}	15^{7}	18^{3}	18^{0}	18^{0}

Eurovision twice as a performer and, by writing the song himself, he equalled the singer/ songwriter record first set by Udo Jürgens in 1966. He was also the first winner to be engaged to be married to a Turkish belly dancer at the time. Remarkably, since Jürgens's win twenty-one years earlier, the only solo male performer to have won Eurovision had been Logan himself, and he had now done it twice. Since 1987, Toto Cutugno has joined that remarkably short list (André Claveau, Jean-Claude Pascal, Udo Jürgens, Johnny Logan and Toto Cutugno) of male soloists to have won the Contest, if any proof was needed that women are more likely to win than men, that list is it.

W. Germany	Cyprus	Finland	Denmark	Ireland	Yugoslavia	Switzerland	**Position**
46^{7}	49^{3}	54^{5}	57^{3}	59^{2}	59^{0}	65^{6}	9
53^{8}	53^{0}	60^{7}	60^{0}	65^{5}	65^{0}	73^{8}	8
8^{0}	8^{0}	8^{0}	8^{0}	8^{0}	8^{0}	8^{0}	20
28^{10}	28^{0}	28^{0}	28^{0}	28^{0}	28^{0}	28^{0}	16
44^{4}	49^{5}	52^{3}	52^{0}	52^{0}	56^{4}	56^{0}	11
36^{0}	43^{7}	43^{0}	50^{7}	50^{0}	50^{0}	50^{0}	12
67^{12}	68^{1}	72^{4}	72^{0}	84^{12}	96^{12}	103^{7}	3
15^{2}	15^{0}	15^{0}	15^{0}	15^{0}	15^{0}	15^{0}	18
10^{0}	10^{0}	10^{0}	10^{0}	10^{0}	10^{0}	10^{0}	19
0^{0}	0^{0}	0^{0}	0^{0}	0^{0}	0^{0}	0^{0}	22
41^{0}	53^{12}	53^{0}	59^{6}	59^{0}	64^{5}	64^{0}	10
55^{0}	55^{0}	57^{2}	59^{2}	65^{6}	73^{8}	83^{1}	5=
4^{0}	4^{0}	4^{0}	4^{0}	4^{0}	4^{0}	4^{0}	21
30^{0}	32^{2}	33^{1}	37^{4}	40^{3}	42^{2}	47^{5}	13
32^{5}	32^{0}	32^{0}	32^{0}	42^{10}	42^{0}	44^{2}	14
98^{x}	104^{6}	114^{10}	126^{12}	133^{7}	140^{7}	141^{1}	2
42^{3}	42^{x}	48^{6}	58^{10}	66^{8}	76^{10}	80^{4}	7
31^{1}	31^{0}	31^{x}	31^{0}	31^{0}	32^{1}	32^{0}	15
68^{0}	68^{0}	76^{8}	76^{x}	80^{4}	80^{0}	83^{3}	5=
129^{6}	**137^{8}**	**149^{12}**	**154^{5}**	**154^{x}**	**160^{6}**	**172^{12}**	**1**
73^{0}	83^{10}	83^{0}	91^{8}	92^{1}	92^{x}	92^{0}	4
18^{0}	22^{4}	22^{0}	23^{1}	23^{0}	26^{3}	26^{x}	17

Second to Logan was Wind, the German group that had come second two years earlier when Bobbysocks had won for Norway. Never before had two performers who had previously been first and second topped the votes, and in all Eurovision history there are only five acts that have twice appeared in the top two positions. Apart from Johnny Logan and Wind, they are Lys Assia (winner in 1956, second in 1958), Gigliola Cinquetti (winner in 1964, second in 1974) and Linda Martin (second in 1984, winner in 1992).

There were more entrants than ever before – twenty-two – but no countries completely new to the competition. Since 1986, Italy and Greece had returned to the fray, bringing the numbers up from the previous year's twenty. It was almost only twenty-one, because the Israeli Minister of Culture felt that his country's entry, 'Shir Habatlanim', was in some way unsuitable as an example of Israeli popular music. What a Minister of Culture should know about Eurovision is anybody's guess, but fortunately the Minister's views were not allowed to prevail, and Datner and Kushnir were able to perform. They did so very well, with huge energy and a typically Eurovisual lack of subtlety, to gain a respectable eighth place.

Defending champions Belgium's entry was a Flemish song with an English title, performed by Liliane St Pierre, who is now married to the widower of Ann Christy. Christy sang for Belgium in 1975, coming fifteenth with 'Gelukkig Zijn'/'Be Happy'. Her biggest hit in Belgium was called 'Ik Leef Voor Jou'/'I Live For You', which was the last before her death from cancer on 7 August 1984. Belgium's entrants have had a perilous time. Louis Neefs, who sang twice for Belgium (in 1967 and 1969) was killed with his wife in a car crash on Christmas Eve 1980. Perhaps that is why Belgian punk Plastic Bertrand, who had had a worldwide hit with his brilliant 'Ça Plane Pour Moi' in 1978, chose to represent Luxembourg at

1987 EUROVISION SONG CONTEST

Host country: Belgium ★ *Venue:* Palais de Centenaire, Brussels
Date: 9 May ★ *Presenter:* Viktor Laszlo
Voting structure: Each country awarded 12 to its top song, 10 to the second, 8 to the third and 7, 6, 5, 4, 3, 2 and 1 point for the next seven
Total entries: 22 ★ *Debut countries:* None

Country	Performer	Song	Pts	Pos.
Norway	Kate Gulbrandsen	Mitt Liv	65	9
Israel	Datner and Kushnir	Shir Habatlanim	73	8
Austria	Gary Lux	Nur Noch Gefühl	8	20
Iceland	Halla Margaret	Hægt Og Hljótt	28	16
Belgium	Liliane St Pierre	Soldiers Of Love	56	11
Sweden	Lotta Engberg	Boogaloo	50	12
Italy	Umberto Tozzi and Raf	Gente Di Mare	103	3
Portugal	Nevada	Neste Barco A Vela	15	18
Spain	Patricia Kraus	No Estas Solo	10	19
Turkey	Seyyal Taner and Locomotif	Sarkim Sevgi Üstüne	0	22
Greece	Bang	Stop	64	10
Netherlands	Marcha	Rechtop In De Wind	83	5
Luxembourg	Plastic Bertrand	Amour Amour	4	21
United Kingdom	Rikki	Only The Light	47	13
France	Christine Minier	Les Mots D'Amour N'ont Pas De Dimanche	44	14
Germany	Wind	Lass Die Sonne In Dein Herz	141	2
Cyprus	Alexia	Aspro Mavro	80	7
Finland	Vicky Rosti	Sata Salamaa	32	15
Denmark	Anne Cathrine Herdorf and Bandjo	En Lille Melodi	83	5
Ireland	**Johnny Logan**	**Hold Me Now**	**172**	**1**
Yugoslavia	Novi Fosili	Ja Sam Za Ples	92	4
Switzerland	Carol Rich	Moitié, Moitié	26	17

Eurovision in 1987. He came last but one, ahead of the zero-points Turkish entry, and just behind Gary Lux, whose second attempt for Austria, with a song called 'Nur Noch Gefühl', was far less successful than his first.

The year 1987 also marked the lowest placing ever recorded by a UK entry. 'Only The Light' by Rikki (real name Ricky Peebles) came thirteenth. Rikki still beat Finland who have never come higher than the UK in thirty-four attempts.

WHERE'S THE BEST DRAW?

More than half of all winners have been drawn in one of five positions. There has been an average of nearly nineteen competing countries and, including ties, there have been forty-six winners. Thus, on average, each position should yield roughly two winners. The following five positions are therefore those most favoured with wins. Dividing the draw into thirds (i.e. top third, middle third and bottom third) it would seem to be best to be drawn in the last third as 43.5 per cent of the winners come from this section. The middle section attracts 39.1 per cent of winners; while only a paltry 17.4 per cent of winners have come from the first third of the draw. Note also that no song drawn second or fourth has ever won the contest to date.

Position	No. of winners	Year	Country	Song	Performer
Last	6	1960	France	Tom Pillibi	Jacqueline Boyer
		1970	Ireland	All Kinds Of Everything	Dana
		1977	France	L'Oiseau Et L'Enfant	Marie Myriam
		1982	Germany	Ein Bisschen Frieden	Nicole
		1983	Luxembourg	Si La Vie Est Cadeau	Corinne Hermès
		1989	Yugoslavia	Rock Me	Riva
Third from last	6	1961	Luxembourg	Nous Les Amoureux	Jean Claude-Pascal
		1968	Spain	La La La	Massiel
		1969	France	Un Jour, Un Enfant	Frida Boccara
		1978	Israel	A-Ba-Ni-Bi	Izhar Cohen and Alphabeta
		1980	Ireland	What's Another Year?	Johnny Logan
		1987	Ireland	Hold Me Now	Johnny Logan
Exactly half-way	5	1957	Netherlands	Net Als Toen	Corrie Brokken
		1962	France	Un Premier Amour	Isabelle Aubret
		1963	Denmark	Dansevise	Grethe and Jørgen Ingmann
		1966	Austria	Mercie Chérie	Udo Jürgens
		1979	Israel	Hallelujah	Milk and Honey featuring Gali Atari
Third	4	1958	France	Dors, Mon Amour	André Claveau
		1969	Spain	Vivo Cantando	Salomé
		1971	Monaco	Un Banc, Un Arbre, Une Rue	Séverine
		1994	Ireland	Rock 'N' Roll Kids	Paul Harrington with Charlie McGettigan
First	3	1975	Netherlands	Ding Dinge Dong	Teach-In
		1976	UK	Save Your Kisses For Me	Brotherhood of Man
		1984	Sweden	Diggi-Loo Diggi-Ley	Herreys

★ ★

THE EUROVISION SONG CONTEST

1988

Won by Switzerland: 'Ne Partez Pas Sans Moi'

Written by Nella Martinetti and Atilla Seraftug

Performed by Céline Dion

Orchestra conducted by Atilla Seraftug

Quite remarkably, the pre-tournament favourite won. Switzerland's entry, sung by the French-Canadian Céline Dion, squeezed home by one vote from Britain's Scott Fitzgerald, thanks

1988	Iceland	Sweden	Finland	UK	Turkey	Spain	Netherlands	Israel	Switzerland	Ireland	W. Germany	Austria	Denmark	Greece
Iceland	0^{x}	1^{1}	1^{0}	1^{0}	1^{0}	1^{0}	5^{4}	5^{0}	5^{0}	5^{0}	5^{0}	5^{0}	9^{4}	9^{0}
Sweden	3^{3}	3^{x}	3^{0}	5^{2}	5^{0}	5^{0}	13^{8}	13^{0}	13^{0}	18^{5}	18^{0}	18^{0}	26^{8}	26^{0}
Finland	0^{0}	0^{0}	0^{x}	0^{0}	0^{0}	0^{0}	0^{0}	3^{3}	3^{0}	3^{0}	3^{0}	3^{0}	3^{0}	3^{0}
UK	1^{1}	6^{5}	16^{10}	16^{x}	28^{12}	38^{10}	38^{0}	48^{10}	53^{5}	60^{7}	70^{10}	80^{10}	**90^{10}**	96^{6}
Turkey	0^{0}	4^{4}	4^{0}	5^{1}	5^{x}	10^{5}	11^{1}	19^{8}	19^{0}	19^{0}	27^{8}	27^{0}	27^{0}	27^{0}
Spain	2^{2}	2^{0}	2^{0}	2^{0}	7^{5}	7^{x}	7^{0}	9^{2}	15^{6}	15^{0}	15^{0}	23^{8}	24^{1}	32^{8}
Netherlands	0^{0}	0^{0}	0^{0}	6^{6}	12^{6}	12^{0}	12^{x}	19^{7}	26^{7}	28^{2}	34^{6}	34^{0}	34^{0}	46^{12}
Israel	6^{6}	6^{0}	12^{6}	16^{4}	16^{0}	22^{6}	25^{3}	25^{x}	35^{10}	36^{1}	41^{5}	43^{2}	43^{0}	46^{3}
Switzerland	7^{7}	**19^{12}**	24^{5}	**34^{10}**	**44^{10}**	**52^{8}**	**62^{10}**	**66^{4}**	**66^{x}**	**76^{10}**	**88^{12}**	**88^{0}**	88^{0}	**98^{10}**
Ireland	0^{0}	7^{7}	9^{2}	12^{3}	14^{2}	26^{12}	32^{6}	32^{0}	36^{4}	36^{x}	43^{7}	49^{6}	56^{7}	56^{0}
W. Germany	8^{8}	8^{0}	8^{0}	13^{5}	14^{1}	17^{3}	17^{0}	22^{5}	22^{0}	28^{6}	28^{x}	28^{0}	34^{6}	34^{0}
Austria	0^{0}	0^{0}	0^{0}	0^{0}	0^{0}	0^{0}	0^{0}	0^{0}	0^{0}	0^{0}	0^{0}	0^{x}	0^{0}	0^{0}
Denmark	10^{10}	13^{3}	17^{4}	17^{0}	17^{0}	18^{1}	30^{12}	36^{6}	37^{1}	41^{4}	45^{4}	57^{12}	57^{x}	57^{0}
Greece	0^{0}	0^{0}	0^{0}	0^{0}	3^{3}	3^{0}	3^{0}	3^{0}	3^{0}	3^{0}	3^{0}	3^{0}	3^{0}	3^{x}
Norway	5^{5}	13^{8}	20^{7}	32^{12}	32^{0}	32^{0}	39^{7}	40^{1}	40^{0}	48^{8}	49^{1}	52^{3}	57^{5}	64^{7}
Belgium	0^{0}	0^{0}	0^{0}	0^{0}	0^{0}	0^{0}	0^{0}	0^{0}	0^{0}	0^{0}	0^{0}	0^{0}	0^{0}	0^{0}
Luxembourg	4^{4}	14^{4}	**26^{12}**	33^{7}	33^{0}	33^{0}	38^{5}	38^{0}	50^{12}	62^{12}	62^{0}	63^{1}	65^{2}	67^{2}
Italy	0^{0}	0^{0}	8^{8}	8^{0}	12^{4}	19^{7}	19^{0}	19^{0}	27^{8}	27^{0}	29^{2}	34^{5}	34^{0}	34^{0}
France	0^{0}	2^{2}	5^{3}	5^{0}	13^{8}	15^{2}	17^{2}	17^{0}	20^{3}	20^{0}	23^{3}	30^{7}	33^{3}	38^{5}
Portugal	0^{0}	0^{0}	0^{0}	0^{0}	0^{0}	4^{4}	4^{0}	4^{0}	4^{0}	4^{0}	4^{0}	4^{0}	4^{0}	5^{1}
Yugoslavia	**12^{12}**	18^{6}	19^{1}	27^{8}	34^{7}	34^{0}	34^{0}	46^{12}	48^{2}	51^{3}	51^{0}	55^{4}	67^{12}	71^{4}

to the final vote from Yugoslavia, which gave Switzerland six points, while ignoring the British entry altogether. This was the basest ingratitude, seeing that Britain had given Yugoslavia eight points, but Switzerland had given it only two. Yugoslavia finished in sixth place, with a very jolly number called 'Mangup', but there was little doubt that the best song won. Céline Dion's career was launched, even if that of her dress designer was not.

The other major voting breakthrough was the awarding of three points by Turkey to Greece, especially as France was the only other country to give the simply terrible Greek entry any points at all. Greece did not return the compliment, but as there was no Cyprus to vote for this year, found itself giving its twelve points to the Netherlands. There was no Cyprus this year because, after the draw had been made (and Cyprus was drawn second, the no-hope position, from which nobody has ever won Eurovision), it was revealed that its song, 'Thimamai' was not original. 'Thimamai' means 'I Remember', and the writer rather belatedly remembered having actually written the song in 1984, so Cyprus had to withdraw. This is the only case so far of a song that was scheduled to be performed having to be withdrawn at a late stage on the grounds of unoriginality. Critics of the Eurovision Song Contest would argue that very few of the songs are even remotely original, but 'Thimamai' is still the only one to have been removed for that reason. The 600 million watching probably did not notice the resulting improvement in originality.

The voting was very close throughout. No fewer than five different countries each received three top votes, and although in the end Switzerland and the UK finished well ahead of the pack, no clear voting pattern was established. Austria, usually a good neighbour of Switzerland, was one of only two nations not to award it any votes at all, but then nobody gave any votes at all to Austria, so it had no favours to repay. Finland's only votes came from Israel, of all places. As might be more generally expected, Norway gave twelve points to Sweden and ten to Denmark.

Looking back at the 1988 Contest from almost ten years on, the overall impression is of huge padded shoulders on everybody's outfits, the lights and the staging, which identified it as a late 1980s broadcast almost as precisely as carbon dating would have done. We also remember the predominance of black-and-white outfits and the comparatively small number of women performing. Israel's Yardena Arazi, singing eighth, was the first female lead vocalist of the night,

Norway	Belgium	Luxembourg	Italy	France	Portugal	Yugoslavia	**Position**
9^{0}	9^{0}	9^{0}	10^{1}	12^{2}	20^{8}	20^{0}	16
38^{12}	39^{1}	42^{3}	52^{10}	52^{0}	52^{0}	52^{0}	12=
3^{0}	3^{0}	3^{0}	3^{0}	3^{0}	3^{0}	3^{0}	20
101^{5}	**113^{12}**	**121^{8}**	**133^{12}**	**133^{0}**	**136^{3}**	136^{0}	2
27^{0}	27^{0}	31^{4}	31^{0}	37^{6}	37^{0}	37^{0}	15
34^{2}	40^{6}	46^{6}	54^{8}	54^{0}	54^{0}	58^{4}	11
46^{0}	46^{0}	58^{12}	63^{5}	63^{0}	63^{0}	70^{7}	9
46^{0}	56^{10}	61^{5}	64^{3}	74^{10}	84^{10}	85^{1}	7
106^{8}	110^{4}	111^{1}	118^{7}	119^{1}	131^{12}	**137^{6}**	**1**
63^{7}	68^{5}	68^{0}	68^{0}	72^{4}	77^{5}	79^{2}	8
38^{4}	38^{0}	38^{0}	38^{0}	38^{0}	40^{2}	48^{8}	14
0^{0}	0^{0}	0^{0}	0^{0}	0^{0}	0^{0}	0^{0}	21
67^{10}	74^{7}	74^{0}	74^{0}	86^{12}	92^{6}	92^{0}	3
3^{0}	3^{0}	3^{0}	3^{0}	10^{7}	10^{0}	10^{0}	17
64^{x}	67^{3}	67^{0}	71^{4}	71^{0}	78^{7}	88^{10}	5
0^{0}	0^{x}	0^{0}	0^{0}	5^{5}	5^{0}	5^{0}	18=
73^{6}	81^{8}	81^{x}	83^{2}	83^{0}	87^{4}	90^{3}	4
37^{3}	37^{0}	39^{2}	39^{x}	47^{8}	47^{0}	52^{5}	12=
39^{1}	41^{2}	51^{10}	51^{0}	51^{x}	52^{1}	64^{12}	10
5^{0}	5^{0}	5^{0}	5^{0}	5^{0}	5^{x}	5^{0}	18=
71^{0}	71^{0}	78^{7}	84^{6}	87^{3}	87^{0}	87^{x}	6

★ ★

1988 EUROVISION SONG CONTEST

Host country: Ireland ★ *Venue:* Royal Dublin Society, Dublin
Date: 30 April ★ *Presenters:* Pat Kenny and Michelle Rocca
Voting structure: Each country awarded 12 to its top song, 10 to the second, 8 to the third and 7, 6, 5, 4, 3, 2 and 1 point for the next seven
Total entries: 21 ★ *Debut countries:* None

Country	Performer	Song	Pts	Pos.
Iceland	Beathoven	Sokrates	20	16
Sweden	Tommy Körberg	Stad I Ljus	52	12
Finland	The Boulevard	Nauravat Silmät Muistetaan	3	20
United Kingdom	Scott Fitzgerald	Go	136	2
Turkey	MFÖ	Sufi (Hey Ya Hey)	37	15
Spain	La Decada	La Chica Que Yo Quiero (Made in Spain)	58	11
Netherlands	Gerard Joling	Shangri-la	70	9
Israel	Yardena Arazi	Ben-Adam	85	7
Switzerland	**Céline Dion**	**Ne Partez Pas Sans Moi**	**137**	**1**
Ireland	Jump The Gun	Take Him Home	79	8
Germany	Maxi and Chris Garden	Lied Für Einen Freund	48	14
Austria	Wilfried	Lisa, Mona Lisa	0	21
Denmark	Hot Eyes	Ka' Du Se Hva' Jeg Sa'	92	3
Greece	Afrodite Fryda	Kloun	10	17
Norway	Karoline Krüger	For Vår Jord	88	5
Belgium	Reynaert	Laissez Briller Le Soleil	5	18
Luxembourg	Lara Fabian	Croire	90	4
Italy	Luca Barbarossa	Ti Scrivo	52	12
France	Gérard Lenorman	Chanteur De Charme	64	10
Portugal	Dora	Voltarei	5	18
Yugoslavia	Silver Wings	Mangup	87	6

although the numbers of women were augmented later on by the first mother and daughter act ever to perform at Eurovision, Maxi and Chris Garden for Germany; and by the very heavily pregnant lead singer of Denmark's Hot Eyes, performing for the third and last time at Eurovision, and finishing higher than ever before, in third place. This made Hot Eyes the top Scandinavian performers, for the first time singing at a Contest not won by one of their close neighbours. Sweden might have won this time as well, had they not been moved up into the disastrous number two slot after Cyprus' withdrawal, and had Tommy Körberg, fresh from his triumphs in the London production of *Chess*, not had a dreadful sore throat all week.

★ ★

WHICH LANGUAGE?

The 772 Eurovision songs have been sung in a total of 29 languages. Of those, only eleven have provided a winner and nearly two thirds of all winners have been in just two tongues – French and English. The Swiss have entered in five languages but only won in French.

Language	Total No. of songs	No. of wins	Countries
French	141	15	France, Belgium, Luxembourg, Switzerland, Monaco
English	97	14	United Kingdom, Ireland, Malta, Sweden, Finland, Norway, Netherlands, Austria, Switzerland, Belgium, Germany
German	85	2	Germany, Switzerland, Austria
Dutch/Flemish	56	3	Netherlands, Belgium
Italian	45	2	Italy, Switzerland
Serbo-Croat	38	1	Yugoslavia, Bosnia-Herzegovina, Croatia
Spanish	37	2	Spain
Greek	36	-	Greece, Cyprus
Swedish	34	2	Sweden
Norwegian	33	2	Norway
Portuguese	33	-	Portugal
Finnish	29	-	Finland
Danish	28	1	Denmark
Hebrew	20	2	Israel
Turkish	19	-	Turkey
Icelandic	12	-	Iceland
Polish	4	-	Poland
Slovenian	4	-	Slovenia
Estonian	3	-	Estonia
Hungarian	3	-	Hungary
Russian	3	-	Russia
Luxembourgeois	2	-	Luxembourg
Maltese	2	-	Malta
Slovakian	2	-	Slovakia
Arabic	1	-	Morocco
Breton	1	-	France
Gaelic	1	-	Ireland
Lithuanian	1	-	Lithuania
Romanian	1	-	Romania
Romansch	1	-	Switzerland

★ ★

THE EUROVISION SONG CONTEST

1989

Won by Yugoslavia: 'Rock Me'

Written by Rajko Dujmic and Stevo Cvikic

Performed by Riva

Orchestra conducted by Nikica Kalogjera

Yugoslavia won Eurovision just in time. In the years that followed the 1989 break-up of Communism and the splintering of the Balkans, many of its component parts entered Eurovision

1989	Italy	Israel	Ireland	Netherlands	Turkey	Belgium	UK	Norway	Portugal	Sweden	Luxembourg	Denmark	Austria	Finland	France
Italy	0^{x}	0^{0}	0^{0}	0^{0}	0^{0}	0^{0}	0^{0}	0^{0}	7^{7}	7^{0}	7^{0}	7^{0}	7^{0}	17^{10}	17^{0}
Israel	1^{1}	1^{x}	8^{7}	11^{3}	11^{0}	11^{0}	13^{2}	13^{0}	13^{0}	18^{5}	18^{0}	23^{5}	23^{0}	28^{5}	28^{0}
Ireland	0^{0}	0^{0}	0^{x}	0^{0}	7^{7}	10^{3}	10^{0}	13^{3}	13^{0}	13^{0}	15^{2}	15^{0}	15^{0}	15^{0}	15^{0}
Netherlands	10^{10}	10^{0}	13^{3}	13^{x}	13^{0}	13^{0}	16^{3}	16^{0}	16^{0}	16^{0}	17^{1}	17^{0}	21^{4}	25^{4}	32^{7}
Turkey	0^{0}	0^{0}	0^{0}	0^{0}	0^{x}	0^{0}	0^{0}	0^{0}	0^{0}	0^{0}	0^{0}	0^{0}	0^{0}	0^{0}	0^{0}
Belgium	0^{0}	0^{0}	5^{5}	10^{5}	10^{0}	10^{x}	10^{0}	12^{2}	12^{0}	12^{0}	12^{0}	12^{0}	12^{0}	12^{0}	12^{0}
UK	6^{6}	13^{7}	17^{4}	24^{7}	25^{1}	25^{0}	25^{x}	37^{12}	49^{12}	59^{10}	71^{12}	72^{1}	80^{8}	86^{6}	98^{12}
Norway	0^{0}	2^{2}	2^{0}	4^{2}	9^{5}	17^{8}	17^{0}	17^{x}	17^{0}	19^{2}	19^{0}	25^{6}	25^{0}	25^{0}	29^{4}
Portugal	0^{0}	0^{0}	0^{0}	0^{0}	4^{4}	6^{2}	6^{0}	7^{1}	7^{x}	10^{3}	17^{7}	17^{0}	23^{6}	25^{2}	25^{0}
Sweden	0^{0}	6^{6}	6^{0}	6^{0}	6^{0}	12^{6}	16^{4}	24^{8}	32^{8}	32^{x}	38^{6}	50^{12}	62^{12}	62^{0}	64^{2}
Luxembourg	0^{0}	0^{0}	0^{0}	0^{0}	0^{0}	0^{0}	0^{0}	0^{0}	0^{0}	0^{0}	0^{x}	0^{0}	0^{0}	0^{0}	5^{5}
Denmark	5^{5}	6^{1}	16^{10}	28^{12}	34^{6}	38^{4}	48^{10}	58^{10}	60^{2}	72^{12}	75^{3}	75^{x}	82^{7}	94^{12}	100^{6}
Austria	**12^{12}**	**20^{8}**	20^{0}	20^{0}	23^{3}	35^{12}	35^{0}	35^{0}	35^{0}	42^{7}	42^{0}	46^{4}	46^{x}	47^{1}	47^{0}
Finland	0^{0}	10^{10}	18^{8}	24^{6}	34^{10}	34^{0}	34^{0}	34^{0}	35^{1}	39^{4}	43^{4}	43^{0}	46^{3}	46^{x}	56^{10}
France	3^{3}	8^{5}	14^{6}	18^{4}	18^{0}	18^{0}	18^{0}	23^{5}	23^{0}	24^{1}	32^{8}	35^{3}	40^{5}	43^{3}	43^{x}
Spain	8^{8}	8^{0}	8^{0}	8^{0}	10^{2}	17^{7}	24^{7}	28^{4}	28^{0}	28^{0}	38^{10}	38^{0}	38^{0}	46^{8}	54^{8}
Cyprus	2^{2}	5^{3}	6^{1}	6^{0}	6^{0}	6^{0}	12^{6}	12^{0}	18^{6}	18^{0}	18^{0}	26^{8}	28^{2}	28^{0}	28^{0}
Switzerland	4^{4}	8^{4}	8^{0}	18^{10}	26^{8}	26^{0}	34^{8}	34^{0}	37^{3}	37^{0}	37^{0}	39^{2}	40^{1}	40^{0}	40^{0}
Greece	0^{0}	0^{0}	0^{0}	1^{1}	1^{0}	2^{1}	7^{5}	13^{6}	23^{10}	23^{0}	23^{0}	23^{0}	23^{0}	23^{0}	24^{1}
Iceland	0^{0}	0^{0}	0^{0}	0^{0}	0^{0}	0^{0}	0^{0}	0^{0}	0^{0}	0^{0}	0^{0}	0^{0}	0^{0}	0^{0}	0^{0}
Germany	7^{7}	7^{0}	9^{2}	9^{0}	9^{0}	14^{5}	15^{1}	15^{0}	20^{5}	26^{6}	26^{0}	33^{7}	33^{0}	33^{0}	33^{0}
Yugoslavia	0^{0}	12^{12}	**24^{12}**	**32^{8}**	**44^{12}**	**54^{10}**	**66^{12}**	**73^{7}**	**77^{4}**	**85^{8}**	**90^{5}**	**100^{10}**	**110^{10}**	**117^{7}**	**120^{3}**

in their own right. In 1992, Yugoslavia participated for the last time, and in 1993, Eurovision debutants Bosnia-Herzegovina, Croatia and Slovenia were allowed to perform. In 1998, Macedonia becomes the fourth country born of the 1989 winners to take part, but whether any of them will win in the near future is more open to debate. They have made use of Eurovision veterans to help them get it right – for instance, Jose Privsek conducted for Yugoslavia in 1961 and 1962, and then three decades later for Slovenia in 1993 – but the new republics have yet to make a serious challenge for the top prize.

Spain	Cyprus	Switzerland	Greece	Iceland	Germany	Yugoslavia	**Position**
29^{12}	35^{6}	37^{2}	41^{4}	41^{0}	48^{7}	56^{8}	9=
28^{0}	28^{0}	35^{7}	35^{0}	40^{5}	43^{3}	50^{7}	12
15^{0}	15^{0}	15^{0}	15^{0}	15^{0}	19^{4}	21^{2}	18
38^{6}	38^{0}	38^{0}	39^{1}	39^{0}	45^{6}	45^{0}	15
1^{1}	1^{0}	1^{0}	1^{0}	1^{0}	1^{0}	5^{4}	21
12^{0}	12^{0}	12^{0}	12^{0}	13^{1}	13^{0}	13^{0}	19
108^{10}	110^{2}	110^{0}	112^{2}	112^{0}	124^{12}	130^{6}	2
29^{0}	29^{0}	30^{1}	30^{0}	30^{0}	30^{0}	30^{0}	17
33^{8}	33^{0}	33^{0}	39^{6}	39^{0}	39^{0}	39^{0}	16
69^{5}	77^{8}	80^{3}	88^{8}	90^{2}	98^{8}	110^{12}	4
8^{3}	8^{0}	8^{0}	8^{0}	8^{0}	8^{0}	8^{0}	20
100^{0}	100^{0}	100^{0}	100^{0}	110^{10}	110^{0}	111^{1}	3
49^{2}	59^{10}	67^{8}	79^{12}	87^{8}	92^{5}	97^{5}	5
63^{7}	66^{3}	66^{0}	66^{0}	66^{0}	66^{0}	76^{10}	7
43^{0}	50^{7}	50^{0}	55^{5}	55^{0}	57^{2}	60^{3}	8
54^{x}	58^{4}	68^{10}	78^{10}	78^{0}	88^{10}	88^{0}	6
28^{0}	28^{x}	32^{4}	39^{7}	51^{12}	51^{0}	51^{0}	11
40^{0}	40^{0}	40^{x}	40^{0}	47^{7}	47^{0}	47^{0}	13
28^{4}	40^{12}	52^{12}	52^{x}	56^{4}	56^{0}	56^{0}	9=
0^{0}	0^{0}	0^{0}	0^{0}	0^{x}	0^{0}	0^{0}	22^{d}
33^{0}	34^{1}	40^{6}	43^{3}	46^{3}	46^{x}	46^{0}	14
120^{0}	**125^{5}**	**130^{5}**	**130^{0}**	**136^{6}**	**137^{1}**	**137^{x}**	**1**

VOTING BIAS

YUGOSLAVIA

Countries most likely to vote for Yugoslavia:

Turkey
Cyprus
Israel
Iceland
Denmark

Countries least likely to vote for Yugoslavia:

Portugal
Switzerland
Germany
Italy
Luxembourg

Countries for whom Yugoslavia is most likely to vote:

Turkey
Cyprus
Italy
France
Netherlands

★ ★ ★

Countries for whom Yugoslavia is least likely to vote:

Denmark
Ireland
Germany
Spain
Norway

Before Yugoslavia's departure in 1992, Turkish and Yugoslav juries were inclined to vote for each other. But since the break-up, Turkey has tended to favour only the predominantly Islamic Bosnia.

★ ★

1989 EUROVISION SONG CONTEST

Host country: Switzerland ★ *Venue:* Palais de Beaulieu, Lausanne
Date: 6 May ★ *Presenters:* Lolita Morena and Jacques Deschenaux
Voting structure: Each country awarded 12 to its top song, 10 to the second, 8 to the third and 7, 6, 5, 4, 3, 2 and 1 point for the next seven
Total entries: 22 ★ *Debut countries:* None

Country	Performer	Song	Pts	Pos.
Italy	Anna Oxa and Fausto Leali	Avrei Voluto	56	9
Israel	Gili and Galit	Derech Ha'melech	50	12
Ireland	Kiev Connolly and the Missing Passengers	The Real Me	21	18
Netherlands	Justine Palmelay	Blijf Zoals Je Bent	45	15
Turkey	Pan	Bana Bana	5	21
Belgium	Ingeborg	Door De Wind	13	19
United Kingdom	Live Report	Why Do I Always Get It Wrong?	130	2
Norway	Britt Synnøve Johansen	Venners Nærhet	30	17
Portugal	Da Vinci	Conquistador	39	16
Sweden	Tommy Nilsson	En Dag	110	4
Luxembourg	Park Café	Monsieur	8	20
Denmark	Birthe Kjaer	Vi Maler Byen Rød	111	3
Austria	Thomas Forstner	Nur Ein Lied	97	5
Finland	Anneli Saaristo	La Dolce Vita	76	7
France	Nathalie Pâque	J'ai Volé La Vie	60	8
Spain	Nina	Nacida Para Amar	88	6
Cyprus	Yiannis Savidakis and Fanny Polymeri	Apopse As Vrethoume	51	11
Switzerland	Furbaz	Viver Senza Tei	47	13
Greece	Marianna Efstratiou	To Diko Sou Asteri	56	9
Iceland	Daniel	Pad Sem Enginn Sér	0	22
Germany	Nino de Angelo	Flieger	46	14
Yugoslavia	**Riva**	**Rock Me**	**137**	**1**

Yugoslavia first entered in 1961, so it took twenty-eight years to take the Grand Prix. Perhaps we will have to wait as long for one of the new Balkan States to achieve victory.

The commercialization of Eurovision had moved a long way in thirty years. This time the show opened, as was traditional, with a reprise of last year's winning song, Céline Dion's 'Ne Partez Pas Sans Moi', but then – in a much less traditional move – it was followed by Céline singing her latest single, 'Where Does My Heart Beat Now?'. Despite 600 or 700 million potential

★ ★

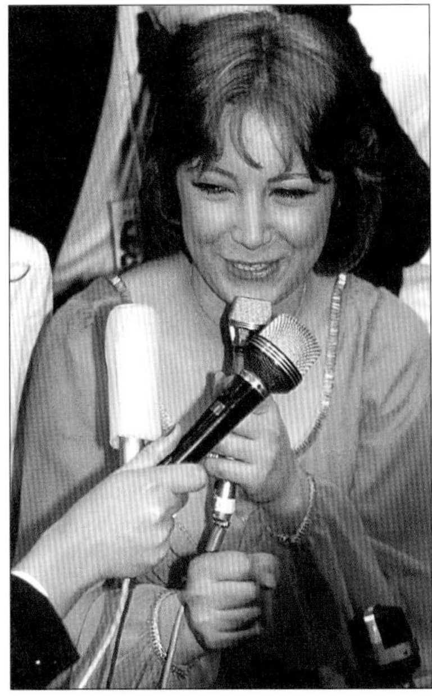

▲ *1977 The good news was that* Marie Myriam *gave France its fifth victory in twenty-two Contests. The bad news is that the country has not won since – proof as positive as the charts that French popular music has made few concessions to international taste.*

▶▲ *1976 'Save Your Kisses For Me' by* Brotherhood of Man *is, in one important sense, the most successful Eurovision song ever: it leads the table of percentage of possible votes obtained with a whopping 80.4 per cent* *(see page 158).*

▶ *1977* Lynsey de Paul and Mike Moran *finished nearly as far from 'Rock Bottom' as could be imagined, coming in second only to Marie Myriam.*

★ ★

▶ ***1978*** *Izhar Cohen was upset that, after his victory, the first for Israel, Terry Wogan teased him on Radio 2,* Top of the Pops *would not have him on, and Capital Radio broke a copy of 'A-Ba-Ni-Bi' on air.*

▼ ***1979*** *Only one country had won the Contest outright twice in succession before, when Luxembourg emerged victorious in both 1972 and 1973, but Israel's winning artists – Izhar Cohen and Milk and Honey – were actually citizens of the nation for which they performed.*

▲ **1981** *Buck's Fizz had more British chart success after their victory than any other United Kingdom winners, enjoying three number ones.*

◀ **1982** *Often a bridesmaid, and once a bride: Germany. It has finished second four times, but won on only one occasion, when Nicole performed 'Ein Bisschen Frieden'. As 'A Little Peace', the song topped the British chart.*

▶ **1983** *The victory of Corinne Hermès gave Luxembourg its fifth win, temporarily tying it with France for most victories.*

▲ *1984* *THE HERREYS were Sweden's first victors since Abba, but did not go on to duplicate their success. Brothers Per, Richard and Lewis had already broken out of their home country, being resident in the United States.*

◀ *1985* *BOBBYSOCKS ended Norway's quarter century of frustration and avenged two recent 'nul points' performances by winning with 'La Det Swinge'.*

▶ *1986* *Belgium has only won once in forty attempts, but did so in historic fashion. At thirteen years of age, SANDRA KIM was, and still is, the youngest Contest winner.*

◀ *1987* JOHNNY LOGAN *was the first, and to date only, performer to win Eurovision twice. He was also the first artist to triumph with a song he wrote unassisted, although Toto Cutugno joined him in this exclusive category three years later.*

▶ *1988 The country-of-origin curiosity that is Eurovision reached new heights when the Canadian artist* CÉLINE DION *won representing Switzerland.*

▼ *1989 Members of* RIVA *hold plaques that resemble a television test card, a bit of a comedown from Jacqueline Boyer's 'silver gilt vase'.*

*▲ **1990** Italy's Eurovision drought had lasted just over a quarter of a century when TOTO CUTUGNO brought the prize back home with his song 'Insieme: 1992'. He and Italy's other winner, Gigliola Cinquetti, hosted together in 1991.*

*◀ **1991** It was not known which of her personal qualities caused the Italian producers of the TV show to liken CAROLA to the Trevi Fountain. Perhaps the writer of Sweden's entry threw three coins at her: eight years after finishing third, Carola won it all.*

*▶ **1992** Just as Carola won eight years after coming close, LINDA MARTIN led the field eight years after finishing second.*

▲ ***1994*** *Paul Harrington and Charlie McGettigan were the first male duo to win Eurovision. Grethe and Jørgen Ingmann (1963) were a female and male pair, and Bobbysocks (1985) were both women.*

◀ ***1993*** *Hygiene be damned, Niamh Kavanagh kisses her trophy, which resembles, but is not, a sheaf of asparagus.*

▼ ***1995*** *Secret Garden won with the fewest lyric lines of any Contest champ. 'Nocturne' was basically an instrumental.*

◀ ***1997*** *Katrina and the Waves enjoyed the largest points victory in the history of the Contest with 'Love Shine A Light', which led second place finisher Ireland's 'Mysterious Woman', performed by Marc Roberts, by a whopping seventy points.*

▼ ***1996*** *When Eimear Quinn and 'The Voice' won for Ireland, it was the country's seventh title and the fourth in five years – both unprecedented achievements. However, the international hit to emerge from the Contest was 'Ooh Aah … Just a Little Bit' by Gina G.*

customers for her new record, Céline did not trouble the international charts for another couple of years or so, and in the early 1990s, 'Where Does My Heart Beat Now?' suffered the ignominious fate of having to be re-released to cash in on Céline's now burgeoning fame.

It was another black-and-white night. Presenter Lolita Morena, wearing a bizarre creation that looked as though she was sitting in a wicker chair even when she was standing up, set the tone with her soberly evening-suited co-presenter Jacques Deschenaux. Italy, Holland, Turkey, the United Kingdom, Portugal and many of the subsequent acts took their cue from the presenters' monochrome colour scheme. The performers ranged from Israel's twelve-year-old boy soprano Gili – dressed all in white and performing with a much older woman – to Yannis Savidakis and Fanny Polymeri of Cyprus, who were dressed as bride and groom (also in black and white). After the success of Céline Dion the year before, there were rather too many young women with powerful voices singing soulful ballads, and the highest-placed of them was Spain's Nina, who came sixth. And Céline Dion was not the only act whose example was followed that year. Maxi and Chris Garden of Germany in 1988 had set a cross-generational precedent that Turkey had obviously noticed, because the group Pan featured Hazal Selçuk, whose father Timur had written the song 'Bana Bana' and was conducting on the night. Five points, four of them from Yugoslavia right at the end, was the only reward the family received.

Proof – if proof were needed after all these years – that Eurovision music crosses all national borders came with the revelation that the German and Austrian entries were written by the same people, Dieter Bohlen and lyricist Joachim Horn-Bernges. Many people have written songs for Eurovision more than once, and for more than one country, but this is the only pair to have written two songs performed in a single year. Both songs were big ballads, but Austria's Thomas Forstner, making the first of his two appearances at Eurovision, easily outperformed his German colleague, coming fifth with 'Nur Ein Lied'/'Only A Song'. Germany's Nino de Angelo came fourteenth, but their combined scores gave them 143 points, making them narrowly the most voted-for composers of the night.

Ireland, third to vote, was also the second to give Yugoslavia full marks. The record of the Irish juries in picking the winners is remarkable. If we exclude those years in which the Irish entry has won, so that, by definition, the Irish jury could not have voted for the eventual winner, it has, on average, awarded over nine points to the winning entry each year. Only Switzerland has a record of picking the winners that can match that. In 1989, however, Switzerland failed to live up to its reputation of picking winners, as it gave only five points to Yugoslavia and lavished its twelve on the Greek entry, Marianna Efstratiou singing 'To Diko Sou Asteri', which finished ninth. However, overall, the Irish and Swiss juries have proved the most consistent over the longest period in identifying the winners. The least successful jury in spotting the eventual winners is Malta. The Maltese juries have, over the years, given fewer than six points to the winning song. They have picked the winner three times, in 1975, 1992 and 1993, but in other years their voting has been bizarre. This is clearly not tactical voting, as only in 1992 has Malta been within striking distance of a win, and it did its cause no good by giving full marks to Ireland, the eventual winners. It must just be that Maltese tastes in music are very much different from those of their mainland European counterparts.

Riva's 'Rock Me', performed last, was like a compilation of all the fashions that had gone before: black-and-white outfits, big ear-rings, orange gloves, dyed hair and Status Quo dance movements. The only difference was that it was a more up tempo song amid a clutch of ballads.

1990

Won by Italy: 'Insieme: 1992'

Written by Toto Cutugno

Performed by Toto Cutugno

Orchestra conducted by Gianni Madanini

It was in 1989 that Eastern Europe started dismantling itself. The Berlin Wall came down and Communism admitted defeat. So it was inevitable that in 1990, when the contest was being held for the first time in a country that had been a part of the bad old order, the songwriters of Europe would grab the opportunity to sing about the most momentous events they had experienced since the war. Some did it well, some did it badly, and some did not bother at all.

It all began with a false start. There was a long pause, followed by a lengthy musical introduction, then suddenly it all stopped. Apparently the problem was that Eduardo Leiva, the Spanish conductor, could not hear anything through his headphones, and singer Azucar Moreno had no idea when they were supposed to come in. Eventually – second time lucky – they got it right. The Spanish ladies were followed by a clutch of songs that might all have shared the Greek entry's title, 'Horis Skopo', which means 'Without A Purpose'. The bottom end of the voting table had been well and truly filled by the time that the first real contender came on stage, fifteen-year-old Emma singing for the UK. She was the youngest soloist to represent Britain, but not the first from Wales. She was clearly chasing the Nicole constituency, singing a tale of peace and love, which usually goes down well at Eurovision. Unfortunately, it was a bad song and there were many others with the same theme in 1990, so Emma could only manage sixth place.

At this point, presenter Helga Vlahovic told the audience, in as unemotional a tone as could be imagined, 'Well, we are obviously having a great time.' Weren't we just! This pronouncement was followed by the party political broadcasts on behalf of New Europe. Norway's contribution was 'Brandenburger Tor', which may be remembered less for its political message and more for the baggy trousers that singer/songwriter Ketil Stokkan wore. Switzerland reminded us that 'Music Rings Around The World', but again it was Egon Egemann's baggy trousers (and violin) that caught the attention. Germany's song, written inevitably by Ralph Siegel, told us we were 'Free To Live', while France covered racial harmony in a song written by the 1965 winning lyricist, Serge Gainsbourg, still involved with Eurovision after a quarter of a century. Many would say that the song, with African drums and an accordion, was the most original of the night, although the lyrical idea had been used in 1981 by Denmark, for one. The song got five first-place votes, more than any other, but ended equal second.

Spain, Ireland and Cyprus were the only juries to give Italy twelve points. Ireland picked the winner for the second year in a row, but for Spain and Cyprus it was a much rarer event for their juries to pick the winner. Spain's juries have over the years been the second worst, after Malta, in finding the winner, striking lucky only four times in the twenty-three years since the current voting system came in. Spain picked the Netherlands in

★ ★

1990 EUROVISION SONG CONTEST

Host country: Yugoslavia ★ *Venue:* Vatroslav Lisinki Hall, Zagreb
Date: 5 May ★ *Presenters:* Helga Vlahovic and Oliver Mlakar
Voting structure: Each country awarded 12 to its top song, 10 to the second, 8 to the third and 7, 6, 5, 4, 3, 2 and 1 point for the next seven
Total entries: 22 ★ *Debut countries:* None

Country	Performer	Song	Pts	Pos.
Spain	Azucar Moreno	Bandido	96	5
Greece	Christos Callow	Horis Skopo	11	19
Belgium	Philippe Lafontaine	Macédomienne	46	12
Turkey	Kayahan	Gözlerinin Hapsindeyim	21	17
Netherlands	Maywood	Ik Wil Alles Met Je Delen	25	15
Luxembourg	Céline Carzo	Quand Je Te Rêve	38	13
United Kingdom	Emma	Give A Little Love Back To The World	87	6
Iceland	Stjornin	Eitt Lag Enn	124	4
Norway	Ketil Stokkan	Brandenburger Tor	8	21
Israel	Rita	Shara Barechovot	16	18
Denmark	Lonnie Devantier	Hallo Hallo	64	8
Switzerland	Egon Egemann	Musik Klingt In Die Welt Hinaus	51	11
Germany	Chris Kempers and Daniel Kovac	Frei Zu Leben	60	9
France	Joëlle Ursull	White And Black Blues	132	2
Yugoslavia	Tajci	Hajde Da Ludujemo	81	7
Portugal	Nucha	Ha Sempre Alguem	9	20
Ireland	Liam Reilly	Somewhere In Europe	132	2
Sweden	Edin and Ådahl	Som En Vind	24	16
Italy	**Toto Cutugno**	**Insieme: 1992**	**149**	**1**
Austria	Simone	Keine Mauern Mehr	58	10
Cyprus	Anastasio	Milas Poli	36	14
Finland	Beat	Fri?	8	21

1975 and the UK in 1976, showing a sympathy with the Eurovision mood that could not last. Since then, Spain had only approved of Nicole's 'A Little Peace' in 1982 before casting its twelve in the direction of Toto Cutugno in 1990. In the interim, it had given maximum points to such unlikely contenders as Greece in 1983 (it finished fourteenth), Italy in 1984, 1987 and 1989 (it came fifth, third and ninth), and Ireland in 1988 (which was one of the very few years when it did not win). One of the reasons that Spain's juries have not picked the winner often is clearly because Italy has not won very often. By giving their top marks to Italy four times in seven contests, they were in danger of being accused of favouritism, but they then transferred their affections to other long shots, such as the entries from Croatia, Malta and Turkey. The Eurovision voting preferences never cease to amaze. With the exception of the Greece/Cyprus relationship, of course. Cyprus only gave six points to the Greek entry in 1990, but it have given full marks to Greece so often, and received high marks in return so often, that it is no surprise that its track record for picking winners is weak. Neither Greece nor Cyprus has yet won the competition.

Ireland's was the other song in second place, another political message delivered 'Somewhere In Europe'. Italy's 'Insieme: 1992' was a song of hope for a united Europe, as was Austria's plea for 'No More Walls'. Toto Cutugno's song won quite easily, despite Terry Wogan's view that it was one of the weakest of the night.

The political correctness of all these entries was offset by the presence of Eurocat, a cartoon cat that cropped up between each song, on a postcard

1990	Spain	Greece	Belgium	Turkey	Netherlands	Luxembourg	UK	Iceland	Norway	Israel	Denmark	Switzerland	Germany	France	Yugoslavia
Spain	0^{x}	8^{8}	9^{1}	19^{10}	21^{2}	21^{0}	22^{1}	26^{4}	31^{5}	31^{0}	31^{0}	37^{6}	49^{12}	54^{5}	57^{3}
Greece	0^{0}	0^{x}	0^{0}	0^{0}	5^{5}	5^{0}	5^{0}	5^{0}	5^{0}	5^{0}	5^{0}	5^{0}	5^{0}	5^{0}	5^{0}
Belgium	0^{0}	0^{0}	0^{x}	0^{0}	7^{7}	11^{4}	11^{0}	11^{0}	12^{1}	12^{0}	12^{0}	16^{4}	24^{8}	32^{8}	32^{0}
Turkey	0^{0}	0^{0}	0^{0}	0^{x}	3^{3}	3^{0}	3^{0}	5^{2}	9^{4}	9^{0}	9^{0}	9^{0}	14^{5}	14^{0}	21^{7}
Netherlands	0^{0}	1^{1}	1^{0}	4^{3}	4^{x}	5^{1}	9^{4}	9^{0}	9^{0}	11^{2}	11^{0}	14^{3}	14^{0}	20^{6}	20^{0}
Luxembourg	0^{0}	4^{4}	4^{0}	4^{0}	4^{0}	4^{x}	7^{3}	7^{0}	7^{0}	7^{0}	7^{0}	7^{0}	10^{3}	22^{12}	24^{2}
UK	7^{7}	12^{5}	24^{12}	24^{0}	24^{0}	27^{3}	27^{x}	27^{0}	27^{0}	37^{10}	40^{3}	50^{10}	51^{1}	61^{10}	71^{10}
Iceland	4^{4}	7^{3}	17^{10}	18^{1}	18^{0}	26^{8}	38^{12}	38^{x}	48^{10}	56^{8}	66^{10}	73^{7}	73^{0}	73^{0}	77^{4}
Norway	0^{0}	0^{0}	0^{0}	0^{0}	0^{0}	0^{0}	0^{0}	0^{0}	0^{x}	4^{4}	5^{1}	5^{0}	5^{0}	5^{0}	5^{0}
Israel	0^{0}	0^{0}	0^{0}	0^{0}	4^{4}	4^{0}	4^{0}	4^{0}	4^{0}	4^{x}	4^{0}	6^{2}	10^{4}	10^{0}	11^{1}
Denmark	6^{6}	6^{0}	9^{3}	11^{2}	11^{0}	11^{0}	11^{0}	18^{7}	25^{7}	32^{7}	32^{x}	33^{1}	33^{0}	33^{0}	33^{0}
Switzerland	1^{1}	13^{12}	13^{0}	19^{6}	19^{0}	21^{2}	21^{0}	21^{0}	21^{0}	21^{0}	33^{12}	33^{x}	33^{0}	34^{1}	39^{5}
Germany	8^{8}	8^{0}	14^{6}	14^{0}	14^{0}	26^{12}	33^{7}	34^{1}	34^{0}	34^{0}	38^{4}	38^{0}	38^{x}	38^{0}	38^{0}
France	5^{5}	5^{0}	9^{4}	13^{4}	25^{12}	25^{0}	25^{0}	37^{12}	49^{12}	55^{6}	60^{5}	72^{12}	82^{10}	82^{x}	94^{12}
Yugoslavia	3^{3}	3^{0}	3^{0}	15^{12}	15^{0}	15^{0}	20^{5}	30^{10}	33^{3}	45^{12}	52^{7}	52^{0}	52^{0}	54^{2}	54^{x}
Portugal	0^{0}	0^{0}	0^{0}	0^{0}	0^{0}	7^{7}	9^{2}	9^{0}	9^{0}	9^{0}	9^{0}	9^{0}	9^{0}	9^{0}	9^{0}
Ireland	10^{10}	17^{7}	24^{7}	29^{5}	39^{10}	45^{6}	55^{10}	**63^{8}**	**71^{8}**	**71^{0}**	**79^{8}**	**84^{5}**	**91^{7}**	**98^{7}**	**98^{0}**
Sweden	2^{2}	4^{2}	4^{0}	4^{0}	10^{6}	10^{0}	16^{6}	16^{0}	22^{6}	22^{0}	22^{0}	22^{0}	24^{2}	24^{0}	24^{0}
Italy	**12^{12}**	**22^{10}**	**30^{8}**	**38^{8}**	**46^{8}**	**56^{10}**	**56^{0}**	59^{3}	59^{0}	60^{1}	66^{6}	74^{8}	80^{6}	84^{4}	90^{6}
Austria	0^{0}	0^{0}	2^{2}	9^{7}	10^{1}	15^{5}	23^{8}	29^{6}	29^{0}	29^{0}	29^{0}	29^{0}	29^{0}	32^{3}	40^{8}
Cyprus	0^{0}	6^{6}	11^{5}	11^{0}	11^{0}	11^{0}	11^{0}	11^{0}	13^{2}	18^{5}	20^{2}	20^{0}	20^{0}	20^{0}	20^{0}
Finland	0^{0}	0^{0}	0^{0}	0^{0}	0^{0}	0^{0}	0^{0}	5^{5}	5^{0}	8^{3}	8^{0}	8^{0}	8^{0}	8^{0}	8^{0}

showing Eurocat and a stereotypical item from the country about to perform. So we saw Eurocat and a plate of spaghetti for Italy; Eurocat and a pub for Ireland; and so on. One day Eurovision will update the image of its member states, but we certainly should not hold our breath waiting for this to happen.

The songs ended with Finland's entry, a song called 'Fri?' performed by Beat. The name was appropriate as they were, by every other entry. The Finns only received votes from the Icelandic and Israeli juries.

Portugal	Ireland	Sweden	Italy	Austria	Cyprus	Finland	**Position**
62^{5}	62^{0}	62^{0}	70^{8}	78^{8}	86^{8}	96^{10}	5
5^{0}	5^{0}	5^{0}	5^{0}	5^{0}	11^{6}	11^{0}	19
34^{2}	35^{1}	42^{7}	42^{0}	46^{4}	46^{0}	46^{0}	12
21^{0}	21^{0}	21^{0}	21^{0}	21^{0}	21^{0}	21^{0}	17
21^{1}	21^{0}	21^{0}	23^{2}	23^{0}	25^{2}	25^{0}	15
27^{3}	27^{0}	27^{0}	28^{1}	33^{5}	38^{5}	38^{0}	13
71^{0}	77^{6}	77^{0}	83^{6}	84^{1}	87^{3}	87^{0}	6
89^{12}	96^{7}	104^{8}	107^{3}	117^{10}	117^{0}	124^{7}	4
5^{0}	8^{3}	8^{0}	8^{0}	8^{0}	8^{0}	8^{0}	21=
11^{0}	11^{0}	11^{0}	11^{0}	11^{0}	11^{0}	16^{5}	18
40^{7}	44^{4}	47^{3}	54^{7}	60^{6}	64^{4}	64^{0}	8
47^{8}	47^{0}	47^{0}	47^{0}	47^{0}	48^{1}	51^{3}	11
38^{0}	48^{10}	52^{4}	57^{5}	60^{3}	60^{0}	60^{0}	9
98^{4}	106^{8}	111^{5}	111^{0}	113^{2}	120^{7}	132^{12}	2=
54^{0}	59^{5}	60^{1}	70^{10}	70^{0}	80^{10}	81^{1}	7
9^{x}	9^{0}	9^{0}	9^{0}	9^{0}	9^{0}	9^{0}	20
104^{6}	104^{x}	116^{12}	116^{0}	128^{12}	128^{0}	132^{4}	2=
24^{0}	24^{0}	24^{x}	24^{0}	24^{0}	24^{0}	24^{0}	16
100^{10}	**112^{12}**	**122^{10}**	**122^{x}**	**129^{7}**	**141^{12}**	**149^{8}**	**1**
40^{0}	42^{2}	44^{2}	56^{12}	56^{x}	56^{0}	58^{2}	10
20^{0}	20^{0}	26^{6}	30^{4}	30^{0}	30^{x}	36^{6}	14
8^{0}	8^{0}	8^{0}	8^{0}	8^{0}	8^{0}	8^{x}	21=

VOTING BIAS

ICELAND

Countries most likely to vote for Iceland:

Sweden
UK
Denmark
Portugal
Ireland

Countries least likely to vote for Iceland:

Turkey
Cyprus
France
Malta
Finland

Countries for whom Iceland is most likely to vote:

Denmark
Yugoslavia
Sweden
Finland
Norway

★ ★ ★

Countries for whom Iceland is least likely to vote:

UK
Ireland
Spain
Malta
Greece

Icelandic is remarkably similar to Old Norse, the language of the Vikings brought to Iceland in the ninth century. Consequently Iceland has an affinity with the Scandinavian countries.

★ ★

THE EUROVISION SONG CONTEST

1991

Won by Sweden: 'Fångad Av En Stormvind'
Written by Stephan Berg
Performed by Carola
Orchestra conducted by Anders Berglund

Eurovision came to Rome for the first time as a result of Toto Cutugno's surprise victory the year before. As a reward, Toto was given the job of co-presenting the 1991 Contest with Italy's only other previous Eurovision winner, Gigliola Cinquetti. They opened the show by reprising their winning songs, but from then on for Toto it was all downhill. 'It was a sorry day for all of us when this man won last year' was Terry Wogan's comment for the BBC, and few who watched would have disagreed. His main failing seemed to be that he did not understand either the scoring system nor any other language besides Italian. This did not make him entirely qualified for the job in hand. Miss Cinquetti tried her hardest, but found it difficult to control her co-host, whose incompetence spread across the whole Contest.

The songs were performed by twenty-two different acts which tried to paper over their musical differences by all wearing either blue or purple, from Yugoslavia's Baby Doll who opened the show onwards. The host country's presentation gimmick idea this year was for each act to be introduced by being compared to famous sights of Italy, which were supposed to 'best represent their personality'. This was just an excuse for a quick travelogue of Italy, because why Atlantis 2000, performing for Germany, should be like the Pantheon, or Carola of Sweden like the Trevi Fountain, nobody either knew or cared. The performers were also asked to sing a snippet of an Italian song as they posed in front of 'their' monument, which made for the curious sound of Ireland's Kim Jackson singing 'Volare, wo-ho-ho-ho', in tribute to Italy's best-known failure at Eurovision.

The show began with a 'la la la' verse from Yugoslavia's Baby Doll, who sang the intrinsically un-European song 'Brazil' while her male chorus line did cartwheels behind her, and the night tried to climb upwards from there. Choreography in the background soon proved to be a well-used idea, as Malta, Sweden, Turkey, Finland and several others tried to turn the night into the Eurovision Song and Dance Contest. The usual clutch of perennial Eurovision themes were there. References to the weather proved to be either enormously successful (Carola's 'Storm Wind' taking the title) or a total failure (Thomas Forstner's 'Venice In The Rain' scoring no points at all), but most of the songs were lovelorn power ballads in the Eurovision mode. Malta marked its return after sixteen years away by coming a very respectable sixth with a classic piano-based belter, and Switzerland took fifth place with a pale imitation of Céline Dion's winner of three years before. However, both the winner and the runner-up were a little different – Carola (who had come third in 1983) performing a more upbeat number than most on show that night, and France's Amina coming up with a sensual song, more in the style of Enya than of Eurovision. Amina's performance came immediately after the high energy of Carola, and the contrast was stark. There is usually little

1991 EUROVISION SONG CONTEST

Host country: Italy ★ *Venue:* Cinecitta Studio 15, Rome
Date: 4 May ★ *Presenters:* Gigliola Cinquetti and Toto Cutugno
Voting structure: Each country awarded 12 to its top song, 10 to the second, 8 to the third and 7, 6, 5, 4, 3, 2 and 1 point for the next seven
Total entries: 22 ★ *Debut countries:* None

Country	Performer	Song	Pts	Pos.
Yugoslavia	Baby Doll	Brazil	1	21
Iceland	Stefan and Eyfi	Nina	26	15
Malta	Georgina and Paul Giordimaina	Could It Be	106	6
Greece	Sofia Vossou	Anixi	36	13
Switzerland	Sandra Simo	Canzone Per Te	118	5
Austria	Thomas Forstner	Venedig Im Regen	0	22
Luxembourg	Sarah Bray	Un Baiser Volé	29	14
Sweden	**Carola**	**Fångad Av En Stormvind**	**146**	**1**
France	Amina	C'est Le Dernier Qui A Parlé Qui A Raison	146	2
Turkey	Izel Celiköz, Reyhan Soykarci and Can Ugurluer	Iki Dakika	44	12
Ireland	Kim Jackson	Could It Be That I'm In Love	47	10
Portugal	Dulce	Lusitana Paixão	62	8
Denmark	Anders Frandsen	Lige Der Hvor Hjertet Slår	8	19
Norway	Just 4 Fun	Mrs Thompson	14	17
Israel	Duo Datz	Kaan	139	3
Finland	Kaija Kärkinen	Hullu Yö	6	20
Germany	Atlantis 2000	Dieser Traum Darf Niemals Sterben	10	18
Belgium	Clouseau	Geef Het Op	23	16
Spain	Sergio Dalma	Bailar Pegados	119	4
United Kingdom	Samantha Janus	A Message To Your Heart	47	10
Cyprus	Elena Patroklou	SOS	60	9
Italy	Peppino di Capri	Comme E Ddoce 'O Mare	89	7

to be said for coming on immediately after a very good performance, because the audience have had their expectations raised and now demand something that will maintain the quality. Only five times in the history of the competition have the top two songs been performed one after the other, but 1991 was one of those years, thanks to the sensuality of Amina's performance (the other years, for reference, were 1957, 1961, 1966 and the following year, 1992).

The voting was the usual chaotic process, the chaos added to by the need to bring an extra language, Italian, into play. By the time the Turkish jury was giving its votes, the technical difficulties of keeping Ankara on the line led Toto Cutugno to cry, 'Mr Naef, Mr Naef' pleadingly to the long-serving and long-suffering EBU scrutineer Frank Naef. From then on the votes were generally announced in English by Mr Naef, in French by the long-suffering Gigliola Cinquetti and then – occasionally – in Italian by her co-host Toto. The end result of all this tomfoolery left Sweden and France tied for first place, thanks to the final jury, Italy, giving twelve points to France, but none to either Sweden or Israel. Rules had been put in place since the débâcle of 1969 to allow for an outright winner to be determined, by counting the number of first-place and second-place votes awarded. Both countries had received four first-place votes, but Sweden had five second-place votes, compared to France's two. It was interesting to note that of the four juries that gave top marks to the French song, two gave second-place votes to Sweden, but none of the

1991	Yugoslavia	Iceland	Malta	Greece	Switzerland	Austria	Luxembourg	Sweden	France	Turkey	Ireland	Portugal	Denmark	Norway	Israel
Yugoslavia	0^{x}	0^{0}	1^{1}	1^{0}	1^{0}	1^{0}	1^{0}	1^{0}	1^{0}	1^{0}	1^{0}	1^{0}	1^{0}	1^{0}	1^{0}
Iceland	0^{0}	0^{x}	0^{0}	0^{0}	4^{4}	4^{0}	4^{0}	14^{10}	14^{0}	14^{0}	14^{0}	14^{0}	14^{0}	14^{0}	14^{0}
Malta	1^{1}	1^{0}	1^{x}	3^{2}	9^{6}	13^{4}	23^{10}	35^{12}	37^{2}	44^{7}	56^{12}	63^{7}	63^{0}	69^{6}	69^{0}
Greece	4^{4}	4^{0}	9^{5}	9^{x}	9^{0}	11^{2}	11^{0}	11^{0}	11^{0}	11^{0}	12^{1}	12^{0}	12^{0}	13^{1}	17^{4}
Switzerland	5^{5}	10^{5}	10^{0}	17^{7}	17^{x}	25^{8}	37^{12}	45^{8}	49^{4}	51^{2}	53^{2}	59^{6}	64^{5}	67^{3}	75^{8}
Austria	0^{0}	0^{0}	0^{0}	0^{0}	0^{0}	0^{x}	0^{0}	0^{0}	0^{0}	0^{0}	0^{0}	0^{0}	0^{0}	0^{0}	0^{0}
Luxembourg	0^{0}	4^{4}	4^{0}	4^{0}	4^{0}	9^{5}	9^{x}	10^{1}	10^{0}	13^{3}	13^{0}	15^{2}	19^{4}	19^{0}	19^{0}
Sweden	6^{6}	18^{12}	18^{0}	18^{0}	28^{10}	38^{10}	45^{7}	45^{x}	45^{0}	51^{6}	54^{3}	64^{10}	76^{12}	84^{8}	94^{10}
France	10^{10}	17^{7}	20^{3}	28^{8}	35^{7}	**47^{12}**	47^{0}	52^{5}	52^{x}	52^{0}	59^{7}	64^{5}	64^{0}	76^{12}	88^{12}
Turkey	0^{0}	0^{0}	7^{7}	7^{0}	7^{0}	7^{0}	7^{0}	7^{0}	14^{7}	14^{x}	14^{0}	14^{0}	22^{8}	22^{0}	29^{7}
Ireland	3^{3}	3^{0}	7^{4}	7^{0}	10^{3}	11^{1}	19^{8}	19^{0}	19^{0}	23^{4}	23^{x}	23^{0}	30^{7}	30^{0}	31^{1}
Portugal	0^{0}	8^{8}	8^{0}	12^{4}	13^{1}	13^{0}	15^{2}	22^{7}	32^{10}	37^{5}	37^{0}	37^{x}	38^{1}	40^{2}	40^{0}
Denmark	0^{0}	0^{0}	0^{0}	0^{0}	0^{0}	0^{0}	0^{0}	3^{3}	3^{0}	3^{0}	3^{0}	3^{0}	3^{x}	8^{5}	8^{0}
Norway	0^{0}	6^{6}	6^{0}	6^{0}	6^{0}	6^{0}	7^{1}	7^{0}	7^{0}	8^{1}	8^{0}	8^{0}	10^{2}	10^{x}	10^{0}
Israel	**12^{12}**	**22^{10}**	**30^{8}**	**35^{5}**	**43^{8}**	43^{0}	48^{5}	54^{6}	57^{3}	**69^{12}**	**77^{8}**	81^{4}	**91^{10}**	**98^{7}**	**98^{x}**
Finland	0^{0}	1^{1}	1^{0}	2^{1}	2^{0}	2^{0}	2^{0}	2^{0}	2^{0}	2^{0}	6^{4}	6^{0}	6^{0}	6^{0}	6^{0}
Germany	0^{0}	0^{0}	0^{0}	0^{0}	0^{0}	0^{0}	0^{0}	0^{0}	0^{0}	0^{0}	0^{0}	0^{0}	6^{6}	6^{0}	6^{0}
Belgium	0^{0}	0^{0}	0^{0}	0^{0}	0^{0}	3^{3}	3^{0}	5^{2}	10^{5}	10^{0}	10^{0}	10^{0}	10^{0}	10^{0}	10^{0}
Spain	8^{8}	10^{2}	16^{6}	26^{10}	38^{12}	45^{7}	**51^{6}**	**55^{4}**	**61^{6}**	**69^{8}**	75^{6}	**83^{8}**	83^{0}	87^{4}	89^{2}
UK	0^{0}	0^{0}	10^{10}	13^{3}	18^{5}	24^{6}	27^{3}	27^{0}	28^{1}	28^{0}	28^{0}	29^{1}	32^{3}	32^{0}	37^{5}
Cyprus	2^{2}	5^{3}	17^{12}	29^{12}	29^{0}	29^{0}	33^{4}	33^{0}	45^{12}	45^{0}	50^{5}	53^{3}	53^{0}	53^{0}	59^{6}
Italy	7^{7}	7^{0}	9^{2}	15^{6}	17^{2}	17^{0}	17^{0}	17^{0}	25^{8}	35^{10}	45^{10}	57^{12}	57^{0}	67^{10}	70^{3}

four who voted for Sweden gave second-place votes to France. It was a night notable for very little of the usual favouritism in the voting: Norway gave twelve points to France, not Sweden, and Cyprus awarded its twelve points to Spain, not Greece.

The Swiss continued to avoid giving any points to Germany, but as everybody else except Denmark, Spain and Cyprus avoided the German song, too, this proved little. Could it be that, at long last, the music was indeed overcoming national prejudices?

Finland	Germany	Belgium	Spain	UK	Cyprus	Italy	**Position**
1^{0}	1^{0}	1^{0}	1^{0}	1^{0}	1^{0}	1^{0}	21
14^{0}	19^{5}	19^{0}	19^{0}	19^{0}	19^{0}	26^{7}	15
69^{0}	79^{10}	83^{4}	89^{6}	96^{7}	96^{0}	106^{10}	6
18^{1}	18^{0}	19^{1}	24^{5}	24^{0}	34^{10}	36^{2}	13
80^{5}	86^{6}	98^{12}	98^{0}	106^{8}	114^{8}	118^{4}	5
0^{0}	0^{0}	0^{0}	0^{0}	0^{0}	0^{0}	0^{0}	22
19^{0}	22^{3}	24^{2}	24^{0}	27^{3}	29^{2}	29^{0}	14
102^{8}	**114^{12}**	**124^{10}**	**128^{4}**	**140^{12}**	**146^{6}**	**146^{0}**	1
98^{10}	106^{8}	113^{7}	121^{8}	127^{6}	134^{7}	**146^{12}**	2
29^{0}	29^{0}	29^{0}	31^{2}	36^{5}	36^{0}	44^{8}	12
33^{2}	35^{2}	40^{5}	40^{0}	44^{4}	44^{0}	47^{3}	$10^{=}$
47^{7}	47^{0}	47^{0}	57^{10}	57^{0}	61^{4}	62^{1}	8
8^{0}	8^{0}	8^{0}	8^{0}	8^{0}	8^{0}	8^{0}	19
10^{0}	14^{4}	14^{0}	14^{0}	14^{0}	14^{0}	14^{0}	17
104^{6}	104^{0}	112^{8}	124^{12}	134^{10}	139^{5}	139^{0}	3
6^{x}	6^{0}	6^{0}	6^{0}	6^{0}	6^{0}	6^{0}	20
6^{0}	6^{x}	6^{0}	7^{1}	7^{0}	10^{3}	10^{0}	18
13^{3}	13^{0}	13^{x}	16^{3}	18^{2}	18^{0}	23^{5}	16
93^{4}	100^{7}	106^{6}	106^{x}	107^{1}	119^{12}	119^{0}	4
37^{0}	37^{0}	40^{3}	40^{0}	40^{x}	41^{1}	47^{6}	10
59^{0}	60^{1}	60^{0}	60^{0}	60^{0}	60^{x}	60^{0}	9
82^{12}	82^{0}	82^{0}	89^{7}	89^{0}	89^{0}	89^{x}	7

VOTING BIAS

SWEDEN

Countries most likely to vote for Sweden:

Norway
Denmark
Germany
Iceland
Austria

Countries least likely to vote for Sweden:

Spain
Turkey
Italy
Greece
Malta

Countries for whom Sweden is most likely to vote:

Ireland
Denmark
Iceland
Norway
Germany

Countries for whom Sweden is least likely to vote:

Spain
Switzerland
Italy
Cyprus
Greece

The year 1991 was unusual in that the winners, Sweden, failed to give any points at all to Ireland. Over the years, Sweden has awarded a total of sixty more votes over and above Ireland's average score.

★ ★

THE EUROVISION SONG CONTEST

1992

Won by Ireland: 'Why Me?'
Written by Johnny Logan
Performed by Linda Martin
Orchestra conducted by Noel Kelehan

This year's Contest was notable for a number of reasons. Johnny Logan, having performed two winners, confirmed his position as master of Eurovision by writing his second winner (he had also written 'Hold Me Now', the second of his two winners as a performer). As he had also written Linda Martin's earlier Eurovision entry, 'Terminal Three', which had come second in 1984, he now joined the likes of Ralph Siegel on the short list of those who have written three songs that have come first or second in Eurovision. With 'Why Me?' Linda Martin became the third woman, after Lys Assia and Gigliola Cinquetti, to have come both first and second in Eurovision, and the first to come second first and first second.

It was also Frank Naef's final Contest as scrutineer. The quality of the sound links had improved dramatically since he took over from Clifford Brown many years before, but there were still plenty of opportunities for the scores to be misheard or drowned out by applause and for Mr Naef to be called upon to scrutinize the proceedings. His final Contest was not a controversial one to deal with, even though twenty-three participating nations was a record number at the time.

The top three songs in the final voting were all performed in English. The language of each song has increasingly become an issue over the years, as most nations feel that it is a great advantage to be able to sing in the most widely understood language of all, English. Many entrants have tried to get round the language issue by singing songs of the 'Bonjour, Good Evening, Guten Abend' variety, or – as Iceland did in 1988 – just listing names of famous international people ('Socrates, Hercules, John Wayne, Michael Caine', and so on). This way, the song is not really sung in any one language and you hope everybody understands a bit of it, at least. It looks like a clever idea, but there is little evidence that it has ever worked. Juries don't really care what the words are: they are just looking for a shape and a sound to vote for. In 1992, the usual plots cropped up in similar titles again, which even the unilinguists could understand. Music was the theme for Spain ('Todo Esto Es La Musica'), Belgium ('Nous On Veut Des Violons'), Switzerland ('Mister Music Man') and Italy ('Rapsodia'), although only the Italian job paid off in votes. There were songs about dreams (Norway and Germany), a song with a nonsense title from Finland and the usual clutch of love songs. Israel got sport into their song, which made a change, but most of the others were a variation on a theme. To be fair to Eurovision composers, what else can we expect? The songs on display this year were the 629th to 651st songs performed at Eurovision, say 50 albums' worth, and we would not criticize any major performer for coming up with plenty of love songs or songs of environmental awareness in their songs over a 40-year career, so why should we criticize Eurovision for not always being original? The object of the Contest is to create a song that will appeal to more

1992 EUROVISION SONG CONTEST

Host country: Sweden ★ *Venue:* Malmomässan, Malmö
Date: 9 May ★ *Presenters:* Harald Treutiger and Lydia Capolicchio
Voting structure: Each country awarded 12 to its top song, 10 to the second, 8 to the third and 7, 6, 5, 4, 3, 2 and 1 point for the next seven
Total entries: 23 ★ *Debut countries:* None

Country	Performer	Song	Pts	Pos.
Spain	Serafin	Todo Esto Es La Musica	37	14
Belgium	Morgane	Nous On Veut Des Violons	11	20
Israel	Dafna	Ze Rak Sport	85	6
Turkey	Aylin Vatankos	Yaz Bitti	17	19
Greece	Cleopatra	Olou Tou Kosmou I Elpida	94	5
France	Kali	Monté La Riviè	73	8
Sweden	Christer Björkman	Imorgon Är En Annan Dag	9	22
Portugal	Dina	Amor d'Agua Fresca	26	17
Cyprus	Evridiki	Tairiazoume	57	11
Malta	Mary Spiteri	Little Child	123	3
Iceland	Heart 2 Heart	Nei Eda Ja	80	7
Finland	Pave Maijanen	Yamma Yamma	4	23
Switzerland	Daisy Auvray	Mister Music Man	32	15
Luxembourg	Marion Welter and Kontinent	Sou Frai	10	21
Austria	Tony Wegas	Zusammen Geh'n	63	10
United Kingdom	Michael Ball	One Step Out Of Time	139	2
Ireland	**Linda Martin**	**Why Me?**	**155**	**1**
Denmark	Lotte Nilsson and Kenny Lübcke	Alt Det Som Ingen Ser	47	12
Italy	Mia Martini	Rapsodia	111	4
Yugoslavia	Extra Nena	Ljubim Te Pesmama	44	13
Norway	Merethe Trøan	Visjoner	23	18
Germany	Wind	Traüme Sind Für Alle Da	27	16
Netherlands	Humphrey Campbell	Wijs Me De Weg	67	9

people across a wide range of cultures than any other on the night, and that goal, almost by definition, excludes too much originality. Familiarity in themes, rhythms and lyrics will be far more likely to win than anything too different.

Although there have been years in which a country could sing in any language it liked, in recent years, singers have been allowed to perform only in a language native to their homeland. This has been taken to odd extremes by the French, for example, who performed in a kind of Romany patois in 1992 and in Breton in 1996, or by the Irish with an entry in Gaelic in 1972. However, the Swiss and the Belgians, who have a variety of languages to choose from, have always been scrupulously fair to the different sections of their populations in choosing the language of that year's Eurovision entrant. For Belgium, 1992 was a French year, but for Switzerland, with four languages to juggle, things were a little more complicated.

The Swiss selection process in 1992 was won by a song called 'Soleil, Soleil'. The song had originally been performed in French, but failed to get to the final, so the lyrics were translated into German. It then won the German heats and went on to win the national final. It was duly chosen as the Swiss entry, but the French-speaking Swiss, who had already voted against 'Soleil, Soleil', complained and so the second-placed song in the finals, 'Mister Music Man' (which was not in English, despite its title, but in French), took its

1992	Spain	Belgium	Israel	Turkey	Greece	France	Sweden	Portugal	Cyprus	Malta	Iceland	Finland	Switzerland	Luxembourg	Austria	UK
Spain	0^{x}	1^{1}	1^{0}	2^{1}	6^{4}	12^{6}	12^{0}	12^{0}	12^{0}	14^{2}	14^{0}	17^{3}	17^{0}	20^{3}	22^{2}	23^{1}
Belgium	3^{3}	3^{x}	3^{0}	7^{4}	7^{0}	10^{3}	10^{0}	10^{0}	10^{0}	10^{0}	10^{0}	10^{0}	10^{0}	11^{1}	11^{0}	11^{0}
Israel	10^{10}	10^{0}	10^{x}	12^{2}	12^{0}	20^{8}	24^{4}	31^{7}	35^{4}	42^{7}	42^{0}	42^{0}	46^{4}	54^{8}	55^{1}	62^{7}
Turkey	0^{0}	0^{0}	0^{0}	0^{x}	0^{0}	0^{0}	0^{0}	0^{0}	0^{0}	8^{8}	8^{0}	8^{0}	8^{0}	8^{0}	8^{0}	8^{0}
Greece	0^{0}	0^{0}	7^{7}	15^{8}	15^{x}	22^{7}	25^{3}	30^{5}	42^{12}	42^{0}	44^{2}	49^{5}	59^{10}	59^{0}	63^{4}	63^{0}
France	6^{6}	6^{0}	18^{12}	21^{3}	21^{0}	21^{x}	21^{0}	21^{0}	24^{3}	24^{0}	24^{0}	31^{7}	43^{12}	43^{0}	43^{0}	43^{0}
Sweden	0^{0}	0^{0}	0^{0}	0^{0}	0^{0}	1^{1}	1^{x}	1^{0}	1^{0}	1^{0}	1^{0}	1^{0}	1^{0}	1^{0}	1^{0}	1^{0}
Portugal	0^{0}	0^{0}	8^{8}	8^{0}	10^{2}	10^{0}	10^{0}	10^{x}	10^{0}	10^{0}	10^{0}	12^{2}	12^{0}	12^{0}	12^{0}	12^{0}
Cyprus	0^{0}	0^{0}	3^{3}	3^{0}	13^{10}	15^{2}	15^{0}	17^{2}	17^{x}	18^{1}	18^{0}	26^{8}	28^{2}	28^{0}	28^{0}	28^{0}
Malta	**12^{12}**	**22^{10}**	**22^{0}**	22^{0}	29^{7}	29^{0}	41^{12}	**53^{12}**	**54^{1}**	54^{x}	62^{8}	62^{0}	67^{5}	79^{12}	87^{8}	87^{0}
Iceland	8^{8}	12^{4}	16^{4}	16^{0}	22^{6}	22^{0}	28^{6}	34^{6}	34^{0}	34^{0}	34^{x}	34^{0}	37^{3}	42^{5}	49^{7}	61^{12}
Finland	0^{0}	0^{0}	1^{1}	1^{0}	1^{0}	1^{0}	1^{0}	1^{0}	1^{0}	1^{0}	1^{0}	1^{x}	1^{0}	1^{0}	1^{0}	1^{0}
Switzerland	0^{0}	5^{5}	5^{0}	5^{0}	5^{0}	5^{0}	5^{0}	5^{0}	5^{0}	5^{0}	17^{12}	17^{0}	17^{x}	17^{0}	17^{0}	21^{4}
Luxembourg	0^{0}	0^{0}	0^{0}	0^{0}	0^{0}	0^{0}	0^{0}	0^{0}	0^{0}	10^{10}	10^{0}	10^{0}	10^{0}	10^{x}	10^{0}	10^{0}
Austria	2^{2}	10^{9}	10^{0}	10^{0}	18^{8}	18^{0}	19^{1}	22^{3}	30^{8}	34^{4}	34^{0}	34^{0}	34^{0}	34^{0}	34^{x}	44^{10}
UK	5^{5}	17^{12}	19^{2}	**29^{10}**	29^{0}	**39^{10}**	**44^{5}**	44^{0}	50^{6}	56^{6}	60^{4}	66^{6}	74^{8}	81^{7}	93^{12}	93^{x}
Ireland	1^{1}	8^{7}	8^{0}	20^{12}	**32^{12}**	32^{0}	42^{10}	47^{4}	51^{5}	**63^{12}**	**70^{7}**	**80^{10}**	**86^{6}**	**96^{10}**	**106^{10}**	**114^{8}**
Denmark	4^{4}	4^{0}	10^{6}	10^{0}	10^{0}	10^{0}	17^{7}	18^{1}	18^{0}	18^{0}	24^{6}	24^{0}	24^{0}	30^{6}	33^{3}	36^{3}
Italy	0^{0}	0^{0}	0^{0}	5^{5}	8^{3}	20^{12}	28^{8}	36^{8}	46^{10}	51^{5}	61^{10}	73^{12}	80^{7}	80^{0}	86^{6}	86^{0}
Yugoslavia	0^{0}	0^{0}	10^{10}	16^{6}	17^{1}	22^{5}	22^{0}	22^{0}	24^{2}	27^{3}	32^{5}	36^{4}	36^{0}	38^{2}	38^{0}	38^{0}
Norway	0^{0}	3^{3}	3^{0}	3^{0}	3^{0}	3^{0}	5^{2}	5^{0}	5^{0}	5^{0}	6^{1}	7^{1}	7^{0}	11^{4}	11^{0}	16^{5}
Germany	0^{0}	6^{6}	6^{0}	6^{0}	6^{0}	6^{0}	6^{0}	16^{10}	16^{0}	16^{0}	16^{0}	16^{0}	16^{0}	16^{0}	16^{0}	22^{6}
Netherlands	7^{7}	9^{2}	14^{5}	21^{7}	26^{5}	30^{4}	30^{0}	30^{0}	37^{7}	37^{0}	40^{3}	40^{0}	41^{1}	41^{0}	46^{5}	48^{2}

place at Malmö. It came fifteenth. As a result Switzerland has not chosen a German song as its entry since then.

Ireland won the contest with only three first-place votes, one fewer than each of the next three songs – the UK, which finished sixteen points adrift, Malta, which was a further sixteen points behind in third place, and Italy twelve votes further away in fourth. The Irish did, however, collect seven second-place votes, compared with three for Malta, two for Britain and only one for Italy.

Ireland	Denmark	Italy	Yugoslavia	Norway	Germany	Netherlands	**Position**
23^{0}	24^{1}	31^{7}	31^{0}	36^{5}	36^{0}	37^{1}	14
11^{0}	11^{0}	11^{0}	11^{0}	11^{0}	11^{0}	11^{0}	20
62^{0}	64^{2}	64^{0}	76^{12}	78^{2}	82^{4}	85^{3}	6
11^{3}	11^{0}	11^{0}	17^{6}	17^{0}	17^{0}	17^{0}	19
63^{0}	63^{0}	75^{12}	82^{7}	90^{8}	90^{0}	94^{4}	5
48^{5}	48^{0}	54^{6}	54^{0}	64^{10}	67^{3}	73^{6}	8
1^{0}	5^{4}	5^{0}	9^{4}	9^{0}	9^{0}	9^{0}	22
12^{0}	12^{0}	13^{1}	18^{5}	18^{0}	26^{8}	26^{0}	17
34^{6}	34^{0}	38^{4}	46^{8}	49^{3}	49^{0}	57^{8}	11
97^{10}	105^{8}	108^{3}	118^{10}	118^{0}	118^{0}	123^{5}	3
61^{0}	66^{5}	71^{5}	71^{0}	72^{1}	78^{6}	80^{2}	7
1^{0}	1^{0}	1^{0}	4^{3}	4^{0}	4^{0}	4^{0}	23
22^{1}	22^{0}	32^{10}	32^{0}	32^{0}	32^{0}	32^{0}	15
10^{0}	10^{0}	10^{0}	10^{0}	10^{0}	10^{0}	10^{0}	21
56^{12}	63^{7}	63^{0}	63^{0}	63^{0}	63^{0}	63^{0}	10
100^{7}	112^{12}	120^{8}	120^{0}	120^{0}	132^{12}	139^{7}	2
$\mathbf{114^{x}}$	$\mathbf{124^{10}}$	$\mathbf{126^{2}}$	$\mathbf{128^{2}}$	$\mathbf{135^{7}}$	$\mathbf{145^{10}}$	$\mathbf{155^{10}}$	**1**
36^{0}	36^{x}	36^{0}	36^{0}	42^{6}	47^{5}	47^{0}	12
86^{0}	86^{0}	86^{x}	86^{0}	98^{12}	99^{1}	111^{12}	4
42^{4}	42^{0}	42^{0}	42^{x}	42^{0}	44^{2}	44^{0}	13
16^{0}	22^{6}	22^{0}	23^{1}	23^{x}	23^{0}	23^{0}	18
24^{2}	27^{3}	27^{0}	27^{0}	27^{0}	27^{x}	27^{0}	16
56^{8}	56^{0}	56^{0}	56^{0}	60^{4}	67^{7}	67^{x}	9

VOTING BIAS

IRELAND

Countries most likely to vote for Ireland:
Sweden
Austria
Belgium
Switzerland
Denmark

Countries least likely to vote for Ireland:
Portugal
Finland
Iceland
Israel
France

Countries for whom Ireland is most likely to vote:
Luxembourg
Austria
Norway
Malta
France

Countries for whom Ireland is least likely to vote:
Spain
Greece
Portugal
Turkey
UK

Ireland awards an average of 9.2 votes to the winning song in Eurovision, more than any other country. Add to that its record seven victories and it can be seen just how expert the Irish are at spotting a good tune.

★ ★

THE EUROVISION SONG CONTEST

1993

Won by Ireland: 'In Your Eyes'
Written by Jimmy Walsh
Performed by Niamh Kavanagh
Orchestra conducted by Noel Kelehan

There were three new countries participating this year, but the same old result. After a preliminary contest in Ljubljana, Bosnia-Herzegovina, Croatia and Slovenia made their first appearances at the Eurovision final, comprising the largest number of new participants since the very first year of the Contest. A year later, there would be seven more debutants, the largest number ever, equalling the record set in the inaugural Contest in 1956.

There were now, as presenter Fionnuala Sweeney pointed out, twenty-one pages of rules for the Contest, and one can assume that one of the rules that year stipulated that every entrant must wear either black or white, or at least something that looked purple or maroon, but was officially described as 'aubergine'. This is a good Euro-colour, much more romantic than the American translation 'eggplant', and it was what Niamh Kavanagh was wearing to win the Contest. So were Spain, Israel and Norway (among others), while almost all the rest of the competitors settled for black or white or both. The Swedish competitors, a four-man group called Arvingarna, had black-and-white letters all over their black-and-white shirts and jackets, which may have spelt 'Arvingarna', if they had stood still, in the correct order, long enough for their message to be read.

Messages were the order of the night. Perhaps there were not quite as many as in 1990, but with the three new Balkan entrants, there were many songs of peace and understanding. Croatia's chorus was in English, 'Don't ever cry, don't say goodbye, my Croatian sky'. Bosnia-Herzegovina's entry was hampered by the fact that its official conductor had been unable to leave his homeland, because he could not get through the unfriendly fire to the flight, but it got Eurovision's most successful conductor, Ireland's Noel Kelehan, to conduct instead. Slovenia was the least successful of the three new entrants, perhaps because it ignored the rule about dress colour, the band preferring to dress in assorted bright colours. One of its backing singers wore a pair of flares of a width not seen at Eurovision for about twenty years, and not seen again until Ruth Jacott pranced on stage to sing for the Netherlands four songs later. Flares did not light up the night that night.

Not all the messages emanating from Millstreet that night were as wholesome as Croatia's chorus. There were very strong, if officially unsubstantiated rumours, that some juries were communicating directly with each other, in strict contravention of Eurovision rules. One jury spokesperson was alleged to have been offering his country's twelve points to any nation that would give them at least six in return. There is no evidence that any such deal was actually struck, but the fact that it was apparently on offer shows the importance that a good performance at Eurovision holds for some nations.

The women really dominated the Millstreet final. Only one of the top six songs was not performed by a solo female vocalist, and even the

1993 EUROVISION SONG CONTEST

Host country: Ireland ★ *Venue:* Green Glens Arena, Millstreet
Date: 15 May ★ *Presenter:* Fionnuala Sweeney
Voting structure: Each country awarded 12 to its top song, 10 to the second, 8 to the third and 7, 6, 5, 4, 3, 2 and 1 point for the next seven
Total entries: 25 ★ *Debut countries:* Bosnia-Herzegovina, Croatia, Slovenia

Country	Performer	Song	Pts	Pos.
Italy	Enrico Ruggeri	Sole d'Europa	45	12
Turkey	Burak Aydos	Esmer Yarim	10	21
Germany	Münchener Freiheit	Viel Zu Weit	18	18
Switzerland	Annie Cotton	Moi, Tout Simplement	148	3
Denmark	Tommy Seebach Band	Under Stjernerne På Himlen	9	22
Greece	Katerina Garbi	Ellada, Hora Tou Photos	64	9
Belgium	Barbara	Iemand Als Jij	3	25
Malta	William Mangion	This Time	69	8
Iceland	Inga	Pa Veistu Svarid	42	13
Austria	Tony Wegas	Maria Magdalena	32	14
Portugal	Anabela	A Cidade Ate Ser Dia	60	10
France	Patrick Fiori	Mama Corsica	121	4
Sweden	Arvingarna	Eloise	89	7
Ireland	**Niamh Kavanagh**	**In Your Eyes**	**187**	**1**
Luxembourg	Modern Times	Donne-Moi Une Chance	11	20
Slovenia	1X Band	Tih Dezeven Dan	9	22
Finland	Katri-Helena	Tule Luo	20	17
Bosnia-Herzegovina	Fazla	Sva Bol Svijeta	27	16
United Kingdom	Sonia	Better The Devil You Know	164	2
Netherlands	Ruth Jacott	Vrede	92	6
Croatia	Put	Don't Ever Cry	31	15
Spain	Eva Santamaria	Hombres	58	11
Cyprus	Zymboulakis and Van Beke	Mi Stamatas	17	19
Israel	Lahakat Shiru	Shiru	4	24
Norway	Silje Vige	Alle Mine Tankar	120	5

odd one out, France's Patrick Fiori, had a song about a woman – 'Mama Corsica', his motherland. But the rest of the top performances were by women: Sonia for the UK, Annie Cotton for Switzerland, Silje Vige for Norway and Ruth Jacott for the Netherlands. It was not as though women outnumbered the men on the night, either. Four of the first five songs were presented by male vocalists, but the only one of those five to finish in the top ten was the odd one out – Annie Cotton, who sang fourth. Several male groups were on show – Turkey's Burak Aydos, Germany's Münchener Freiheit, Sweden's Arvingarna and Slovenia's 1X Band, as well as the Cypriot answer to Wham!, Zymboulakis and Van Beke. None of them scored even half the number of votes that Niamh Kavanagh earned for Ireland.

Twenty-five-year-old Niamh Kavanagh worked for Allied Irish Banks at the time, and sang a strong and emotional ballad about the glories of love. She actually won very easily, but the EBU managed to keep us all on tenterhooks by failing to get through to Malta the first time around, so that when it finally voted, the Irish lead over

1993	Italy	Turkey	Germany	Switzerland	Denmark	Greece	Belgium	Iceland	Austria	Portugal	France	Sweden	Ireland	Luxembourg	Slovenia	Finland	Bosnia-Herz.	UK
Italy	0^{x}	0^{0}	0^{0}	1^{1}	1^{0}	1^{0}	1^{0}	1^{0}	1^{0}	11^{10}	16^{5}	16^{0}	16^{0}	26^{10}	26^{0}	34^{8}	34^{0}	34^{0}
Turkey	0^{0}	0^{x}	0^{0}	0^{0}	0^{0}	0^{0}	0^{0}	1^{1}	1^{0}	1^{0}	1^{0}	1^{0}	1^{0}	1^{0}	1^{0}	1^{0}	3^{2}	3^{0}
Germany	8^{8}	8^{0}	8^{x}	10^{2}	13^{3}	13^{0}	13^{0}	13^{0}	13^{0}	13^{0}	13^{0}	13^{0}	17^{4}	17^{0}	17^{0}	17^{0}	17^{0}	17^{0}
Switzerland	10^{10}	10^{0}	**22^{12}**	22^{x}	32^{10}	39^{7}	47^{8}	51^{4}	57^{6}	58^{1}	70^{12}	76^{6}	83^{7}	95^{12}	103^{8}	107^{4}	107^{0}	117^{10}
Denmark	0^{0}	0^{0}	0^{0}	0^{0}	0^{x}	0^{0}	0^{0}	0^{0}	0^{0}	0^{0}	0^{0}	1^{1}	1^{0}	4^{3}	4^{0}	4^{0}	9^{5}	9^{0}
Greece	2^{2}	4^{2}	6^{2}	6^{0}	6^{0}	6^{x}	6^{0}	6^{0}	6^{0}	6^{0}	13^{7}	13^{0}	13^{0}	13^{0}	13^{0}	19^{6}	19^{0}	19^{0}
Belgium	0^{0}	0^{0}	3^{3}	3^{0}	3^{0}	3^{0}	3^{x}	3^{0}	3^{0}	3^{0}	3^{0}	3^{0}	3^{0}	3^{0}	3^{0}	3^{0}	3^{0}	3^{0}
Malta	7^{7}	12^{5}	16^{4}	23^{7}	28^{5}	33^{5}	33^{0}	33^{0}	37^{4}	39^{2}	41^{2}	45^{4}	47^{2}	47^{0}	47^{0}	47^{0}	51^{4}	57^{6}
Iceland	0^{0}	0^{0}	0^{0}	0^{0}	4^{4}	8^{4}	8^{0}	8^{x}	9^{1}	9^{0}	9^{0}	16^{7}	17^{1}	17^{0}	22^{5}	22^{0}	22^{0}	24^{2}
Austria	0^{0}	4^{4}	4^{0}	4^{0}	4^{0}	5^{1}	8^{3}	8^{0}	8^{x}	8^{0}	11^{3}	11^{0}	17^{6}	17^{0}	17^{0}	17^{0}	29^{12}	32^{3}
Portugal	0^{0}	0^{0}	1^{1}	1^{0}	2^{1}	4^{2}	4^{0}	6^{2}	11^{5}	11^{x}	19^{8}	21^{2}	21^{0}	25^{4}	25^{0}	27^{2}	27^{0}	28^{1}
France	0^{0}	7^{7}	7^{0}	11^{4}	23^{12}	26^{3}	26^{0}	34^{8}	41^{7}	53^{12}	53^{x}	61^{8}	71^{10}	77^{6}	81^{4}	82^{1}	82^{0}	86^{4}
Sweden	0^{0}	0^{0}	8^{8}	16^{8}	23^{7}	23^{0}	33^{10}	40^{7}	50^{10}	54^{4}	54^{0}	54^{x}	54^{0}	59^{5}	65^{6}	72^{7}	72^{0}	79^{7}
Ireland	**12^{12}**	13^{1}	18^{5}	**30^{12}**	**36^{6}**	**42^{6}**	44^{2}	47^{3}	55^{8}	61^{6}	71^{10}	83^{12}	83^{x}	90^{7}	102^{12}	105^{3}	113^{8}	**125^{12}**
Luxembourg	0^{0}	0^{0}	0^{0}	0^{0}	0^{0}	0^{0}	0^{0}	0^{0}	0^{0}	0^{0}	0^{0}	0^{0}	0^{0}	0^{x}	1^{1}	1^{0}	1^{0}	1^{0}
Slovenia	4^{4}	4^{0}	4^{0}	4^{0}	4^{0}	4^{0}	4^{0}	4^{0}	4^{0}	4^{0}	4^{0}	7^{3}	7^{0}	7^{0}	7^{x}	7^{0}	8^{1}	8^{0}
Finland	0^{0}	3^{3}	3^{0}	3^{0}	3^{0}	11^{8}	11^{0}	16^{5}	16^{0}	16^{0}	16^{0}	16^{0}	16^{0}	18^{2}	18^{0}	18^{x}	18^{0}	18^{0}
Bosnia-Herz.	3^{3}	**15^{12}**	15^{0}	15^{0}	15^{0}	15^{0}	16^{1}	16^{0}	16^{0}	16^{0}	20^{4}	20^{0}	23^{3}	23^{0}	23^{0}	23^{0}	23^{x}	23^{0}
UK	1^{1}	9^{8}	15^{6}	20^{5}	28^{8}	28^{0}	40^{12}	52^{12}	**64^{12}**	**71^{7}**	**77^{6}**	**87^{10}**	**95^{8}**	**103^{8}**	**113^{10}**	**118^{5}**	**121^{3}**	121^{x}
Netherlands	6^{6}	12^{6}	19^{7}	19^{0}	19^{0}	19^{0}	26^{7}	32^{6}	35^{3}	35^{0}	35^{0}	40^{5}	52^{12}	52^{0}	59^{7}	59^{0}	69^{10}	69^{0}
Croatia	0^{0}	0^{0}	0^{0}	3^{3}	3^{0}	3^{0}	7^{4}	7^{0}	7^{0}	12^{5}	12^{0}	12^{0}	12^{0}	12^{0}	12^{0}	12^{0}	12^{0}	20^{8}
Spain	5^{5}	5^{0}	5^{0}	11^{6}	11^{0}	11^{0}	16^{5}	16^{0}	18^{2}	18^{0}	18^{0}	18^{0}	18^{0}	18^{0}	20^{2}	30^{10}	36^{6}	36^{0}
Cyprus	0^{0}	0^{0}	0^{0}	0^{0}	2^{2}	12^{10}	12^{0}	12^{0}	12^{0}	12^{0}	12^{0}	12^{0}	12^{0}	12^{0}	12^{0}	12^{0}	12^{0}	17^{5}
Israel	0^{0}	0^{0}	0^{0}	0^{0}	0^{0}	0^{0}	0^{0}	0^{0}	0^{0}	3^{3}	4^{1}	4^{0}	4^{0}	4^{0}	4^{0}	4^{0}	4^{0}	4^{0}
Norway	0^{0}	10^{10}	20^{10}	**30^{10}**	30^{0}	**42^{12}**	**48^{6}**	**58^{10}**	58^{0}	66^{8}	66^{0}	66^{0}	71^{5}	72^{1}	75^{3}	87^{12}	94^{7}	94^{0}

Britain's Sonia was only eleven points. Malta gave Ireland full marks and the UK none, but if that score had been known much earlier, Ireland would have been uncatchable from an early stage. As it was, it only took the lead when the UK jury gave the Irish entry twelve points. Be a woman, wear the right colour and sing with feeling about the positive side of love, and you have a great chance of victory. And it helps if you are Irish.

Netherlands	Croatia	Spain	Cyprus	Israel	Norway	Malta	**Position**
36^{2}	36^{0}	38^{2}	38^{0}	38^{0}	38^{0}	45^{7}	12
3^{0}	4^{1}	10^{6}	10^{0}	10^{0}	10^{0}	10^{0}	21
18^{1}	18^{0}	18^{0}	18^{0}	18^{0}	18^{0}	18^{0}	18
125^{8}	127^{2}	130^{3}	136^{6}	140^{4}	143^{3}	148^{5}	3
9^{0}	9^{0}	9^{0}	9^{0}	9^{0}	9^{0}	9^{0}	22=
24^{5}	24^{0}	32^{8}	44^{12}	51^{7}	58^{7}	64^{4}	9
3^{0}	3^{0}	3^{0}	3^{0}	3^{0}	3^{0}	3^{0}	25
57^{0}	61^{4}	65^{4}	66^{1}	69^{3}	69^{0}	69^{x}	8
31^{7}	36^{5}	36^{0}	38^{2}	40^{2}	42^{2}	42^{0}	13
32^{0}	32^{0}	32^{0}	32^{0}	32^{0}	32^{0}	32^{0}	14
40^{12}	40^{0}	52^{12}	55^{3}	55^{0}	60^{5}	60^{0}	10
89^{3}	97^{8}	97^{0}	107^{10}	115^{8}	121^{6}	121^{0}	4
79^{0}	79^{0}	79^{0}	79^{0}	89^{10}	89^{0}	89^{0}	7
135^{10}	**141^{6}**	**151^{10}**	**158^{7}**	**163^{5}**	**175^{12}**	**187^{12}**	**1**
1^{0}	1^{0}	1^{0}	1^{0}	1^{0}	1^{0}	11^{10}	20
8^{0}	8^{0}	8^{0}	8^{0}	8^{0}	8^{0}	9^{1}	22=
18^{0}	18^{0}	18^{0}	18^{0}	18^{0}	18^{0}	20^{2}	17
23^{0}	23^{0}	23^{0}	23^{0}	23^{0}	23^{0}	27^{4}	16
125^{4}	135^{10}	140^{5}	144^{4}	156^{12}	164^{8}	164^{0}	2
69^{x}	72^{3}	79^{7}	79^{0}	79^{0}	89^{10}	92^{3}	6
20^{0}	20^{x}	21^{1}	21^{0}	27^{6}	31^{4}	31^{0}	15
36^{0}	43^{7}	43^{x}	48^{5}	49^{1}	50^{1}	58^{8}	11
17^{0}	17^{0}	17^{0}	17^{x}	17^{0}	17^{0}	17^{0}	19
4^{0}	4^{0}	4^{0}	4^{0}	4^{x}	4^{0}	4^{0}	24
100^{6}	112^{12}	112^{0}	120^{8}	120^{0}	120^{x}	120^{0}	5

VOTING BIAS

BOSNIA-HERZEGOVINA

Countries most likely to vote for Bosnia:

Turkey
Croatia
France
Malta
Slovakia

Countries least likely to vote for Bosnia:

Cyprus
Greece
Iceland
Norway
Portugal

Countries for whom Bosnia is most likely to vote:

Malta
Slovenia
Croatia
Ireland
Turkey

Countries for whom Bosnia is least likely to vote:

Cyprus
France
Greece
Sweden
Portugal

Six countries voted for Bosnia on her debut in 1993. Only three of them competed in 1994 (Malta, Ireland, France), and they were rewarded for their generosity.

★ ★

THE EUROVISION SONG CONTEST

1994

Won by Ireland: 'Rock 'N' Roll Kids'

Written by Brendan Graham

Performed by Paul Harrington with Charlie McGettigan

Orchestra conducted by ???

The song Rock 'N' Roll Kids' was a surprise winner. It was widely seen by commentators – both inside and outside Ireland – as a gentle attempt *not* to win Eurovision, as the Irish had won it for the past two years and were not overly enthusiastic about the costs involved in staging another contest. However, despite a very strong start to the voting by Hungary, and consistently strong scores awarded to Poland, the gentle and definitely un-rock'n'roll-y Irish entry stormed home with the highest score yet recorded and sixty votes to spare, upsetting the bookies and the RTE organizers in equal measures.

After three rounds of voting, it looked as though the Irish would not win again because they were in a modest fourth place, behind the Hungarian entry, which had taken twelve votes each time, and the equally unrated Maltese and Portuguese entries. However, it soon became clear that these outsiders would not be able to hold the Irish, who only four times received a worse than eight points for a third-place vote. Finland gave them just seven points, Slovakia six and Malta five. Greece, of course awarded its twelve to Cyprus and none at all to the 'Rock 'N' Roll Kids', but then also gave no points to the Polish, German and Hungarian entries that finished second, third and fourth, to complete a bravura performance of musical unappreciation that will take some beating.

In 1994, there were seven countries appearing for the first time in the Contest – the largest group of new contestants since the very first year. Their first efforts produced very varied results. Lithuania was last with no votes at all, and Estonia ran a close second last. At the other end of the scale, Poland came second. Indeed, Poland's was the strongest debut ever recorded, because even Switzerland's victory in the very first Eurovision was with the second song it performed that night. Until 1994, no country had ever been placed higher than third in its first Contest, a record set by Denmark in 1957.

However, the 1994 contest is not remembered for its debutants nor for 'Rock 'N' Roll Kids'. The show is remembered for the real Irish winner of the night, *Riverdance.* The performance by Irish folk dancers, under the leadership of Michael Flatley, dancing to music by Eurovision veteran Bill Whelan, was staged during the interval while the juries made up their minds. But it was more than just a variety act to fill the screens for a few minutes – it became the basis of a global phenomenon that toured the world, breaking box office records in theatres everywhere it went, and reshaping modern popular dance on the way. *Riverdance* is probably the biggest money-spinner ever created by Eurovision, with the single exception of Abba.

This was a far cry from the first attempts by Eurovision producers to fill those blank moments while jurors voted and millions made cups of tea across the Continent. In early years, little thought went into a creative solution to the problem. We've seen all kinds of everything, including a

1994 EUROVISION SONG CONTEST

Host country: Ireland ✶ *Venue:* The Point, Dublin
Date: 30 April ✶ *Presenters:* Cynthia Ni Mhurchu and Gerry Ryan
Voting structure: Each country awarded 12 to its top song, 10 to the second, 8 to the third and 7, 6, 5, 4, 3, 2 and 1 point for the next seven ✶ *Total entries:* 25
Debut countries: Estonia, Hungary, Lithuania, Poland, Romania, Russian Federation, Slovakia

Country	Performer	Song	Pts	Pos.
Sweden	Marie Bergman and Roger Pontare	Stjärnorna	48	13
Finland	CatCat	Bye Bye Baby	11	22
Ireland	**Paul Harrington with Charlie McGettigan**	**Rock 'N' Roll Kids**	**226**	**1**
Cyprus	Evridiki	Eimai Anthropos Ki Ego	51	11
Iceland	Sigga	Nætur	49	12
United Kingdom	Frances Ruffelle	We Will Be Free (Lonely Symphony)	63	10
Croatia	Toni Cetinski	Nek 'Ti Bude Ljubav Sva	27	16
Portugal	Sara Tavares	Chamar A Musica	73	8
Switzerland	Duilio	Sto Pregando	15	19
Estonia	Silvi Vrait	Nagu Merelaine	2	24
Romania	Dan Bittman	Dincolo De Nori	14	21
Malta	Chris and Moira	More Than Love	97	5
Netherlands	Willeke Alberti	Waar Is De Zon	4	23
Germany	Mekado	Wir Geben 'Ne Party	128	3
Slovakia	Martin Durinda and Tublatanka	Nekonecna Piesen	15	19
Lithuania	Ovidijus Vysniauskas	Lopisine Mylimaj	0	25
Norway	Elisabeth Andreassen and Jan Werner Danielsen	Duett	76	6
Bosnia-Herzegovina	Alma and Dejan	Ostani Kraj Mene	39	15
Greece	Costas Bigalis and the Sea Lovers	To Trehantiri (Diri-Diri)	44	14
Austria	Petra Frey	Für Den Frieden Der Welt	19	17
Spain	Alejandro Abad	Ella No Es Ella	17	18
Hungary	Friderika	Kinek Mondjam El Vetkeimet	122	4
Russian Federation	Youddiph	Vechni Stranik	70	9
Poland	Edyta Gorniak	To Nie Ja!	166	2
France	Nina Morato	Je Suis Un Vrai Garçon	74	7

performance of the tune 'Ceilito Lindo' by the orchestra in 1958; a short ballet in 1961; Achille Zavatta swallowing the reed from his oboe in 1962; the Vienna Boys' Choir in 1967; 'A London Medley' by Norrie Paramor and the orchestra in 1968; the Don Lurio Dancers in 1970; Stephane Grappelli, Yehudi Menuhin and Oscar Peterson playing jazz in 1978; the Shalom 79 Israeli folk dance troupe in 1979; the orchestra playing simple tunes while we watch a tourist film of Yorkshire in 1982 and Guy Tell, the crossbow man, in 1989. The most unspeakably bizarre interlude probably came in 1963, when the BBC paid Ola and Barbro, a Swedish bicycle act, to pedal round and round the stage on unicycles and other trick cycles. The urge in those who watch at a safe distance of thirty-five years and more to shout 'On yer bike!' is almost overwhelming, but

1994	Sweden	Finland	Ireland	Cyprus	Iceland	UK	Croatia	Portugal	Switzerland	Estonia	Romania	Malta	Netherlands	Germany	Slovakia	Lithuania	Norway	Bosnia-Herz.
Sweden	0^{x}	0^{0}	0^{0}	0^{0}	2^{2}	2^{0}	2^{0}	2^{0}	9^{7}	11^{2}	11^{0}	14^{3}	20^{6}	25^{5}	25^{0}	30^{5}	40^{10}	40^{0}
Finland	0^{0}	0^{x}	0^{0}	0^{0}	0^{0}	0^{0}	0^{0}	0^{0}	0^{0}	0^{0}	0^{0}	0^{0}	0^{0}	0^{0}	0^{0}	0^{0}	0^{0}	1^{1}
Ireland	**10^{10}**	**17^{7}**	**17^{x}**	**25^{8}**	**37^{12}**	**47^{10}**	**59^{12}**	**71^{12}**	**83^{12}**	**93^{10}**	**101^{8}**	**106^{5}**	**118^{12}**	**130^{12}**	**136^{6}**	**146^{10}**	**158^{12}**	**168^{10}**
Cyprus	0^{0}	10^{10}	10^{0}	10^{x}	13^{3}	13^{0}	13^{0}	18^{5}	20^{2}	20^{0}	20^{0}	20^{0}	20^{0}	20^{0}	20^{0}	20^{0}	25^{5}	25^{0}
Iceland	8^{8}	9^{1}	15^{6}	15^{0}	15^{x}	21^{6}	21^{0}	24^{3}	27^{3}	27^{0}	27^{0}	27^{0}	27^{0}	27^{0}	28^{1}	31^{3}	31^{0}	31^{0}
UK	0^{0}	0^{0}	1^{1}	6^{5}	6^{0}	6^{x}	12^{6}	20^{8}	28^{8}	33^{5}	33^{0}	33^{0}	35^{2}	39^{4}	42^{3}	42^{0}	44^{2}	48^{4}
Croatia	0^{0}	0^{0}	0^{0}	0^{0}	0^{0}	0^{0}	0^{x}	0^{0}	0^{0}	0^{0}	0^{0}	10^{10}	10^{0}	10^{0}	22^{12}	22^{0}	22^{0}	22^{0}
Portugal	5^{5}	10^{5}	18^{8}	18^{0}	26^{8}	34^{8}	34^{0}	34^{x}	39^{5}	39^{0}	39^{0}	40^{1}	43^{3}	43^{0}	43^{0}	43^{0}	43^{0}	43^{0}
Switzerland	0^{0}	0^{0}	0^{0}	0^{0}	0^{0}	0^{0}	0^{0}	0^{0}	0^{x}	0^{0}	0^{0}	8^{8}	8^{0}	8^{0}	8^{0}	8^{0}	8^{0}	8^{0}
Estonia	0^{0}	0^{0}	0^{0}	0^{0}	0^{0}	0^{0}	0^{0}	0^{0}	0^{0}	0^{x}	0^{0}	0^{0}	0^{0}	0^{0}	0^{0}	0^{0}	0^{0}	0^{0}
Romania	0^{0}	0^{0}	0^{0}	0^{0}	0^{0}	0^{0}	0^{0}	0^{0}	0^{0}	0^{0}	0^{x}	6^{6}	6^{0}	6^{0}	6^{0}	8^{2}	8^{0}	8^{0}
Malta	4^{4}	10^{6}	20^{10}	22^{2}	22^{0}	23^{1}	30^{7}	34^{4}	40^{6}	47^{7}	57^{10}	57^{x}	58^{1}	61^{3}	71^{10}	78^{7}	78^{0}	90^{12}
Netherlands	0^{0}	0^{0}	0^{0}	0^{0}	0^{0}	0^{0}	0^{0}	0^{0}	0^{0}	0^{0}	0^{0}	0^{0}	0^{x}	0^{0}	0^{0}	0^{0}	0^{0}	0^{0}
Germany	6^{6}	9^{3}	14^{5}	20^{6}	27^{7}	34^{7}	44^{10}	54^{10}	54^{0}	57^{3}	69^{12}	69^{0}	73^{4}	73^{x}	80^{7}	84^{4}	85^{1}	92^{7}
Slovakia	0^{0}	0^{0}	0^{0}	0^{0}	0^{0}	0^{0}	0^{0}	0^{0}	0^{0}	0^{0}	0^{0}	12^{12}	12^{0}	12^{0}	12^{x}	12^{0}	12^{0}	12^{0}
Lithuania	0^{0}	0^{0}	0^{0}	0^{0}	0^{0}	0^{0}	0^{0}	0^{0}	0^{0}	0^{0}	0^{0}	0^{0}	0^{0}	0^{0}	0^{0}	0^{x}	0^{0}	0^{0}
Norway	7^{7}	7^{0}	10^{3}	20^{10}	21^{1}	25^{4}	28^{3}	28^{0}	29^{1}	37^{8}	41^{4}	41^{0}	48^{7}	50^{2}	50^{0}	51^{1}	51^{x}	57^{6}
Bosnia-Herz.	0^{0}	2^{2}	2^{0}	2^{0}	2^{0}	2^{0}	6^{4}	6^{0}	6^{0}	6^{0}	6^{0}	13^{7}	13^{0}	13^{0}	21^{8}	21^{0}	21^{0}	21^{x}
Greece	2^{2}	6^{4}	6^{0}	18^{12}	18^{0}	18^{0}	18^{0}	18^{0}	18^{0}	18^{0}	24^{6}	28^{4}	28^{0}	29^{1}	34^{5}	34^{0}	38^{4}	38^{0}
Austria	1^{1}	1^{0}	1^{0}	8^{7}	8^{0}	11^{3}	13^{2}	13^{0}	13^{0}	13^{0}	14^{1}	14^{0}	14^{0}	14^{0}	14^{0}	14^{0}	14^{0}	19^{5}
Spain	0^{0}	0^{0}	0^{0}	0^{0}	0^{0}	0^{0}	0^{0}	0^{0}	0^{0}	0^{0}	5^{5}	5^{0}	5^{0}	5^{0}	7^{2}	7^{0}	7^{0}	7^{0}
Hungary	**12^{12}**	**24^{12}**	**36^{12}**	**36^{0}**	**46^{10}**	**48^{2}**	53^{5}	54^{1}	58^{4}	62^{4}	64^{2}	64^{0}	74^{10}	81^{7}	81^{0}	81^{0}	89^{8}	92^{3}
Russia	0^{0}	0^{0}	4^{4}	7^{3}	11^{4}	16^{5}	17^{1}	19^{2}	19^{0}	20^{1}	23^{3}	23^{0}	28^{5}	34^{6}	34^{0}	40^{6}	43^{3}	43^{0}
Poland	0^{0}	8^{8}	15^{7}	16^{1}	22^{6}	34^{12}	42^{8}	49^{7}	59^{10}	71^{12}	78^{7}	80^{2}	88^{8}	98^{10}	102^{4}	114^{12}	120^{6}	128^{8}
France	3^{3}	3^{0}	5^{2}	9^{4}	14^{5}	14^{0}	14^{0}	20^{6}	20^{0}	26^{6}	26^{0}	26^{0}	26^{0}	34^{8}	34^{0}	42^{8}	49^{7}	51^{2}

at the time Ola and Barbro seemed to attract no adverse comment.

Since the success of *Riverdance*, the attitude of organizers and producers to the 'middle bit' ought to have changed. But as Ireland has kept on winning and has hosted two of the three Contests since 1994, it is difficult to tell exactly how these few minutes of light relief from the tension of the Contest might develop. Watch this space.

Greece	Austria	Spain	Hungary	Russia	Poland	France	**Position**
40^{0}	45^{5}	46^{1}	48^{2}	48^{0}	48^{0}	48^{0}	13
11^{10}	11^{0}	11^{0}	11^{0}	11^{0}	11^{0}	11^{0}	22
$\mathbf{168^{0}}$	$\mathbf{178^{10}}$	$\mathbf{188^{10}}$	$\mathbf{198^{10}}$	$\mathbf{210^{12}}$	$\mathbf{218^{8}}$	$\mathbf{226^{8}}$	**1**
37^{12}	37^{0}	41^{4}	41^{0}	43^{2}	48^{5}	51^{3}	11
31^{0}	34^{3}	40^{6}	40^{0}	41^{1}	45^{4}	49^{4}	12
48^{0}	49^{1}	52^{3}	55^{3}	60^{5}	63^{3}	63^{0}	10
27^{5}	27^{0}	27^{0}	27^{0}	27^{0}	27^{0}	27^{0}	16
43^{0}	43^{0}	55^{12}	62^{7}	66^{4}	67^{1}	73^{6}	8
8^{0}	8^{0}	10^{2}	10^{0}	10^{0}	10^{0}	15^{5}	19=
2^{2}	2^{0}	2^{0}	2^{0}	2^{0}	2^{0}	2^{0}	24
14^{6}	14^{0}	14^{0}	14^{0}	14^{0}	14^{0}	14^{0}	21
97^{7}	97^{0}	97^{0}	97^{0}	97^{0}	97^{0}	97^{0}	5
0^{0}	4^{4}	4^{0}	4^{0}	4^{0}	4^{0}	4^{0}	23
92^{0}	94^{2}	102^{8}	114^{12}	121^{7}	128^{7}	128^{0}	3
15^{3}	15^{0}	15^{0}	15^{0}	15^{0}	15^{0}	15^{0}	19=
0^{0}	0^{0}	0^{0}	0^{0}	0^{0}	0^{0}	0^{0}	25
58^{1}	58^{0}	63^{5}	68^{5}	76^{8}	76^{0}	76^{0}	6
21^{0}	21^{0}	28^{7}	29^{1}	29^{0}	29^{0}	39^{10}	15
38^{x}	38^{0}	38^{0}	42^{4}	42^{0}	44^{2}	44^{0}	14
19^{0}	19^{x}	19^{0}	19^{0}	19^{0}	19^{0}	19^{0}	17
15^{8}	15^{0}	15^{x}	15^{0}	15^{0}	15^{0}	17^{2}	18
92^{0}	100^{8}	100^{0}	100^{x}	103^{3}	115^{12}	122^{7}	4
47^{4}	53^{6}	53^{0}	59^{6}	59^{x}	69^{10}	70^{1}	9
128^{0}	140^{12}	140^{0}	148^{8}	154^{6}	154^{x}	166^{12}	2
51^{0}	58^{7}	58^{0}	58^{0}	68^{10}	74^{6}	74^{x}	7

VOTING BIAS

POLAND

Countries most likely to vote for Poland:

Austria
Bosnia
Germany
Hungary
Estonia

Countries least likely to vote for Poland:

Sweden
Malta
Cyprus
Ireland
Spain

Countries for whom Poland is most likely to vote:

France
Hungary
Estonia
Russia
Austria

Countries for whom Poland is least likely to vote:

Malta
Cyprus
Portugal
Croatia
Bosnia

With the obvious exception of the first contest in 1956, Poland's second position in 1994 marked the first time a debut country had managed to finish in one of the top two placings.

★ ★

THE EUROVISION SONG CONTEST

1995

Won by Norway: 'Nocturne'
Written by Rolf Lovland and Peter Skavlan
Performed by Secret Garden
Orchestra conducted by Geir Lanslet

After three consecutive victories, there was a great deal of press speculation about Ireland's desire definitely not to win Eurovision again. The Contest was held at the Point, in Dublin, for the second consecutive year, the only time so far that the same venue has been used twice in succession. The hosts, Ireland, were drawn to sing second – from their point of view a wonderful opportunity as no country singing second had ever won the Contest. Their entrant this year, Eddie Friel with 'Dreamin'', stormed home a safe fourteenth out of twenty-three.

This was also the first year that Jonathan King had been in charge of Britain's entry, and he made the elementary mistake of trying to find a hit song for the Contest. He was given a free hand by the BBC to find a strong contender after thirteen years without a British winner, and 'I thought if I find a hit as our entry, we'll win,' he said later. 'I found a hit – "Love City Groove" – but we didn't win because it was not representative of the tastes of the entire population.' Many Eurofans could have told him that well before the Contest began. The French jury gave 'Love City Groove' twelve points, though, an unusual event in Eurovision voting.

The Norwegian entry won, by following many of the well-tried Eurovision rules for victory, but also breaking just as many. The secret seems to be knowing which rules to break and which traditions to follow. 'Nocturne' was virtually an instrumental, with just eight short lines of lyric. In this it was clearly a major departure from the standard Eurovision song, but of course it got over the major hurdle of too many lyrics, often put across with emotion and much body language, which only a handful of juries can understand at all. No lyrics, no misunderstandings. It all seems so simple.

It was also unusual in that Norway seemed to be taking Eurovision seriously for a change. After the antics of Jahn Teigen and his then wife Anita Skorgan in the 1970s and 1980s, not to mention some of the songs they had performed even two or three years earlier and the voting idiosyncrasies of some of their juries, we suddenly found ourselves listening to a credible Norwegian entry, and it was too good an opportunity to miss. But Norway followed some of the rules closely. 'Nocturne' was, in Jonathan King's view, clearly modelled on the Irish *Riverdance* of the year before (although a bit less dance, and a bit more river), and it featured an Irish violinist, Fionnuala Murray, in the group. She wore leather trousers, which did their cause no harm.

Norway was also helped by the rest of the music on show that night. There were no new countries welcomed to the Eurovision fold, but all the debutants from the previous two years seemed to have forgotten what they had learnt from their earlier appearances. Poland only collected fifteen votes, perhaps more than the song deserved. Bosnia-Herzegovina's fourteen points were collected largely from neighbours Croatia, which gave them eight. It also gave Russia six of its

★ ★

1995 EUROVISION SONG CONTEST

Host country: Ireland ★ *Venue:* The Point, Dublin
Date: 13 May ★ *Presenter:* Mary Kennedy
Voting structure: Each country awarded 12 to its top song, 10 to the second, 8 to the third and 7, 6, 5, 4, 3, 2 and 1 point for the next seven
Total entries: 23 ★ *Debut countries:* None

Country	Performer	Song	Pts	Pos.
Poland	Justyna Steczkowska	Sama	15	18
Ireland	Eddie Friel	Dreamin'	44	14
Germany	Stone and Stone	Verliebt In Dich	1	23
Bosnia-Herzegovina	Davor Popovic	Dvadeset I Prvi Viijek	14	19
Norway	**Secret Garden**	**Nocturne**	**148**	**1**
Russian Federation	Philipp Kirkorov	Lullaby For A Volcano	17	17
Iceland	Bo Halldorsson	Nuna	31	15
Austria	Stella Jones	Die Welt Dreht Sich Verkehrt	67	13
Spain	Anabel Condé	Vuelve Conmigo	119	2
Turkey	Arzu Ece	Sev	21	16
Croatia	Magazin and Lidija	Nostalgija	91	6
France	Nathalie Santamaria	Il Me Donne Rendez-vous	94	4
Hungary	Csaba Szigetj	Uj Nev A Regi Haz Falan	3	22
Belgium	Frédéric Etherlinck	La Voix Est Libre	8	20
United Kingdom	Love City Groove	Love City Groove	76	10
Portugal	To Cruz	Baunilha E Chocolate	5	21
Cyprus	Alex Panayi	Sti Fotia	79	9
Sweden	Jan Johansen	Se På Mej	100	3
Denmark	Aud Wilken	Fra Mols Til Skagen	92	5
Slovenia	Darja Svajger	Prisluhni Mi	84	7
Israel	Liora	Amen	81	8
Malta	Mike Spiteri	Keep Me In Mind	76	10
Greece	Elina Konstantopoulou	Pia Prosefhi	68	12

seventeen points, ten more of which came from the idiosyncratic Norwegian jury. Hungary could not keep up the pace it set the year before, and gained only three votes, two of them from the new-look Russia. Only Croatia and Slovenia, which finished sixth and seventh, contributed much to the evening's entertainment. With all of the former Eastern Europe not only watching but also competing and voting, the skills required to find a song that catches the imagination across thousands of kilometres and which can break out from underneath tons of cultural baggage are hard to acquire. Norway's success would seem to bear this out. It received maximum votes from Poland, Russia, Iceland, Turkey, Portugal and Greece. None of these countries were part of Eurovision in the early years and all are, both geographically and culturally, on the very edge of Europe. Yet, without their votes, Norway would not have won. More and more, some would argue, the Contest is becoming a matter of luck.

The main interest seemed to be in the dress worn by Spain's Anabel Condé (who came second) and in the fact that Belgium's Frédéric Etherlinck was reportedly the adopted grandchild of Count Maurice Maeterlinck, winner of the Nobel Prize for Literature in 1911. Etherlinck is not the only grandchild of a Nobel laureate to compete in Eurovision. He shares this odd distinction with Olivia Newton-John, Britain's entrant in 1974, whose grandfather Max Born had won the Nobel Prize for Physics in 1954.

1995	Poland	Ireland	Germany	Bosnia-Herz.	Norway	Russia	Iceland	Austria	Spain	Turkey	Croatia	France	Hungary	Belgium	UK	Portugal
Poland	0^{x}	0^{0}	0^{0}	0^{0}	4^{4}	4^{0}	10^{6}	10^{0}	10^{0}	10^{0}	10^{0}	10^{0}	11^{1}	11^{0}	11^{0}	12^{1}
Ireland	0^{0}	0^{x}	1^{1}	6^{5}	7^{1}	12^{5}	15^{3}	15^{0}	18^{3}	23^{5}	23^{0}	24^{1}	24^{0}	24^{0}	24^{0}	24^{0}
Germany	0^{0}	0^{0}	0^{x}	0^{0}	0^{0}	0^{0}	0^{0}	0^{0}	0^{0}	0^{0}	0^{0}	0^{0}	0^{0}	0^{0}	0^{0}	0^{0}
Bosnia-Herz.	0^{0}	0^{0}	0^{0}	0^{x}	0^{0}	0^{0}	0^{0}	0^{0}	0^{0}	3^{3}	11^{8}	11^{0}	11^{0}	11^{0}	11^{0}	11^{0}
Norway	**12^{12}**	**22^{10}**	26^{4}	27^{1}	27^{x}	39^{12}	51^{12}	51^{0}	55^{4}	**67^{12}**	**67^{0}**	**77^{10}**	**83^{6}**	**88^{5}**	**92^{4}**	**104^{12}**
Russia	0^{0}	0^{0}	0^{0}	0^{0}	10^{10}	10^{x}	10^{0}	10^{0}	10^{0}	10^{0}	16^{6}	16^{0}	16^{0}	16^{0}	16^{0}	16^{0}
Iceland	0^{0}	6^{6}	6^{0}	6^{0}	8^{2}	11^{3}	11^{x}	15^{4}	15^{0}	15^{0}	15^{0}	17^{2}	17^{0}	17^{0}	17^{0}	17^{0}
Austria	2^{2}	2^{0}	2^{0}	2^{0}	5^{3}	5^{0}	5^{0}	5^{x}	11^{6}	15^{4}	15^{0}	23^{8}	27^{4}	37^{10}	42^{5}	44^{2}
Spain	8^{8}	10^{2}	16^{6}	24^{8}	24^{0}	24^{0}	29^{5}	29^{0}	29^{x}	37^{8}	47^{10}	54^{7}	56^{2}	68^{12}	76^{8}	83^{7}
Turkey	0^{0}	0^{0}	0^{0}	0^{0}	0^{0}	0^{0}	0^{0}	0^{0}	2^{2}	2^{x}	7^{5}	7^{0}	7^{0}	8^{1}	10^{2}	10^{0}
Croatia	0^{0}	3^{3}	3^{0}	13^{10}	20^{7}	20^{0}	30^{10}	30^{0}	42^{12}	49^{7}	49^{x}	49^{0}	49^{0}	49^{0}	49^{0}	53^{4}
France	7^{7}	12^{5}	20^{8}	20^{0}	26^{6}	26^{0}	34^{8}	44^{10}	44^{0}	46^{2}	49^{3}	49^{x}	59^{10}	65^{6}	66^{1}	66^{0}
Hungary	0^{0}	0^{0}	0^{0}	0^{0}	0^{0}	2^{2}	2^{0}	2^{0}	3^{1}	3^{0}	3^{0}	3^{0}	3^{x}	3^{0}	3^{0}	3^{0}
Belgium	0^{0}	0^{0}	0^{0}	0^{0}	0^{0}	0^{0}	0^{0}	1^{1}	8^{7}	8^{0}	8^{0}	8^{0}	8^{0}	8^{x}	8^{0}	8^{0}
UK	5^{5}	6^{1}	6^{0}	10^{4}	10^{0}	11^{1}	11^{0}	23^{12}	23^{0}	23^{0}	23^{0}	35^{12}	42^{7}	49^{7}	49^{x}	59^{10}
Portugal	0^{0}	0^{0}	0^{0}	0^{0}	0^{0}	0^{0}	0^{0}	0^{0}	0^{0}	0^{0}	0^{0}	4^{4}	4^{0}	4^{0}	4^{0}	4^{x}
Cyprus	1^{1}	1^{0}	4^{3}	4^{0}	9^{5}	13^{4}	15^{2}	15^{0}	20^{5}	20^{0}	21^{1}	21^{0}	33^{12}	41^{8}	44^{3}	44^{0}
Sweden	10^{10}	**22^{12}**	**34^{12}**	**36^{2}**	**44^{8}**	**50^{6}**	**54^{4}**	**62^{8}**	**62^{0}**	63^{1}	63^{0}	66^{3}	66^{0}	66^{0}	72^{6}	80^{8}
Denmark	3^{3}	10^{7}	17^{7}	20^{3}	32^{12}	42^{10}	49^{7}	56^{7}	56^{0}	62^{6}	62^{0}	62^{0}	65^{3}	68^{3}	68^{0}	74^{6}
Slovenia	4^{4}	12^{8}	17^{5}	23^{6}	23^{0}	30^{7}	31^{1}	34^{3}	34^{0}	34^{0}	36^{2}	36^{0}	44^{8}	44^{0}	54^{10}	59^{5}
Israel	0^{0}	0^{0}	10^{10}	17^{7}	17^{0}	25^{8}	25^{0}	31^{6}	31^{0}	31^{0}	35^{4}	35^{0}	40^{5}	44^{4}	56^{12}	56^{0}
Malta	0^{0}	4^{4}	6^{2}	18^{12}	18^{0}	18^{0}	18^{0}	20^{2}	30^{10}	40^{10}	52^{12}	58^{6}	58^{0}	58^{0}	65^{7}	65^{0}
Greece	6^{6}	6^{0}	6^{0}	6^{0}	6^{0}	6^{0}	6^{0}	11^{5}	19^{8}	19^{0}	26^{7}	31^{5}	31^{0}	33^{2}	33^{0}	36^{3}

The 1990s were proving very tough for the original Eurovision entrants: Belgium, France, Germany, Italy, Luxembourg, the Netherlands and Switzerland. Belgium had come last in 1993, and thus missed the 1994 Contest, the first time it had not been represented. Its comeback this year was not spectacular. In 1995, Switzerland was absent for the very first time, and Germany came last with only one vote, and thus did not qualify for the 1996 Contest. This made it the last of the seven original entrants to miss a Contest.

Cyprus	Sweden	Denmark	Slovenia	Israel	Malta	Greece	**Position**
12^{0}	12^{0}	12^{0}	12^{0}	12^{0}	12^{0}	15^{3}	18
24^{0}	34^{10}	35^{1}	40^{5}	40^{0}	40^{0}	44^{4}	14
0^{0}	0^{0}	0^{0}	0^{0}	0^{0}	1^{1}	1^{0}	23
11^{0}	11^{0}	14^{3}	14^{0}	14^{0}	14^{0}	14^{0}	19
111^{7}	**111^{0}**	**113^{2}**	**120^{7}**	**130^{10}**	**136^{6}**	**148^{12}**	**1**
17^{1}	17^{0}	17^{0}	17^{0}	17^{0}	17^{0}	17^{0}	17
17^{0}	23^{6}	31^{8}	31^{0}	31^{0}	31^{0}	31^{0}	15
44^{0}	48^{4}	58^{10}	58^{0}	60^{2}	60^{0}	67^{7}	13
93^{10}	93^{0}	93^{0}	93^{0}	105^{12}	113^{8}	119^{6}	2
10^{0}	10^{0}	10^{0}	13^{3}	14^{1}	21^{7}	21^{0}	16
58^{5}	58^{0}	58^{0}	70^{12}	74^{4}	86^{12}	91^{5}	6
69^{2}	71^{3}	77^{6}	85^{8}	92^{7}	92^{0}	94^{2}	4
3^{0}	3^{0}	3^{0}	3^{0}	3^{0}	3^{0}	3^{0}	22
8^{0}	8^{0}	8^{0}	8^{0}	8^{0}	8^{0}	8^{0}	20
59^{0}	64^{5}	71^{7}	71^{0}	76^{5}	76^{0}	76^{0}	10=
4^{0}	4^{0}	4^{0}	4^{0}	4^{0}	4^{0}	5^{1}	21
44^{x}	52^{8}	57^{5}	61^{4}	67^{6}	71^{4}	79^{8}	9
84^{4}	84^{x}	96^{12}	97^{1}	97^{0}	100^{3}	100^{0}	3
74^{0}	86^{12}	86^{x}	92^{6}	92^{0}	92^{0}	92^{0}	5
62^{3}	69^{7}	69^{0}	69^{x}	72^{3}	74^{2}	84^{10}	7
64^{8}	66^{2}	66^{0}	76^{10}	76^{x}	81^{5}	81^{0}	8
71^{6}	72^{1}	76^{4}	76^{0}	76^{0}	76^{x}	76^{0}	10=
48^{12}	48^{0}	48^{0}	50^{2}	58^{8}	68^{10}	68^{x}	12

VOTING BIAS

SLOVENIA

★ ★ ★

Countries most likely to vote for Slovenia:

Bosnia
Russia
Greece
Croatia
Sweden

★ ★ ★

Countries least likely to vote for Slovenia:

Norway
Denmark
Spain
Belgium
Austria

★ ★ ★

Countries for whom Slovenia is most likely to vote:

Russia
Ireland
Israel
Sweden
Iceland

★ ★ ★

Countries for whom Slovenia is least likely to vote:

Malta
Austria
Greece
Portugal
Turkey

Having competed on just four occasions, Slovenia's voting patterns have yet to be fully established. For example, its disposition towards Russia is entirely explained by the twelve points in 1997.

★ ★

THE EUROVISION SONG CONTEST

1996

Won by Ireland: 'The Voice'
Written by Brendan Graham
Performed by Eimear Quinn
Orchestra conducted by Noel Kelehan

Normal service had been resumed. Ireland won the Eurovision Song Contest for a record seventh time in all, and a record fourth time in five years. It's song was composed for a record-equalling second time by Brendan Graham, who also wrote 1994's 'Rock 'N' Roll Kids'. There have now been four people who have written or part-written at least two Eurovision winners, but nobody has yet written three. Willy van Hemert, Yves Dessca and Johnny Logan are the others on the list that Brendan Graham joined in 1996: Dessca, who co-wrote the 1971 winner for Monaco and 1972's for Luxembourg, is the only person to win the writing trophy two years in a row and for two different nations.

The rules about the nationality of the singers and writers of the songs have always been vague. There seems to be more general agreement that the writers ought to be nationals of the country for which they write, or at least based there. However, there have been many exceptions to that, especially in the case of Monaco and Luxembourg. There are no rules, however, saying that the performers have to be nationals of the country they sing for. Thus we have have had many winners who have not been native to the country they represented (France Gall in 1965, Dana in 1970, Vicky Leandros in 1972, Céline Dion in 1988 and Katrina and the Waves in 1997, for example), and many more entrants from as far apart as Angola and Australia. Britain's entrant in 1996 was one of the Australians.

Gina G had been discovered working in a shop in Hampstead, and the song 'Ooh Aah ... Just A Little Bit' came from Steve Long, then of Puls8 Records in North London. It was put into all the preliminary heats for the British entry and continually failed to win any sort of backing, except from Jonathan King. It was not until the final selection by British TV viewers and radio listeners that the song began to pick up support, and it was a clear winner in the final telephone vote. By the time Eurovision was staged on 18 May, 'Ooh Aah ...' was already a big hit in Britain, and it reached number one the next week. But once again, the difference between the singles market and the Eurovision market was clearly shown. Gina G's single went on to become the first Eurovision hit for many years to reach the top twenty in America, not to mention topping the charts in Britain and many other countries around the world, but it never looked like winning Eurovision. The Irish entry, on the other hand, did. After a slow start in the voting, during which the UK jury gave it no points at all, Eimear Quinn's 'The Voice' pulled ahead, taking over the lead when Switzerland it them twelve points. By the time Ireland came to vote itself, it was too far ahead to be caught.

The host nation, Norway, not only came a very creditable second, but also achieved one of the most accurate votes ever recorded. After years during which the Norwegians have been accused of favouritism in their voting, they now reflected

1996 EUROVISION SONG CONTEST

Host country: Norway ★ *Venue:* Specktrum, Oslo
Date: 18 May ★ *Presenters:* Morten Harket and Ingvild Bryn
Voting structure: Each country awarded 12 to its top song, 10 to the second, 8 to the third and 7, 6, 5, 4, 3, 2 and 1 point for the next seven
Total entries: 23 ★ *Debut countries:* None

Country	Performer	Song	Pts	Pos.
Turkey	Sebnem Paker	Besinci Mevsim	57	12
United Kingdom	Gina G	Ooh Aah ... Just A Little Bit	77	8
Spain	Antonio Carbonell	Ay! Que Deseo!	17	20
Portugal	Lucia Moniz	O Meu Coração Não Tem Cor	92	6
Cyprus	Constantinos	Mono Gia Mas	72	9
Malta	Miriam Christine	In A Woman's Heart	68	10
Croatia	Maja Blagdan	Sveta Ljubav	98	4
Austria	George Nussbaumer	Wiel's Da Güt Gott	68	10
Switzerland	Kathy Leander	Mon Coeur L'Aime	22	16
Greece	Marianna Efstratiou	Emis Forame Ton Himona Anixiatika	36	14
Estonia	Ivo Linna and Marja-Liis Ilus	Kaelakee Hääl	94	5
Norway	Elisabeth Andreassen	I Evighet	114	2
France	Dan Ar Braz and L'Héritage des Celtes	Diwanis Bugale	18	19
Slovenia	Regina	Dan Najlepsih Sanj	16	21
Netherlands	Maxine and Franklin Brown	De Eerste Keer	78	7
Belgium	Lisa Del Bo	Liefde Is Een Kaartspel	22	16
Ireland	**Eimear Quinn**	**The Voice**	**162**	**1**
Finland	Jasmine	Niin Kaunis On Taivas	9	23
Iceland	Anna Mjöll	Sjubidu	51	13
Poland	Kasia Kowalska	Chce Znac Swoj Grzech	31	15
Bosnia-Herzegovina	Amila Glamocak	Za Nasu Ljubav	13	22
Slovakia	Marcel Polander	Kym Nas Mas	19	18
Sweden	One More Time	Den Vilda	100	3

the overall European opinion more accurately than we had seen from one jury for many years, if at all. Norway gave its top five votes to the other five songs that finished in the top six, which must be the ultimate in non-tactical voting. It gave twelve points to Portugal (sixth overall), ten to Ireland, the winners, eight to Estonia (fifth), seven to Croatia (fourth) and six points to Sweden (third). Croatia, which perhaps fancied its chances of victory, voted in a way that appeared much more tactical. It only gave points to Norway and Portugal among any of the leading contenders, and gave its twelve points to Malta (tenth). And local generosity is still alive and well in parts of Europe at least. Finland came last, with a song that did not compare well with Eimear Quinn, who had sung immediately before them, but its only votes came from Norway (two points) and Iceland (seven points). Slovenia managed to scrape in two places higher with sixteen points, thanks mainly to six points from Croatia and eight from Bosnia-Herzegovina. If Slovenia had returned the compliment to its Bosnian neighbours, it would have finished one place lower than it did. France's experiment of presenting a Breton song did not work: its fellow Celts, the Irish, were unimpressed, and the biggest enthusiasm for it came from mainly French-speaking Belgium. Some songs earned all their votes quickly: by the time Greece had finished

1996	Turkey	UK	Spain	Portugal	Cyprus	Malta	Croatia	Austria	Switzerland	Greece	Estonia	Norway	France	Slovenia	Netherlands	Belgium
Turkey	0^{x}	6^{6}	14^{8}	14^{0}	14^{0}	24^{10}	25^{1}	25^{1}	31^{6}	31^{0}	31^{0}	31^{0}	35^{4}	35^{4}	42^{7}	47^{5}
UK	3^{3}	3^{x}	3^{0}	15^{12}	16^{1}	22^{6}	29^{7}	32^{3}	36^{3}	36^{0}	38^{2}	38^{0}	46^{8}	46^{0}	46^{0}	58^{12}
Spain	0^{0}	0^{0}	0^{x}	0^{0}	2^{2}	7^{5}	11^{4}	11^{0}	11^{0}	17^{6}	17^{0}	17^{0}	17^{0}	17^{0}	17^{0}	17^{0}
Portugal	5^{5}	7^{2}	7^{0}	7^{x}	19^{12}	19^{0}	29^{10}	30^{1}	40^{10}	45^{5}	45^{0}	57^{12}	62^{5}	62^{0}	68^{6}	74^{6}
Cyprus	0^{0}	**12^{12}**	19^{7}	22^{3}	22^{x}	24^{2}	32^{8}	34^{2}	39^{5}	51^{12}	51^{0}	51^{0}	53^{2}	53^{0}	53^{0}	53^{0}
Malta	10^{10}	10^{0}	**20^{10}**	20^{0}	20^{0}	20^{x}	32^{12}	32^{0}	32^{0}	40^{8}	40^{0}	41^{1}	41^{0}	45^{4}	45^{0}	45^{0}
Croatia	8^{8}	**12^{4}**	17^{5}	**27^{10}**	**35^{8}**	**42^{7}**	**42^{x}**	**42^{0}**	43^{1}	44^{1}	50^{6}	57^{7}	57^{0}	60^{3}	65^{5}	69^{4}
Austria	4^{4}	4^{0}	4^{0}	9^{5}	9^{0}	21^{12}	21^{0}	21^{x}	21^{0}	23^{2}	30^{7}	30^{0}	42^{12}	43^{1}	43^{0}	43^{0}
Switzerland	0^{0}	3^{3}	3^{0}	3^{0}	3^{0}	3^{0}	3^{0}	3^{0}	3^{x}	3^{0}	3^{0}	3^{0}	3^{0}	5^{2}	9^{4}	11^{2}
Greece	0^{0}	7^{7}	7^{0}	7^{0}	17^{10}	18^{1}	18^{0}	18^{0}	20^{2}	20^{x}	20^{0}	23^{3}	23^{0}	23^{0}	24^{1}	24^{0}
Estonia	0^{0}	10^{10}	14^{4}	14^{0}	21^{7}	21^{0}	21^{0}	26^{5}	26^{0}	26^{0}	26^{x}	34^{8}	35^{1}	43^{8}	46^{3}	46^{0}
Norway	2^{2}	10^{8}	10^{0}	12^{2}	15^{3}	15^{0}	20^{5}	28^{8}	35^{7}	35^{0}	40^{5}	40^{x}	47^{7}	57^{10}	67^{10}	75^{8}
France	0^{0}	1^{1}	1^{0}	2^{1}	2^{0}	2^{0}	2^{0}	2^{0}	2^{0}	2^{0}	5^{3}	9^{4}	9^{x}	9^{0}	9^{0}	16^{7}
Slovenia	0^{0}	0^{0}	1^{1}	1^{0}	1^{0}	1^{0}	7^{6}	7^{0}	7^{0}	7^{0}	7^{0}	7^{0}	7^{0}	7^{x}	7^{0}	7^{0}
Netherlands	1^{1}	1^{0}	7^{6}	14^{7}	19^{5}	19^{0}	19^{0}	31^{12}	34^{3}	34^{0}	38^{4}	38^{0}	48^{10}	53^{5}	53^{x}	54^{1}
Belgium	0^{0}	5^{5}	17^{12}	17^{0}	17^{0}	17^{0}	19^{2}	19^{0}	19^{0}	19^{0}	20^{1}	20^{0}	20^{0}	20^{0}	25^{5}	25^{x}
Ireland	**12^{12}**	**12^{0}**	12^{0}	20^{8}	26^{6}	30^{4}	30^{0}	37^{7}	**49^{12}**	**59^{10}**	**71^{12}**	**81^{10}**	**87^{6}**	**99^{12}**	**111^{12}**	**114^{3}**
Finland	0^{0}	0^{0}	0^{0}	0^{0}	0^{0}	0^{0}	0^{0}	0^{0}	0^{0}	0^{0}	0^{0}	2^{2}	2^{0}	2^{0}	2^{0}	2^{0}
Iceland	0^{0}	0^{0}	3^{3}	9^{6}	9^{0}	9^{0}	9^{0}	15^{6}	15^{0}	18^{3}	26^{8}	31^{5}	31^{0}	37^{6}	37^{0}	37^{0}
Poland	7^{7}	7^{0}	7^{0}	7^{0}	11^{4}	11^{0}	11^{0}	15^{4}	15^{0}	22^{7}	22^{0}	22^{0}	22^{0}	22^{0}	22^{0}	22^{0}
Bosnia-Herz.	6^{6}	6^{0}	6^{0}	6^{0}	6^{0}	9^{3}	12^{3}	12^{0}	12^{0}	12^{0}	12^{0}	12^{0}	12^{0}	12^{0}	12^{0}	12^{0}
Slovakia	0^{0}	0^{0}	2^{2}	2^{0}	2^{0}	10^{8}	10^{0}	10^{0}	10^{0}	14^{4}	14^{0}	14^{0}	14^{0}	14^{0}	14^{0}	14^{0}
Sweden	0^{0}	0^{0}	0^{0}	4^{4}	4^{0}	4^{0}	4^{0}	14^{10}	22^{8}	22^{0}	32^{10}	38^{6}	41^{3}	48^{7}	56^{8}	66^{10}

voting, Spain had collected all the points it would earn all night. Some presented a challenge at the end that nobody had noticed before: the Estonian entry gained forty-six votes from the final six juries, only two fewer than Ireland. Unfortunately, it had been trailing by sixty-six points up to then.

Sweden, which finished third, was represented by a band called One More Time. One of its members was Peter Andersson, son of Benny Andersson of Abba, who had won twenty-three years earlier.

Ireland	Finland	Iceland	Poland	Bosnia-Herz.	Slovakia	Sweden	**Position**
47^{0}	52^{5}	52^{0}	52^{0}	57^{5}	57^{0}	57^{0}	12
61^{3}	61^{0}	65^{4}	65^{0}	65^{0}	71^{6}	77^{6}	8=
17^{0}	17^{0}	17^{0}	17^{0}	17^{0}	17^{0}	17^{0}	20
74^{0}	77^{3}	87^{10}	87^{0}	88^{1}	88^{0}	92^{4}	6
54^{1}	60^{6}	60^{0}	60^{0}	60^{0}	70^{10}	72^{2}	8=
45^{0}	45^{0}	45^{0}	51^{6}	51^{0}	63^{12}	68^{5}	10=
75^{6}	75^{0}	80^{5}	82^{2}	92^{10}	97^{5}	98^{1}	4
51^{8}	51^{0}	51^{0}	59^{8}	65^{6}	68^{3}	68^{0}	10=
15^{4}	19^{4}	22^{3}	22^{0}	22^{0}	22^{0}	22^{0}	17
24^{0}	24^{0}	24^{0}	25^{1}	25^{0}	33^{8}	36^{3}	14
48^{2}	60^{12}	72^{12}	82^{10}	82^{0}	82^{0}	94^{12}	5
82^{7}	89^{7}	97^{8}	101^{4}	104^{3}	104^{0}	114^{10}	2
16^{0}	18^{2}	18^{0}	18^{0}	18^{0}	18^{0}	18^{0}	19
7^{0}	7^{0}	8^{1}	8^{0}	16^{8}	16^{0}	16^{0}	21
59^{5}	59^{0}	61^{2}	68^{7}	70^{2}	70^{0}	78^{8}	7
25^{0}	25^{0}	25^{0}	25^{0}	25^{0}	25^{0}	25^{0}	16
114^{x}	**124^{10}**	**124^{0}**	**136^{12}**	**148^{12}**	**155^{7}**	**162^{7}**	**1**
2^{0}	2^{x}	9^{7}	9^{0}	9^{0}	9^{0}	9^{0}	23
47^{10}	47^{0}	47^{x}	50^{3}	50^{0}	51^{1}	51^{0}	13
22^{0}	22^{0}	22^{0}	22^{x}	29^{7}	31^{2}	31^{0}	15
12^{0}	13^{1}	13^{0}	13^{0}	13^{x}	13^{0}	13^{0}	22
14^{0}	14^{0}	14^{0}	19^{5}	19^{0}	19^{x}	19^{0}	18
78^{12}	86^{8}	92^{6}	92^{0}	96^{4}	100^{4}	100^{x}	3

VOTING BIAS

CROATIA

Countries most likely to vote for Croatia:

Malta
Slovakia
Bosnia
Portugal
Norway

Countries least likely to vote for Croatia:

Austria
France
Finland
Germany
Denmark

Countries for whom Croatia is most likely to vote:

Malta
Bosnia
UK
Germany
Spain

Countries for whom Croatia is least likely to vote:

Sweden
Ireland
Estonia
Austria
France

Over the last four years, Croatia has given Malta forty-two points from a possible maximum forty-eight. In return Croatia has received an almost equally generous thirty-nine points.

THE EUROVISION SONG CONTEST

1997

Won by United Kingdom: 'Love Shine A Light'
Written by Kimberley Rew
Performed by Katrina and the Waves
Orchestra conducted by Don Airey

When the United Kingdom wins, it wins big. Taking a song originally written for the Samaritans' thirtieth birthday celebrations, performed by an American resident of Newmarket (where the horses come from), Britain achieved the rare distinction of receiving votes from every one of the twenty-four other juries, including ten top votes and five second places, and won at a canter, leaving even the Irish entry a length and seventy votes behind in second place. Norway returned to old form by failing to secure a single vote, but it was Denmark that brought the house down with a rap by a man who called himself Kølig Kai. The song was remarkable not only for the daring involved in performing a rap in Danish for Eurovision, but also for the appalling quality of the rap. Some rap is good, some is bad. This was bad.

Katrina Leskanich, the thirty-seven-year-old leader of the winning band, who last had a hit in 1986, had decided to do Eurovision because they had nothing left to lose. After ten years of ever-deepening obscurity, with just one glorious record, 'Walking On Sunshine', in their back catalogue (not to mention an impressive version of 'Torn' which Natalie Imbruglia would have a massive hit with a year later), Katrina and the Waves thought of Gina G, thought of the European record sales and decided that their street credibility was less important than a revived career. 'I knew we had a winner with Katrina,' said Jonathan King, 'when my eighty-two-year-old mother said, "That will win with no trouble at all".' At long last he was learning that hits and Eurovision winners are two different things: 'Love Shine A Light' reached the top ten in Britain, but it did not top the charts and it did not sell nearly as many copies around the world as 'Ooh Aah ... Just A Little Bit'.

The arrival of telephone voting will make a big difference. The Iceland entry – which not even Paul Oscar's silver-haired grandmother would have described as a potential winner – scored well in the UK telephone vote because, in Terry Wogan's theory, people came back from the pub to watch Katrina singing second to last and the only other song they even heard through their beery haze was the one from Iceland that rounded off proceedings. So they voted for it. You will note that the UK jury gave Iceland six points, more even than it was given by Norway, Finland and Denmark (no points from any of them), and only two fewer than it got from Sweden. Happy accidents such as this, on a larger scale, will soon be deciding the outcome of the entire Contest. Imagine what it will be like when all the juries are created out of anybody still sober enough to dial the necessary numbers.

Norway and Portugal both scored no points, bringing to an end a good Eurovision run by both countries. Norway had been in the top ten in each of the previous four contests, and had won it only two years earlier. Portugal had also been among the top ten nations more often than not in the 1990s, but it was not a new experience for either

1997 EUROVISION SONG CONTEST

Host country: Ireland ★ *Venue:* The Point, Dublin
Date: 3 May ★ *Presenters:* Ronan Keating and Carrie Crowley
Voting structure: Each country awarded 12 to its top song, 10 to the second, 8 to the third and 7, 6, 5, 4, 3, 2 and 1 point for the next seven
Total entries: 25 ★ *Debut countries:* None

Country	Performer	Song	Pts	Pos.
Cyprus	Hara and Andreas Constantinou	Mana Mou	98	5
Turkey	Sebnem Paker	Dinle	121	3
Norway	Tor Endresen	San Francisco	0	24
Austria	Bettina Soriat	One Step	12	21
Ireland	Marc Roberts	Mysterious Woman	157	2
Slovenia	Tanja Ribic	Zbudi Se	60	10
Switzerland	Barbara Berta	Dentro Di Me	5	22
Netherlands	Mrs Einstein	Niemand Heeft Nog Tijd	5	22
Italy	Jalisse	Fiumi Di Parole	114	4
Spain	Marcos Llunas	Sin Rencor	96	6
Germany	Bianca Shomburg	Zeit	22	18
Poland	Anna-Maria Jopek	Ale Jestem	54	11
Estonia	Maarja-Liis Ilus	Keelatud Maa	82	8
Bosnia-Herzegovina	Alma Cardzic	Goodbye	22	18
Portugal	Celia Lawson	Antes Do Adeus	0	24
Sweden	Blond	Bara Hon Alskar Moj	36	14
Greece	Marianna Zorba	Horepse	39	12
Malta	Debbie Scerri	Let Me Fly	66	9
Hungary	VIP	Miert Kell Hogy Elmenj?	39	12
Russian Federation	Alla Pugachova	Prima Donna	33	15
Denmark	Kølig Kaj	Stemmen I Mit Liv	25	16
France	Fanny	Sentiment Songes	95	7
Croatia	ENI	Probudi Mi	24	17
United Kingdom	**Katrina and the Waves**	**Love Shine A Light**	**227**	**1**
Iceland	Paul Oscar	Minn Hinsti Dans	18	20

country to end up with nothing to show for the night. For Norway, it was its record-breaking fourth 'nul points', and for Portugal its second, thirty-three years after their first. However, neither of them are as unsuccessful as Lithuania, which gained no votes at all in its only appearance, in 1994. Even if it came back into the competition in 1999, it will have taken at least five years from its first appearance to earn its first vote – a desperately unimpressive record.

The overall impression of the 1997 Contest, however, was of a show that did not quite know in which direction it ought to be going. With the splitting of popular music into many mutually exclusive factions – from rap to heavy metal, to jungle, to soul, to jazz, to plain old Eurovision corn – it is hard to work out what European audiences want. In a strange way, Europe as a political and economic concept has become more universally accepted and as more states queue up to join this culturally neutral entity, its musical cultures become more tribal, more mutually exclusive. The dead hand of American music is being lifted as memories of the American Forces

1997	Cyprus	Turkey	Norway	Austria	Ireland	Slovenia	Switzerland	Netherlands	Italy	Spain	Germany	Poland	Estonia	Bosnia-Herz.	Portugal	Sweden	Greece	Malta
Cyprus	0^{x}	0^{0}	2^{2}	2^{0}	5^{3}	9^{4}	13^{4}	23^{10}	27^{4}	37^{10}	42^{5}	42^{0}	43^{1}	43^{0}	46^{3}	46^{0}	58^{12}	65^{7}
Turkey	0^{0}	0^{x}	0^{0}	7^{7}	9^{2}	9^{0}	15^{6}	17^{2}	24^{7}	36^{12}	48^{12}	48^{0}	54^{6}	66^{12}	71^{5}	77^{6}	84^{7}	94^{10}
Norway	0^{0}	0^{0}	0^{x}	0^{0}	0^{0}	0^{0}	0^{0}	0^{0}	0^{0}	0^{0}	0^{0}	0^{0}	0^{0}	0^{0}	0^{0}	0^{0}	0^{0}	0^{0}
Austria	0^{0}	0^{0}	0^{0}	0^{x}	0^{0}	0^{0}	0^{0}	3^{3}	3^{0}	3^{0}	3^{0}	4^{1}	4^{0}	4^{0}	4^{0}	4^{0}	4^{0}	4^{0}
Ireland	8^{8}	14^{6}	17^{3}	27^{10}	27^{x}	28^{1}	35^{7}	39^{4}	49^{10}	56^{7}	63^{7}	70^{7}	78^{8}	86^{8}	96^{10}	106^{10}	106^{0}	106^{0}
Slovenia	2^{2}	12^{10}	12^{0}	12^{0}	12^{0}	12^{x}	12^{0}	12^{0}	12^{0}	12^{0}	12^{0}	14^{2}	18^{4}	25^{7}	29^{4}	29^{0}	32^{3}	37^{5}
Switzerland	0^{0}	0^{0}	0^{0}	0^{0}	0^{0}	0^{0}	0^{x}	0^{0}	2^{2}	5^{3}	5^{0}	5^{0}	5^{0}	5^{0}	5^{0}	5^{0}	5^{0}	5^{0}
Netherlands	0^{0}	1^{1}	1^{0}	1^{0}	1^{0}	1^{0}	1^{0}	1^{x}	1^{0}	1^{0}	1^{0}	1^{0}	1^{0}	1^{0}	1^{0}	1^{0}	1^{0}	5^{4}
Italy	6^{6}	11^{5}	11^{0}	12^{1}	13^{1}	23^{10}	33^{10}	40^{7}	40^{x}	48^{8}	52^{4}	60^{8}	60^{0}	66^{6}	78^{12}	81^{3}	86^{5}	86^{0}
Spain	10^{10}	14^{4}	14^{0}	14^{0}	20^{6}	25^{5}	33^{8}	39^{6}	42^{3}	42^{x}	44^{2}	48^{4}	48^{0}	48^{0}	56^{8}	56^{0}	62^{6}	74^{12}
Germany	0^{0}	0^{0}	0^{0}	3^{3}	3^{0}	3^{0}	8^{5}	8^{0}	13^{5}	13^{0}	13^{x}	13^{0}	13^{0}	13^{0}	13^{0}	13^{0}	13^{0}	16^{3}
Poland	0^{0}	0^{0}	4^{4}	12^{8}	12^{0}	19^{7}	19^{0}	20^{1}	21^{1}	23^{2}	29^{6}	29^{x}	32^{3}	36^{4}	38^{2}	38^{0}	39^{1}	39^{0}
Estonia	1^{1}	1^{0}	1^{0}	7^{6}	15^{8}	18^{3}	18^{0}	18^{0}	30^{12}	34^{4}	41^{7}	47^{6}	47^{x}	48^{1}	49^{1}	50^{1}	50^{0}	50^{0}
Bosnia-Herz.	0^{0}	8^{8}	8^{0}	12^{4}	12^{0}	12^{0}	14^{2}	14^{0}	14^{0}	14^{0}	17^{3}	17^{0}	17^{0}	17^{x}	17^{0}	21^{4}	21^{0}	21^{0}
Portugal	0^{0}	0^{0}	0^{0}	0^{0}	0^{0}	0^{0}	0^{0}	0^{0}	0^{0}	0^{0}	0^{0}	0^{0}	0^{0}	0^{0}	0^{x}	0^{0}	0^{0}	0^{0}
Sweden	0^{0}	0^{0}	8^{8}	8^{0}	13^{5}	19^{6}	19^{0}	19^{0}	19^{0}	19^{0}	19^{0}	19^{0}	19^{0}	19^{0}	19^{0}	19^{x}	19^{0}	19^{0}
Greece	**12^{12}**	12^{0}	17^{5}	17^{0}	17^{0}	17^{0}	17^{0}	17^{0}	17^{0}	24^{7}	24^{0}	24^{0}	24^{0}	24^{0}	24^{0}	24^{0}	24^{x}	30^{6}
Malta	5^{5}	**17^{12}**	**27^{10}**	27^{0}	34^{7}	34^{0}	34^{0}	34^{0}	40^{6}	41^{1}	41^{0}	41^{0}	41^{0}	46^{5}	46^{0}	46^{0}	54^{8}	54^{x}
Hungary	0^{0}	3^{3}	3^{0}	3^{0}	7^{4}	7^{0}	7^{0}	7^{0}	7^{0}	7^{0}	7^{0}	12^{5}	17^{5}	17^{0}	17^{0}	17^{0}	17^{0}	19^{2}
Russia	0^{0}	0^{0}	1^{1}	6^{5}	6^{0}	18^{12}	18^{0}	26^{8}	26^{0}	26^{0}	26^{0}	26^{0}	33^{7}	33^{0}	33^{0}	33^{0}	33^{0}	33^{0}
Denmark	0^{0}	0^{0}	7^{7}	7^{0}	7^{0}	7^{0}	8^{1}	8^{0}	8^{0}	8^{0}	8^{0}	8^{0}	8^{0}	8^{0}	8^{0}	15^{7}	17^{2}	17^{0}
France	3^{3}	5^{2}	17^{12}	17^{0}	27^{10}	29^{2}	32^{3}	37^{5}	37^{0}	37^{0}	37^{0}	49^{12}	61^{12}	64^{3}	70^{6}	72^{2}	76^{4}	76^{0}
Croatia	4^{4}	4^{0}	4^{0}	4^{0}	4^{0}	4^{0}	4^{0}	4^{0}	4^{0}	4^{0}	5^{1}	8^{3}	8^{0}	10^{2}	10^{0}	15^{5}	15^{0}	23^{8}
UK	7^{7}	14^{7}	20^{6}	**32^{12}**	**44^{12}**	**52^{8}**	**64^{12}**	**76^{12}**	**84^{8}**	**89^{5}**	**99^{10}**	**109^{10}**	**119^{10}**	**129^{10}**	**136^{7}**	**148^{12}**	**158^{10}**	**159^{1}**
Iceland	0^{0}	0^{0}	0^{0}	2^{2}	2^{0}	2^{0}	2^{0}	2^{0}	2^{0}	2^{0}	2^{0}	2^{0}	4^{2}	4^{0}	4^{0}	12^{8}	12^{0}	12^{0}

Network fade and new countries from the old Eastern bloc come into the competition. MTV, the cultural glue of the younger generation of European music followers, is nothing to do with Eurovision: the culture gap seems to be not between Estonian and French but between those over thirty and under thirty. The over-thirties still rule Eurovision, but they can't quite work out where they ought to be taking it.

Hungary	Russia	Denmark	France	Croatia	UK	Iceland	**Position**
65^{0}	66^{1}	73^{7}	77^{4}	81^{4}	86^{5}	98^{12}	5
100^{6}	104^{4}	104^{0}	110^{6}	110^{0}	114^{4}	121^{7}	3
0^{0}	0^{0}	0^{0}	0^{0}	0^{0}	0^{0}	0^{0}	24=
9^{5}	12^{3}	12^{0}	12^{0}	12^{0}	12^{0}	12^{0}	21
114^{8}	119^{5}	129^{10}	139^{10}	145^{6}	157^{12}	157^{0}	2
37^{0}	47^{10}	47^{0}	54^{7}	57^{3}	57^{0}	60^{3}	10
5^{0}	5^{0}	5^{0}	5^{0}	5^{0}	5^{0}	5^{0}	22=
5^{0}	5^{0}	5^{0}	5^{0}	5^{0}	5^{0}	5^{0}	22=
89^{3}	96^{7}	100^{4}	100^{0}	110^{10}	113^{3}	114^{1}	4
84^{10}	92^{8}	94^{2}	96^{2}	96^{0}	96^{0}	96^{0}	6
17^{1}	17^{0}	17^{0}	17^{0}	22^{5}	22^{0}	22^{0}	18=
46^{7}	46^{0}	51^{5}	54^{3}	54^{0}	54^{0}	54^{0}	11
54^{4}	54^{0}	62^{8}	70^{8}	70^{0}	80^{10}	82^{2}	8
21^{0}	21^{0}	21^{0}	21^{0}	22^{1}	22^{0}	22^{0}	18=
0^{0}	0^{0}	0^{0}	0^{0}	0^{0}	0^{0}	0^{0}	24=
19^{0}	19^{0}	25^{6}	25^{0}	25^{0}	32^{7}	36^{4}	14
30^{0}	32^{2}	32^{0}	32^{0}	39^{7}	39^{0}	39^{0}	12=
54^{0}	54^{0}	57^{3}	58^{1}	66^{8}	66^{0}	66^{0}	9
19^{x}	19^{0}	19^{0}	24^{5}	26^{2}	34^{8}	39^{5}	12=
33^{0}	33^{0}	33^{0}	33^{0}	33^{0}	33^{0}	33^{0}	15
17^{0}	17^{0}	17^{0}	17^{0}	17^{0}	19^{2}	25^{6}	16
78^{2}	84^{6}	85^{1}	85^{0}	85^{0}	85^{0}	95^{10}	7
23^{0}	23^{0}	23^{0}	23^{0}	23^{0}	24^{1}	24^{1}	17
171^{12}	**183^{12}**	**195^{12}**	**207^{12}**	**219^{12}**	**219^{x}**	**227^{8}**	**1**
12^{0}	12^{0}	12^{0}	12^{0}	12^{0}	18^{6}	18^{x}	20

VOTING BIAS

TURKEY

Countries most likely to vote for Turkey:

Malta
Yugoslavia
Switzerland
Spain
Germany

Countries least likely to vote for Turkey:

Cyprus
Portugal
Norway
Denmark
Ireland

★ ★ ★

Countries for whom Turkey is most likely to vote:

Spain
Yugoslavia
Bosnia
Malta
Italy

Countries for whom Turkey is least likely to vote:

Cyprus
France
Sweden
Israel
Denmark

Turkey has never fared well in Eurovision; until 1997 it had only once finished in the top ten. This year was exceptional: Turkey received votes from eighteen juries, enough to give it a best-ever placing.

ENTRIES BY COUNTRY

AUSTRIA

36 entries, best placing: 1st in 1966

1957, Bob Martin; *Wohin, Kleines Pony*
1958, Liane Augustin; *Die Ganze Welt Braucht Liebe*
1959, Ferry Graf; *Der K und K Kalypso Aus Wien*
1960, Harry Winter; *Du Hast Mich So Fasziniert*
1961, Jimmy Makulis; *Sehnsucht*
1962, Eleonore Schwarz; *Nur In Der Wiener Luft*
1963, Carmela Corren; *Vielleicht Geschieht Ein Wunder*
1964, Udo Jürgens; *Warum Nur Warum?*
1965, Udo Jürgens; *Sag Ihr, Ich Lass Sie Grüssen*
1966, Udo Jürgens; *Merci Chérie*
1967, Peter Horten; *Warum Es 100,000 Sterne Gibt*
1968, Karel Gott; *Tausend Fenster*
1969–70, No entry
1971, Marianne Mendt; *Musik*
1972, The Milestones; *Falter Im Wind*
1973–5, No entry
1976, Waterloo and Robinson; *My Little World*
1977, Schmetterlinge; *Boom Boom Boomerang*
1978, Springtime; *Mrs Caroline Robinson*
1979, Christine Simon; *Heute In Jerusalem*
1980, Blue Danube; *Du Bist Musik*
1981, Marty Brem; *Wenn Du Da Bist*
1982, Mess; *Sonntag*
1983, Westend; *Hurricane*
1984, Anita; *Einfach Weg*
1985, Gary Lux; *Kinder Dieser Welt*
1986, Timna Brauer; *Die Zeit Ist Einsam*
1987, Gary Lux; *Nur Noch Gefühl*
1988, Wilfried; *Lisa, Mona Lisa*
1989, Thomas Forstner; *Nur Ein Lied*
1990, Simone; *Keine Mauern Mehr*
1991, Thomas Forstner; *Venedig Im Regen*
1992, Tony Wegas; *Zusammen Geh'n*
1993, Tony Wegas; *Maria Magdalena*
1994, Petra Frey; *Für Den Frieden der Welt*
1995, Stella Jones; *Die Welt Dreht Sich Verkehrt*
1996, George Nussbaumer; *Wiel's Da Güt Gott*
1997, Bettina Soriat; *One Step*

BELGIUM

40 entries, best placing: 1st in 1986

1956, Mony Marc; *Le Plus Beau Jour De Ma Vie*
1956, Fud Leclerc; *Messieurs Les Noyés De La Seine*
1957, Bobbejaan Schoepen; *Straatdeuntje*
1958, Fud Leclerc; *Ma Petite Chatte*
1959, Bob Benny; *Hou Toch Van Me*
1960, Fud Leclerc; *Mon Amour Pour Toi*
1961, Bob Benny; *Septembre, Gouden Roos*
1962, Fud Leclerc; *Ton Nom*
1963, Jacques Raymond; *Waarom?*
1964, Robert Cogoi; *Près De Ma Rivière*
1965, Lize Marke; *Als Het Weer Lente Is*
1966, Tonia; *Un Peu De Poivre, Un Peu De Sel*
1967, Louis Neefs; *Ik Heb Zorgen*
1968, Claude Lombard; *Quand Tu Reviendras*
1969, Louis Neefs; *Jennifer Jennings*
1970, Jean Vallée; *Viens L'Oublier*
1971, Lily Castel and Jacques Raymond; *Goeie Morgen, Morgen*
1972, Serge and Christine Ghisoland; *A La Folie Ou Pas Du Tout*
1973, Nicole and Hugo; *Baby Baby*
1974, Jacques Hustin; *Fleur De Liberté*
1975, Ann Christy; *Gelukkig Zijn*
1976, Pierre Rapsat; *Judy et Cie*
1977, Dream Express; *A Million In One, Two, Three*

1978, Jean Vallée; *L'Amour Ça Fait Chanter La Vie*
1979, Micha Marah; *Hey Nana*
1980, Telex; *Eurovision*
1981, Emly Starr; *Samson*
1982, Stella; *Si Tu Aimes Ma Musique*
1983, Pas de Deux; *Rendez-vous*
1984, Jacques Zégers; *Avanti La Vie*
1985, Linda Lepomme; *Laat Me Nu Gaan*
1986, Sandra Kim; *J'Aime La Vie*
1987, Liliane St Pierre; *Soldiers Of Love*
1988, Reynaert; *Laissez Briller Le Soleil*
1989, Ingeborg; *Door de Wind*
1990, Philippe Lafontaine; *Macédomienne*
1991, Clouseau; *Geef Het Op*
1992, Morgane; *Nous On Veut Des Violons*
1993, Barbara; *Iemand Als Jij*
1994, No entry
1995, Frédéric Etherlinck; *La Voix Est Libre*
1996, Lisa Del Bo; *Liefde Is Een Kaartspel*
1997, No entry

BOSNIA-HERZEGOVINA

5 ENTRIES, BEST PLACING: 15TH IN 1994
1993, Fazla; *Sva Bol Svijeta*
1994, Alma and Dejan; *Ostani Kraj Mene*
1995, Davor Popovic; *Dvadeset I Prvi Viijek*
1996, Amila Glamocak; *Za Nasu Ljubav*
1997, Alma Cardzic; *Goodbye*

CROATIA

5 ENTRIES, BEST PLACING: 4TH IN 1996
1993, Put; *Don't Ever Cry*
1994, Toni Cetinski; *Nek 'Ti Bude Ljubav Sva*
1995, Magazin and Lidija; *Nostalgia*
1996, Maja Blagdan; *Sveta Ljubav*
1997, ENI; *Probudi Mi*

CYPRUS

16 ENTRIES, BEST PLACING: 5TH IN 1982 AND 1997
1981, Island; *Monika*
1982, Anna Vissi; *Mono I Agapi*
1983, Stavros and Constantina; *I Agapi Akoma Zi*
1984, Andy Paul; *Anna Maria-Lena*
1985, Lia Vissi; *To Katalava Arga*
1986, Elpida; *Tora Zo*
1987, Alexia; *Aspro Mavro*
1988, No entry
1989, Yiannis Savidakis and Fanny Polymeri; *Apopse As Vrethoume*
1990, Anastazio; *Milas Poli*
1991, Elena Patroklou; *SOS*
1992, Evridiki; *Tairiazoume*
1993, Zymbolakis and Van Beke; *Mi Stamatas*
1994, Evridiki; *Eimai Anthropos Ki Ego*
1995, Alex Panayi; *Sti Fotia*
1996, Constantinos; *Mono Gia Mas*
1997, Hara and Andreas Constantinou; *Mana Mou*

DENMARK

28 ENTRIES, BEST PLACING: 1ST IN 1963
1957, Birthe Wilke and Gustav Winckler; *Skibet Skal Sejle I Nat*
1958, Raquel Rastenni; *Jeg Rev Et Blad Ud Af Min Dagbog*
1959, Birthe Wilke; *Uh-jeg Ville Ønske Jeg Var Dig*
1960, Katy Bødtger; *Det Var En Yndig Tid*
1961, Dario Campeotto; *Angelique*
1962, Ellen Winther; *Vuggevise*
1963, Grethe and Jørgen Ingmann; *Dansevise*
1964, Bjørn Tidmand; *Sangen Om Dig*
1965, Birgit Brüel; *For Din Skyld*
1966, Ulla Pia; *Stop, Mens Legen Er Go*
1967–77, No entries
1978, Mabel; *Boom-Boom*
1979, Tommy Seebach; *Disco Tango*
1980, Bamses Venner; *Tænker Altid På Dig*
1981, Debbie Cameron and Tommy Seebach; *Krøller Eller Ej*
1982, Brixx; *Video Video*
1983, Gry Johansen; *Kloden Drejer*
1984, Hot Eyes; *Det' Lige Det*
1985, Hot Eyes; *Sku' Du Spør Fra No'en*
1986, Trax; *Du Er Fuld Af Løgn*
1987, Anne Cathrine Herdorf and Bandjo; *En Lille Melodi*
1988, Hot Eyes; *Ka' Du Se Hva' Jeg Sa'*

★ ★

1989, Birthe Kjaer; *Vi Maler Byen Rød*
1990, Lonnie Devantier; *Hallo Hallo*
1991, Anders Frandsen; *Lige Der Hvor Hjertet Slår*
1992, Lotte Nilsson and Kenny Lübcke; *Alt Det Som Ingen Ser*
1993, Tommy Seebach Band; *Under Stjernerne På Himlen*
1994, No entry
1995, Aud Wilken; *Fra Mols Til Skagen*
1996, No entry
1997, Kølig Kaj; *Stemmen I Mit Liv*

ESTONIA

3 ENTRIES, BEST PLACING: 5TH IN 1996

1994, Silvi Vrait; *Nagu Merelaine*
1995, No entry
1996, Ivo Linna and Maarja-Liis Ilus; *Kaelakee Hääl*
1997, Maarja-Liis Ilus; *Keelatud Maa*

FINLAND

34 ENTRIES, BEST PLACING: 6TH IN 1973

1961, Laila Kinnunen; *Valoa Ikkunassa*
1962, Marion Rung; *Tipi-tii*
1963, Laila Halme; *Muistojeni Laulu*
1964, Lasse Mårtenson; *Laiskotellen*
1965, Viktor Klimenko; *Aurinko Laskee Lånteen*
1966, Ann Christine Nyström; *Play Boy*
1967, Fredi; *Varjoon-Suojaan*
1968, Kristína Hautala; *Kun Kello Käy*
1969, Jarkko and Laura; *Kuin Silloin Ennen*
1970, No entry
1971, Markuu Aro and the Koivisto Sisters; *Tie Uuteen Päivään*
1972, Päivi Paunu and Kim Floor; *Muistathan*
1973, Marion Rung; *Tom Tom Tom*
1974, Carita; *Keep Me Warm*
1975, Pihasoittajat; *Old Man Fiddle*
1976, Fredi and Friends; *Pump-pump*
1977, Monica Aspelund; *Lapponia*
1978, Seija Simola; *Anna Rakkaudelle Tilaisuus*
1979, Katri Helena; *Katson Sineen Taivaan*
1980, Vesa-Matti Loiri; *Huilumies*
1981, Riki Sorsa; *Reggae OK*
1982, Kojo; *Nuku Pommiin*
1983, Ami Aspelund; *Fantasiaa*
1984, Kirka; *Hengaillaan*
1985, Sonja Lumme; *Eläköön Elämä*
1986, Kari; *Paiva Kahden Ihmisen*
1987, Vicky Rosti; *Sata Salamaa*
1988, The Boulevard; *Nauravat Silmät Muistetaan*
1989, Anneli Saaristo; *La Dolce Vita*
1990, Beat; *Fri?*
1991, Kaija Kärkinen; *Hullu Yö*
1992, Pave Maijanen; *Yamma Yamma*
1993, Katri-Helena; *Tule Luo*
1994, CatCat; *Bye Bye Baby*
1995, No entry
1996, Jasmine; *Niin Kaunis On Taivas*
1997, No entry

FRANCE

41 ENTRIES, BEST PLACING: 1ST IN 1958, 1960, 1962, 1969, 1977

1956, Dany Dauberson; *Il Est Là*
1956, Mathé Altéry; *Le Temps Perdu*
1957, Paule Desjardins; *La Belle Amour*
1958, André Claveau; *Dors, Mon Amour*
1959, Jean Philippe; *Oui Oui Oui Oui*
1960, Jacqueline Boyer; *Tom Pillibi*
1961, Jean-Paul Mauric; *Printemps (Avril Carillonne)*
1962, Isabelle Aubret; *Un Premier Amour*
1963, Alain Barrière; *Elle Etait Si Jolie*
1964, Rachel; *Le Chant De Mallory*
1965, Guy Mardel; *N'Avoue Jamais*
1966, Dominique Walter; *Chez Nous*
1967, Noëlle Cordier; *Il Doit Faire Beau Là-bas*
1968, Isabelle Aubret; *La Source*
1969, Frida Boccara; *Un Jour, Un Enfant*
1970, Guy Bonnet; *Marie Blanche*
1971, Serge Lama; *Un Jardin Sur La Terre*
1972, Betty Mars; *Comé-Comédie*
1973, Martine Clémenceau; *Sans Toi*
1974, No entry
1975, Nicole Rieu; *Et Bonjour A Toi L'Artiste*
1976, Catherine Ferry; *Un, Deux, Trois*
1977, Marie Myriam; *L'Oiseau Et L'Enfant*

★ ★

1978, Joël Prévost; *Il Y Aura Toujours Des Violons*
1979, Anne-Marie David; *Je Suis L'Enfant Soleil*
1980, Profil; *Hé, Hé, M'sieurs Dames*
1981, Jean Gabilou; *Humanahum*
1982, No entry
1983, Guy Bonnet; *Vivre*
1984, Annick Thoumazeau; *Autant D'Amoureux Que D'Etoiles*
1985, Roger Bens; *Femme Dans Ses Rêves Aussi*
1986, Cocktail Chic; *Europiennes*
1987, Christine Minier; *Les Mots D'Amour N'ont Pas De Dimanche*
1988, Gérard Lenorman; *Chanteur De Charme*
1989, Nathalie Pâque; *J'ai Volé La Vie*
1990, Joëlle Ursull; *White And Black Blues*
1991, Amina; *C'est Le Dernier Qui A Parlé Qui A Raison*
1992, Kali; *Monté La Riviè*
1993, Patrick Fiori; *Mama Corsica*
1994, Nina Morato; *Je Suis Un Vrai Garçon*
1995, Nathalie Santamaria; *Il Me Donne Rendez-vous*
1996, Dan Ar Braz et L'Héritage Des Celtes; *Diwanis Bugale*
1997, Fanny; *Sentiment Songes*

GERMANY

42 ENTRIES, BEST PLACING: 1ST IN 1982

1956, Walter Andreas Schwarz; *Im Wartesaal Zum Grossen Glück*
1956, Freddy Quinn; *So Geht Das Jede Nacht*
1957, Margot Hielscher; *Telefon, Telefon*
1958, Margot Hielscher; *Für Zwei Groschen Musik*
1959, Alice and Ellen Kessler; *Heute Abend Woll'n Wir Tanzen Geh'n*
1960, Wyn Hoop; *Bonne Nuit, Ma Chérie*
1961, Lale Andersen; *Einmal Sehen Wir Uns Wieder*
1962, Conny Froböss; *Zwei Kleine Italiener*
1963, Heidi Brühl; *Marcel*
1964, Nora Nova; *Man Gewöhnt Sich So Schnell An Das Schöne*
1965, Ulla Wiesner; *Paradies, Wo Bist Du?*
1966, Margot Eskens; *Die Zeiger Der Uhr*
1967, Inge Brück; *Anouschka*
1968, Wencke Myhre; *Ein Hoch Der Liebe*
1969, Siw Malmqvist; *Prima Ballerina*
1970, Katja Ebstein; *Wunder Gibt Es Immer Wieder*
1971, Katja Ebstein; *Diese Welt*
1972, Mary Roos; *Nur Die Liebe Lässt Uns Leben*
1973, Gitte; *Junger Tag*
1974, Cindy and Bert; *Die Sommermelodie*
1975, Joy Fleming; *Ein Lied Kann Eine Brücke Sein*
1976, Les Humphries Singers; *Sing, Sang, Song*
1977, Silver Convention; *Telegram*
1978, Ireen Sheer; *Feuer*
1979, Dschingis Khan; *Dschingis Khan*
1980, Katja Ebstein; *Theater*
1981, Lena Valaitis; *Johnny Blue*
1982, Nicole; *Ein Bisschen Frieden*
1983, Hoffmann and Hoffmann; *Rücksicht*
1984, Mary Roos; *Aufrecht Geh'n*
1985, Wind; *Für Alle*
1986, Ingrid Peters; *Über Die Brücke Geh'n*
1987, Wind; *Lass Die Sonne In Dein Herz*
1988, Maxi and Chris Garden; *Lied Für Einen Freund*
1989, Nino de Angelo; *Flieger*
1990, Chris Kempers and Daniel Kovac; *Frei Zu Leben*
1991, Atlantis 2000; *Dieser Traum Darf Niemals Sterben*
1992, Wind; *Träume Sind Für Alle Da*
1993, Münchener Freiheit; *Viel Zu Weit*
1994, Mekado; *Wir Geben 'Ne Party*
1995, Stone and Stone; *Verliebt In Dich*
1996, No entry
1997, Bianca Shomburg; *Zeit*

GREECE

20 ENTRIES, BEST PLACING: 5TH IN 1977, 1992

1974, Marinella; Krassi; *Thalassa Ke T'Agori Mou*
1975, No entry
1976, Mariza Koch; *Panaghia Mou, Panaghia Mou*
1977, Pascalis, Marianna, Robert and Bessy; *Mathema Solfege*
1978, Tania Tsanaklidou; *Charlie Chaplin*
1979, Elpida; *Socrates*
1980, Anna Vissi; *Autostop*
1981, Yiannis Dimitras; *Feggari Kalokerino*

★ ★

1982, No entry
1983, Christie; *Mou Les*
1984, No entry
1985, Takis Biniaris; *Miazoume*
1986, No entry
1987, Bang; *Stop*
1988, Afrodite Fryda; *Kloun*
1989, Marianna Efstratiou; *To Diko Sou Asteri*
1990, Christos Callow; *Horis Skopo*
1991, Sofia Vossou; *Anixi*
1992, Cleopatra; *Olou Tou Kosmou I Elpida*
1993, Katerina Garbi; *Ellada, Hora Tou Photos*
1994, Costas Bigalis and the Sea Lovers; *To Trehantiri (Diri-Diri)*
1995, Elina Konstantopoulou; *Pia Prosefhi*
1996, Marianna Efstratiou; *Emis Forame Tom Himona Anixiatika*
1997, Marianna Zorba; *Horepse*

HUNGARY

3 ENTRIES, BEST PLACING: 4TH IN 1994

1994, Friderika; *Kinek Mondjam El Vetkeimet*
1995, Csaba Szigetj; *Uj Nev A Regi Haz Falan*
1996, No entry
1997, VIP; *Miert Kell Hogy Elmenj?*

ICELAND

12 ENTRIES, BEST PLACING: 4TH IN 1990

1986, ICY; *Gledibankinn*
1987, Halla Margaret; *Hægt Og Hljótt*
1988, Beathoven; *Sokrates*
1989, Daniel; *Pad Sem Enginn Sér*
1990, Stjornin; *Eitt Lag Enn*
1991, Stefan and Eyfi; *Nina*
1992, Heart 2 Heart; *Nei Eda Ja*
1993, Inga; *Pa Veistu Svarid*
1994, Sigga; *Nætur*
1995, Bo Halldorsson; *Nuna*
1996, Anna Mjöll; *Sjubidu*
1997, Paul Oscar; *Minn Hinsti Dans*

IRELAND

32 ENTRIES, BEST PLACING: 1ST IN 1970, 1980, 1987, 1992, 1993, 1994, 1996

1965, Butch Moore; *Walking The Streets In The Rain*
1966, Dickie Rock; *Come Back To Stay*
1967, Sean Dunphy; *If I Could Choose*
1968, Pat McGeegan; *Chance Of A Lifetime*
1969, Muriel Day and the Lindsays; *The Wages Of Love*
1970, Dana; *All Kinds Of Everything*
1971, Angela Farrell; *One Day Love*
1972, Sandie Jones; *Ceol An Ghrà*
1973, Maxi; *Do I Dream*
1974, Tina Reynolds; *Cross Your Heart*
1975, The Swarbriggs; *That's What Friends Are For*
1976, Red Hurley; *When*
1977, The Swarbriggs Plus Two; *It's Nice To Be In Love Again*
1978, C. T. Wilkinson; *Born To Sing*
1979, Cathal Dunne; *Happy Man*
1980, Johnny Logan; *What's Another Year?*
1981, Sheeba; *Horoscopes*
1982, The Duskeys; *Here Today, Gone Tomorrow*
1983, No entry
1984, Linda Martin; *Terminal Three*
1985, Maria Christian; *Wait Until The Weekend Comes*
1986, Luv Bug; *You Can Count On Me*
1987, Johnny Logan; *Hold Me Now*
1988, Jump The Gun; *Take Him Home*
1989, Kiev Connolly and the Missing Passengers; *The Real Me*
1990, Liam Reilly; *Somewhere In Europe*
1991, Kim Jackson; *Could It Be That I'm In Love*
1992, Linda Martin; *Why Me?*
1993, Niamh Kavanagh; *In Your Eyes*
1994, Paul Harrington with Charlie McGettigan; *Rock 'N' Roll Kids*
1995, Eddie Friel; *Dreamin'*
1996, Eimear Quinn; *The Voice*
1997, Marc Roberts; *Mysterious Woman*

ISRAEL

20 ENTRIES, BEST PLACING: 1ST IN 1978, 1979

1973, Ilanit; *Ei Sham*

1974, Poogy; *Natati La Khaia*
1975, Shlomo Artzi; *At Ve'Ani*
1976, Chocolate Menta Mastik; *Emor Shalom*
1977, Ilanit; *Ha'ara Hi Shir Lishnayim*
1978, Izhar Cohen and Alphabeta; *A-Ba-Ni-Bi*
1979, Milk and Honey featuring Gali Atari; *Hallelujah*
1980, No entry
1981, Habibi; *Layla*
1982, Avi Toledano; *Hora*
1983, Ofra Haza; *Hi*
1984, No entry
1985, Izhar Cohen and Alphabeta; *Olé Olé*
1986, Moti iladi and Sarai Tzuriel; *Yavoh Yom*
1987, Datner and Kushnir; *Shir Habatlanim*
1988, Yardena Arazi; *Ben-Adam*
1989, Gili and Galit; *Derech Ha'melech*
1990, Rita; *Shara Barechovot*
1991, Duo Datz; *Kaan*
1992, Dafna; *Ze Rak Sport*
1993, Lahakat Shiru; *Shiru*
1994, No entry
1995, Liora; *Amen*
1996–7, No entry

ITALY

37 ENTRIES, BEST PLACING: 1ST IN 1964, 1990

1956, Tonina Torrielli; *Amami Se Vuoi*
1956, Franca Raimondi; *Aprite Le Finestra*
1957, Nunzio Gallo; *Corde Della Mia Chitarra*
1958, Domenico Modugno; *Nel Blu Dipinto Di Blu*
1959, Domenico Modugno; *Piove*
1960, Renato Rascel; *Romantica*
1961, Betty Curtis; *Al Di La*
1962, Claudio Villa; *Addio, Addio*
1963, Emilio Pericoli; *Uno Per Tutte*
1964, Gigliola Cinquetti; *Non Ho L'Eta*
1965, Bobby Solo; *Se Piangi, Se Ridi*
1966, Domenico Modugno; *Dio Come Ti Amo*
1967, Claudio Villa; *Non Andare Piu Lontano*
1968, Sergio Endrigo; *Marianne*
1969, Iva Zanicchi; *Due Grosse Lacrime Bianche*
1970, Gianni Morandi; *Occhi Di Ragazza*
1971, Massimo Ranieri; *L'Amore E Un Attimo*
1972, Nicola di Bari; *I Giorni Dell'Arcobaleno*
1973, Massimo Ranieri; *Chi Sara' Con Te*
1974, Gigliola Cinquetti; *Si*
1975, Wess and Dori Ghezzi; *Era*
1976, Romina Power and Al Bano; *Noi Lo Rivivremo Di Nuovo*
1977, Mia Martini; *Libera*
1978, Ricchi e Poveri; *Questo Amore*
1979, Matia Bazar; *Raggio Di Luna*
1980, Alan Sorrenti; *Non Se Che Darei*
1981–2, No entry
1983, Riccardo Fogli; *Per Lucia*
1984, Alice and Franco Battiato; *I Treni De Tozeur*
1985, Romina Power and Al Bano; *Magic, Oh Magic*
1986, No entry
1987, Umberto Tozzi and Raf; *Gente Di Mare*
1988, Luca Barbarossa; *Ti Scrivo*
1989, Anna Oxa and Fausto Leali; *Avrei Voluto*
1990, Toto Cutugno; *Insieme: 1992*
1991, Peppino di Capri; *Comme E Ddoce 'O Mare*
1992, Mia Martini; *Rapsodia*
1993, Enrico Ruggeri; *Sole d'Europa*
1994–6, No entry
1997, Jalisse; *Fiumi Di Parole*

LITHUANIA

1 ENTRY, BEST PLACING: 25TH IN 1994

1994, Ovidijus Vysniauskas; *Lopisine Mylimaj*

LUXEMBOURG

38 ENTRIES, BEST PLACING: 1ST IN 1961, 1965, 1972, 1973, 1983

1956, Michèle Arnaud; *Les Amants De Minuit*
1956, Michèle Arnaud; *Ne Crois Pas*
1957, Danièle Dupré; *Tant De Peine*
1958, Solange Berry; *Un Grand Amour*
1959, No entry
1960, Camillo Felgen; *So Laang We's Du Do Bast*
1961, Jean-Claude Pascal; *Nous Les Amoureux*
1962, Camillo Felgen; *Petit Bonhomme*
1963, Nana Mouskouri; *A Force De Prier*
1964, Hugues Aufray; *Dès Que Le Printemps Revient*
1965, France Gall; *Poupée De Cire, Poupée De Son*

1966, Michèle Torr; *Ce Soir Je T'Attendais*
1967, Vicky; *L'Amour Est Bleu*
1968, Chris Baldo and Sophie Garel; *Nous Vivrons D'Amour*
1969, Romuald; *Cathérine*
1970, David Alexandre Winter; *Je Suis Tombé Du Ciel*
1971, Monique Melsen; *Pomme, Pomme, Pomme*
1972, Vicky Leandros; *Après Toi*
1973, Anne-Marie David; *Tu Te Reconnaîtras*
1974, Ireen Sheer; *Bye Bye, I Love You*
1975, Géraldine; *Toi*
1976, Jürgen Marcus; *Chansons Pour Ceux Qui S'Aiment*
1977, Anne-Marie B; *Frère Jacques*
1978, Baccara; *Parlez-Vous Français*
1979, Jeane Manson; *J'ai Déjà Vu Ça Dans Tes Yeux*
1980, Sophie and Magaly; *Le Papa Pingouin*
1981, Jean-Claude Pascal; *C'est Peut-être Pas L'Amérique*
1982, Svetlana; *Cours Après Le Temps*
1983, Corinne Hermès; *Si La Vie Est Cadeau*
1984, Sophie Carle; *100% D'Amour*
1985, Ireen Sheer, Margo, Franck Olivier, Chris and Malcolm Roberts, Diane Solomon; *Children, Kinder, Enfants*
1986, Sherisse Laurence; *L'Amour De Ma Vie*
1987, Plastic Bertrand; *Amour Amour*
1988, Lara Fabian; *Croire*
1989, Park Café; *Monsieur*
1990, Céline Carzo; *Quand Je Te Rêve*
1991, Sarah Bray; *Un Baiser Volé*
1992, Marion Welter and Kontinent; *Sou Frai*
1993, Modern Times; *Donne-Moi Une Chance De Te Dire*
1994–7, No entries

MALTA

10 ENTRIES, BEST PLACING: 3RD IN 1992
1971, Joe Grech; *Marija L-Maltija*
1972, Helen and Joseph; *L-Imhabba*
1973–4, No entry
1975, Renato; *Singing This Song*
1976–90, No entries
1991, Georgina and Paul Giordimaina; *Could It Be*
1992, Mary Spiteri; *Little Child*
1993, William Mangion; *This Time*
1994, Chris and Moira; *More Than Love*
1995, Mike Spiteri; *Keep Me In Mind*
1996, Miriam Christine; *In A Woman's Heart*
1997, Debbie Scerri; *Let Me Fly*

MONACO

21 ENTRIES, BEST PLACING: 1ST IN 1971
1959, Jacques Pills; *Mon Ami Pierrot*
1960, François Deguelt; *Ce Soir-là*
1961, Colette Deréal; *Allons, Allons Les Enfants*
1962, François Deguelt; *Dis Rien*
1963, Françoise Hardy; *L'Amour S'En Va*
1964, Romuald; *Où Sont-Elles Passées?*
1965, Marjorie Noël; *Va Dire A L'Amour*
1966, Tereza; *Bien Plus Fort*
1967, Minouche Barelli; *Boum Badaboum*
1968, Line and Willy; *A Chacun Sa Chanson*
1969, Jean-Jacques; *Maman Maman*
1970, Dominique Dussault; *Marlène*
1971, Sèverine; *Un Banc, Un Arbre, Une Rue*
1972, Anne-Marie Godart and Peter McLane; *Comme On S'Aime*
1973, Marie; *Un Train Qui Part*
1974, Romuald; *Celui Qui Reste Et Celui Qui S'en Va*
1975, Sophie; *Une Chanson C'est Une Lettre*
1976, Mary Cristy; *Toi, La Musique Et Moi*
1977, Michèle Torr; *Une Petite Française*
1978, Caline and Olivier Toussaint; *Les Jardins De Monaco*
1979, Laurent Vaguener; *Notre Vie, C'est La Musique*
1980–97, No entries

MOROCCO

1 ENTRY, BEST PLACING: 18TH
1980, Samira Ben Said; *Bitakat Hob*

NETHERLANDS

40 ENTRIES, BEST PLACING: 1ST 1957, 1959, 1969, 1975
1956, Jetty Paerl; *De Vogels Van Holland*
1956, Corry Brokken; *Voor Goed Voor Bij*
1957, Corry Brokken; *Net Als Toen*
1958, Corry Brokken; *Heel De Wereld*

★ ★

1959, Teddy Scholten; *Een Beetje*
1960, Rudi Carrell; *Wat Een Geluk*
1961, Greetje Kauffeld; *Wat Een Dag*
1962, De Spelbrekers; *Katinka*
1963, Annie Palmen; *Een Speeldoos*
1964, Anneke Grönloh; *Jij Bent Mijn Leven*
1965, Conny van den Bos; *'T Het Is Genoeg*
1966, Milly Scott; *Fernando En Philippo*
1967, Thérèse Steinmetz; *Ringe Ding*
1968, Ronnie Tober; *Morgen*
1969, Lennie Kuhr; *De Troubadour*
1970, Patricia and Hearts of Soul; *Waterman*
1971, Saskia and Serge; *De Tijd*
1972, Sandra and Andres; *Als Het Om De Liefde Gaat*
1973, Ben Cramer; *De Oude Muzikant*
1974, Mouth and MacNeal; *I See A Star*
1975, Teach-In; *Ding Dinge Dong*
1976, Sandra Reemer; *The Party's Over*
1977, Heddy Lester; *De Mallemolen*
1978, Harmony; *'T Is OK*
1979, Xandra; *Colorado*
1980, Maggie McNeal; *Amsterdam*
1981, Linda Williams; *Het Is Een Wonder*
1982, Bill van Dijke; *Jij En Ik*
1983, Bernadette; *Sing Me A Song*
1984, Maribelle; *Ik Hou Van Jou*
1985, No entry
1986, Frizzle Sizzle; *Alles Heeft Ritme*
1987, Marcha; *Rechtop In De Wind*
1988, Gerhard Joling; *Shangri-la*
1989, Justine Palmelay; *Blijf Zoals Je Bent*
1990, Maywood; *Ik Wil Alles Met Je Delen*
1991, No entry
1992, Humphrey Campbell; *Wijs Me De Weg*
1993, Ruth Jacott; *Vrede*
1994, Willeke Alberti; *Waar Is De Zon*
1995, No entry
1996, Maxine and Franklin Brown; *De Eerste Keer*
1997, Mrs Einstein; *Niemand Heeft Nog Tijd*

NORWAY

37 ENTRIES, BEST PLACING: 1ST IN 1985, 1995

1960, Nora Brockstedt; *Voi-voi*
1961, Nora Brockstedt; *Sommer I Palma*
1962, Inger Jacobsen; *Kom Sol, Kom Regn*
1963, Anita Thallaug; *Solhverv*
1964, Arne Bendiksen; *Spiral*
1965, Kirsti Sparboe; *Karusell*
1966, Åse Kleveland; *Intet Er Nytt Under Solen*
1967, Kirsti Sparboe; *Dukkemann*
1968, Odd Børre; *Stress*
1969, Kirsti Sparboe; *Oj, Oj, Oj, Så Glad Jeg Skal Bli*
1970, No entry
1971, Hanne Krogh; *Lykken Er ...*
1972, Grethe Kausland and Benny Borg; *Småting*
1973, Bendik Singers; *It's Just A Game*
1974, Anne Karine Strøm and the Bendik Singers; *The First Day Of Love*
1975, Ellen Nikolaysen; *Touch My Life With Summer*
1976, Anne-Karine Strøm; *Mata Hari*
1977, Anita Skorgan; *Casanova*
1978, Jahn Teigen; *Mil Etter Mil*
1979, Anita Skorgan; *Oliver*
1980, Sverre Kjelsberg and Hattis Maetta; *Samiid Aednan*
1981, Finn Kalvik; *Aldri I Livet*
1982, Jahn Teigen and Anita Skorgan; *Adieu*
1983, Jahn Teigen; *Do Re Mi*
1984, Dollie de Luxe; *Lenge Leve Livet*
1985, Bobbysocks; *La Det Swinge*
1986, Ketil Stokkan; *Romeo*
1987, Kate Gulbrandsen; *Mitt Liv*
1988, Karoline Krüger; *For Vår Jord*
1989, Britt Synnøve Johansen; *Venners Nærhet*
1990, Ketil Stokkan; *Brandenburger Tor*
1991, Just 4 Fun; *Mrs Thompson*
1992, Merethe Trøan; *Visjoner*
1993, Silje Vige; *Alle Mine Tankar*
1994, Elisabeth Andreassen and Jan Werner Danielsen; *Duett*
1995, Secret Garden; *Nocturne*
1996, Elisabeth Andreassen; *I Evighet*
1997, Tor Endresen; *San Francisco*

POLAND

4 ENTRIES, BEST PLACING: 2ND IN 1994

1994, Edyta Gorniak; *To Nie Ja!*

1995, Justyna Steczkowska; *Sama*
1996, Kasia Kowalska; *Chce Znac Swoj Grzech*
1997, Anna-Maria Jopek; *Ale Jestem*

PORTUGAL

33 ENTRIES, BEST PLACING: 6TH IN 1996
1964, Antonio Calvario; *Oração*
1965, Simone de Oliveira; *Sol De Inverno*
1966, Madaleña Iglesias; *Ele E Ela*
1967, Eduardo Nascimento; *O Vento Mudou*
1968, Carlos Mendes; *Verão*
1969, Simone de Oliveira; *Desfolhada*
1970, No entry
1971, Tonicha; *Menina*
1972, Carlos Mendes; *A Festa Da Vida*
1973, Fernando Tordo; *Tourada*
1974, Paulo de Cavalho; *E Depois Do Adeus*
1975, Duarte Mendes; *Madrugada*
1976, Carlos do Carmo; *Uma Flor De Verde Pinho*
1977, Os Amigos; *Portugal No Coração*
1978, Gemini; *Dai-Li-Dou*
1979, Manuela Bravo; *Sobe, Sobe Balão Sobe*
1980, José Cid; *Um Grande, Grande Amor*
1981, Carlos Paião; *Play-back*
1982, Doce; *Bem Bom*
1983, Armando Gama; *Esta Balada Que Te Dou*
1984, Maria Guinot; *Silencio E Tanta Gente*
1985, Adelaide; *Penso Em Ti, Eu Sei*
1986, Dora; *Não Sejas Mau P'ra Mim*
1987, Nevada; *Neste Barco A Vela*
1988, Dora; *Voltarei*
1989, Da Vinci; *Conquistador*
1990, Nucha; *Ha Sempre Alguem*
1991, Dulce; *Lusitana Paixão*
1992, Dina; *Amor D'Agua Fresca*
1993, Anabela; *A Cidade Ate Ser Dia*
1994, Sara Tavares; *Chamar A Musica*
1995, To Cruz; *Baunilha E Chocolate*
1996, Lucia Moniz; *O Meu Coração Não Tem Cor*
1997, Celia Lawson; *Antes Do Adeus*

ROMANIA

1 ENTRY, BEST PLACING: 21ST IN 1994
1994, Dan Bittman; *Dincolo Di Nori*

RUSSIAN FEDERATION

3 ENTRIES, BEST PLACING: 9TH IN 1994
1994, Youddiph; *Vechni Stranik*
1995, Philipp Kirkorov; *Kobelnaya Dlya Vulkana*
1996, No entry
1997, Alla Pugachova; *Prima Donna*

SLOVAKIA

2 ENTRIES, BEST PLACING: 18TH IN 1996
1994, Martin Durinda and Tublatanka; *Nekonecna Piesen*
1995, No entry
1996, Marcel Polander; *Kym Nas Mas*
1997, No entry

SLOVENIA

4 ENTRIES, BEST PLACING: 7TH IN 1995
1993, 1X Band; *Tih Dezeven Dan*
1994, No entry
1995, Darja Svajger; *Prisluhni Mi*
1996, Regina; *Dan Najlepsih Sanj*
1997, Tanja Ribic; *Zbudi Se*

SPAIN

37 ENTRIES, BEST PLACING: 1ST IN 1968, 1969
1961, Conchita Bautista; *Estando Contigo*
1962, Victor Balaguer; *Llamame*
1963, José Guardiola and Rosa Mary; *Algo Prodigioso*
1964, Nelly, Tim and Tony; *Caracola*
1965, Conchita Bautista; *Que Bueno, Que Bueno*
1966, Raphael; *Yo Soy Aquel*
1967, Raphael; *Hablemos Del Amor*
1968, Massiel; *La La La*
1969, Salomé; *Vivo Cantando*
1970, Julio Iglesias; *Gwendolyne*
1971, Karina; *En Un Mondo Nuevo*
1972, Jaime Morey; *Amanece*
1973, Mocedades; *Eres Tu*
1974, Peret; *Canta Y Se Feliz*

★ ★

1975, Sergio and Estibaliz; *Tu Volveras*
1976, Braulio; *Sobran Las Palabras*
1977, Micky; *Enseñame A Cantar*
1978, José Velez; *Bailemos Un Vals*
1979, Betty Missiego; *Su Canción*
1980, Trigio Limpio; *Quedate Esta Noche*
1981, Bacchelli; *Y Solo Tu*
1982, Lucia; *El*
1983, Remedios Amaya; *Quién Maneja Mi Barca*
1984, Bravo; *Lady Lady*
1985, Paloma san Basilio; *La Fiesta Terminó*
1986, Cadillac; *Valentino*
1987, Patricia Kraus; *No Estas Solo*
1988, La Decada; *La Chica Que Yo Quiero (Made In Spain)*
1989, Nina; *Nacida Para Amar*
1990, Azucar Moreno; *Bandido*
1991, Sergio Dalma; *Bailar Pegados*
1992, Serafin; *Todo Esto Es La Musica*
1993, Eva Santamaria; *Hombres*
1994, Alejandro Abad; *Ella No Es Ella*
1995, Anabel Condé; *Vuelve Conmigo*
1996, Antonio Carbonell; *Ay! Que Deseo!*
1997, Marcos Llunas; *Sin Rencor*

SWEDEN

37 ENTRIES, BEST PLACING: 1ST IN 1974, 1984, 1991

1958, Alice Babs; *Lilla Stjärna*
1959, Brita Borg; *Augustin*
1960, Siw Malmkvist; *Alla Andra Får Varann*
1961, Lill-Babs; *April April*
1962, Inger Berggren; *Sol Och Vår*
1963, Monica Zetterlund; *En Gång I Stockholm*
1964, No entry
1965, Ingvar Wixell; *Absent Friend*
1966, Lill Lindfors and Svante Thuresson; *Nygammal Vals*
1967, Östen Warnerbring; *Som En Dröm*
1968, Claes-Göran Hederström; *Det Börjar Verka Kärlek Banne Mej*
1969, Tommy Körberg; *Judy Min Vän*
1970, No entry
1971, Family Four; *Vita Vidder*
1972, Family Four; *Härliga Sommardag*
1973, The Nova and the Dolls; *You're Summer*
1974, Abba; *Waterloo*
1975, Lars Berghagen; *Jennie, Jennie*
1976, No entry
1977, Forbes; *Beatles*
1978, Björn Skifs; *Det Blir Alltid Värre Framåt Natten*
1979, Ted Gärdestad; *Satellit*
1980, Tomas Ledin; *Just Nu*
1981, Björn Skifs; *Fångad I En Dröm*
1982, Chips; *Dag Efter Dag*
1983, Carola Häggkvist; *Främling*
1984, Herreys; *Diggi-Loo Diggi-Ley*
1985, Kikki Danielsson; *Bra Vibrationer*
1986, Lasse Holm and Monica Törnell; *E' De' Det Här Du Kallar Kärlek?*
1987, Lotta Engberg; *Boogaloo*
1988, Tommy Körberg; *Stad I Ljus*
1989, Tommy Nilsson; *En Dag*
1990, Edin and Ådahl; *Som En Vind*
1991, Carola; *Fångad Av En Stormvind*
1992, Christer Björkman; *Imorgon Är En Annan Dag*
1993, Arvingarna; *Eloise*
1994, Marie Bergman and Roger Pontare; *Stjärnorna*
1995, Jan Johansen; *Se På Mej*
1996, One More Time; *Den Vilda*
1997, Blond; *Bara Hon Alskar Mig*

SWITZERLAND

42 ENTRIES, BEST PLACING: 1ST IN 1956, 1988

1956, Lys Assia; *Das Alte Karussel*
1956, Lys Assia; *Refrain*
1957, Lys Assia; *L'enfant Que J'etais*
1958, Lys Assia; *Giorgio*
1959, Christa Williams; *Irgendwoher*
1960, Anita Traversi; *Cielo E Terra*
1961, Franca di Rienzo; *Nous Aurons Demain*
1962, Jean Philippe; *Le Retour*
1963, Ester Ofarim; *T'en Va Pas*
1964, Anita Traversi; *I Miei Pensieri*
1965, Yovanna; *Non A Jamais Sans Toi*
1966, Madeleine Pascal; *Ne Vois-tu Pas?*
1967, Géraldine; *Quel Coeur Vas-tu Briser?*

1968, Gianni Mascolo; *Guardando Il Sole*
1969, Paola; *Bonjour Bonjour*
1970, Henri Dès; *Retour*
1971, Peter, Sue and Marc; *Les Illusions De Nos Vingt Ans*
1972, Véronique Müller; *C'Est La Chanson De Mon Amour*
1973, Patrick Juvet; *Je Vais Me Marier, Marie*
1974, Piera Martell; *Mein Ruf Nach Dir*
1975, Simone Drexel; *Mikado*
1976, Peter, Sue and Marc; *Djambo, Djambo*
1977, Pepe Lienhard Band; *Swiss Lady*
1978, Carole Vinci; *Vivre*
1979, Peter, Sue and Marc, and Pfuri, Gorps and Kniri; *Trödler und Co*
1980, Paola; *Cinéma*
1981, Peter, Sue and Marc; *Io Senza Te*
1982, Arlette Zola; *Amour On T'Aime*
1983, Mariella Farré; *Io Cosi Non Ci Sto*
1984, Rainy Day; *Welche Farbe Hat Der Sonnenschein*
1985, Mariella Farré and Pino Gasparini; *Piano Piano*
1986, Daniela Simons; *Pas Pour Moi*
1987, Carol Rich; *Moitié, Moitié*
1988, Céline Dion; *Ne Partez Pas Sans Moi*
1989, Furbaz; *Viver Senza Tei*
1990, Egon Egemann; *Musik Klingt In Die Welt Hinaus*
1991, Sandra Simo; *Canzone Per Te*
1992, Daisy Auvray; *Mister Music Man*
1993, Annie Cotton; *Moi, Tout Simplement*
1994, Duilio; *Sto Pregando*
1995, No entry
1996, Kathy Leander; *Mon Coeur L'Aime*
1997, Barbara Berta; *Dentro Di Me*

TURKEY

19 ENTRIES, BEST PLACING: 3RD IN 1997

1975, Semiha Yanki; *Seninle Bir Dakika*
1976–7, No entry
1978, Nazar; *Sevince*
1979, No entry
1980, Ajda Pekkan; *Petr'oil*
1981, Modern Folk Trio and Aysegül; *Dönme Dolap*
1982, Neco; *Hani*
1983, Cetin Alp and Short Wave; *Opera*
1984, Bes Yil Önce, On Yil Sonra; *Halay*
1985, MFÖ; *Didai Didai Dai*
1986, Klips and Onlar; *Halley*
1987, Seyyal Taner and Locomotif; *Sarkim Sevgi Üstüne*
1988, MFÖ; *Sufi (Hey Ya Hey)*
1989, Pan; *Bana Bana*
1990, Kayahan; *Gözlerinin Hapsindeyim*
1991, Izel Celiköz, Reyhan Soykarci and Can Ugurluer; *Iki Dakika*
1992, Aylin Vatankos; *Yaz Bitti*
1993, Burak Aydos; *Esmer Yarim*
1994, No entry
1995, Arzu Ece; *Sev*
1996, Sebnem Paker; *Besinci Mevsim*
1997, Sebnem Paker; *Dinle*

UNITED KINGDOM

40 ENTRIES, BEST PLACING: 1ST IN 1967, 1969, 1976, 1981, 1997

1957, Patricia Bredin; *All*
1958, No entry
1959, Pearl Carr and Teddy Johnson; *Sing Little Birdie*
1960, Bryan Johnson; *Looking High, High, High*
1961, The Allisons; *Are You Sure?*
1962, Ronnie Carroll; *Ring-a-Ding Girl*
1963, Ronnie Carroll; *Say Wonderful Things*
1964, Matt Monro; *I Love The Little Things*
1965, Kathy Kirby; *I Belong*
1966, Kenneth McKellar; *A Man Without Love*
1967, Sandie Shaw; *Puppet On A String*
1968, Cliff Richard; *Congratulations*
1969, Lulu; *Boom Bang-A-Bang*
1970, Mary Hopkin; *Knock Knock – Who's There?*
1971, Clodagh Rodgers; *Jack In The Box*
1972, The New Seekers; *Beg, Steal Or Borrow*
1973, Cliff Richard; *Power To All Our Friends*
1974, Olivia Newton-John; *Long Live Love*
1975, The Shadows; *Let Me Be The One*
1976, Brotherhood of Man; *Save Your Kisses For Me*
1977, Lynsey de Paul and Mike Moran; *Rock Bottom*
1978, Co-Co; *The Bad Old Days*

★ ★

1979, Black Lace; *Mary Ann*
1980, Prima Donna; *Love Enough For Two*
1981, Buck's Fizz; *Making Your Mind Up*
1982, Bardo; *One Step Further*
1983, Sweet Dreams; *I'm Never Giving Up*
1984, Belle and the Devotions; *Love Games*
1985, Vikki; *Love Is*
1986, Ryder; *Runner In The Night*
1987, Rikki; *Only The Light*
1988, Scott Fitzgerald; *Go*
1989, Live Report; *Why Do I Always Get It Wrong?*
1990, Emma; *Give A Little Love Back To The World*
1991, Samantha Janus; *A Message To Your Heart*
1992, Michael Ball; *One Step Out Of Time*
1993, Sonia; *Better The Devil You Know*
1994, Frances Ruffelle; *We Will Be Free (Lonely Symphony)*
1995, Love City Groove; *Love City Groove*
1996, Gina G; *Ooh Aah ... Just A Little Bit*
1997, Katrina and the Waves; *Love Shine A Light*

YUGOSLAVIA

27 ENTRIES, BEST PLACING: 1ST IN 1989

1961, Ljiljana Petrovic; *Neke Davne Zvezde*
1962, Lola Novakovic; *Ne Pali Svetla U Sumrak*
1963, Vice Vukov; *Brodovi*
1964, Sabahudin Kurt; *Zivot Je Sklopio Krug*
1965, Vice Vukov; *Ceznja*
1966, Berta Ambroz; *Brez Besed*
1967, Lado Leskovar; *Vse Roze Sveta*
1968, Luci Kapurso and Hamo Hajdarhodzic; *Jedan Dan*
1969, Ivan; *Pozdrav Svijetu*
1970, Eva Srsen; *Pridi, Dala Ti Bom Cvet*
1971, Krunoslav Slabinac; *Tvoj Djecak Je Tuzan*
1972, Tereza; *Muzika I Ti*
1973, Zdravko Colic; *Gori Vatra*
1974, Korni; *Generacija '42*
1975, Blood and Ashes; *Dan Ljubezni*
1976, Ambasadori; *Ne Mogu Skriti Svoju Bol*
1977–80, No entries
1981, Seid Memic-Vajta; *Leila*
1982, Aska; *Halo Halo*
1983, Daniel; *Dzuli*
1984, Vlado and Isolda; *Ciao Amore*
1985, No entry
1986, Doris Dragovic; *Zeljo Moja*
1987, Novi Fosili; *Ja Sam Za Ples*
1988, Silver Wings; *Mangup*
1989, Riva; *Rock Me*
1990, Tajci; *Hajde Da Ludujemo*
1991, Baby Doll; *Brazil*
1992, Extra Nena; *Ljubim Te Pesmama*

MOST SUCCESSFUL SONGS

Below is a list of the top fifty most successful Eurovision entries based on the percentage of votes gained.

So, for example, if 'Save Your Kisses For Me' had been awarded a maximum of twelve points from each jury, its total would have been 204. Its actual total of 164 points therefore represents 80.4 per cent of the total votes available.

In the early years, each jury member had a vote and a song could have received a maximum of ten votes from each country. In practice, however, juries generally awarded between three and six votes to their most favoured song. In these instances we have calculated the average highest mark per year and used that figure as the benchmark for a percentage.

Pos.	Title	Artist	Year	Country	% of vote
1	Save Your Kisses for Me	Brotherhood of Man	1976	United Kingdom	80.4
2	Ein Bisschen Frieden	Nicole	1982	Germany	78.9
3	Love Shine A Light	Katrina and the Waves	1997	United Kingdom	78.8
4	Rock 'N' Roll Kids	Paul Harrington with Charlie McGettigan	1994	Ireland	78.5
5	J'Aime La Vie	Sandra Kim	1986	Belgium	77.2
6	Tu Te Reconnaitras	Anne-Marie David	1973	Luxembourg	75.8
7	Puppet On A String	Sandie Shaw	1967	United Kingdom	73.4
8	Eres Tu	Mocedades	1973	Spain	72.7
9	Un, Deux, Trois	Catherine Ferry	1976	France	72.1
10	Net Als Toen	Corrie Brokken	1957	Netherlands	71.8
11	Power To All Our Friends	Cliff Richard	1973	United Kingdom	71.1
12	Ding Dinge Dong	Teach-In	1975	Netherlands	70.4
13	Un Banc, Un Arbre, Une Rue	Sèverine	1971	Monaco	69.1
	Après Toi	Vicky Leandros	1972	Luxembourg	69.1
15	A-Ba-Ni-Bi	Izhar Cohen and Alphabeta	1978	Israel	68.9
16	Hold Me Now	Johnny Logan	1987	Ireland	68.3
17	Diggi-Loo Diggi-Ley	Herreys	1984	Sweden	67.1
18	All Kinds Of Everything	Dana	1970	Ireland	67.1

19	L'Oiseau Et L'Enfant	Marie Myriam	1977	France	66.7
20	What's Another Year?	Johnny Logan	1980	Ireland	66.2
21	Non Ho L'Eta	Gigliola Cinquetti	1964	Italy	65.3
22	In Your Eyes	Niamh Kavanagh	1993	Ireland	64.9
23	Let Me Be The One	The Shadows	1975	United Kingdom	63.9
24	Terminal Three	Linda Martin	1984	Ireland	63.4
25	Si La Vie Est Cadeau	Corinne Hermès	1983	Luxembourg	62.3
26	Tom Pillibi	Jacqueline Boyer	1960	France	62.0
27	Pas Pour Moi	Daniela Simons	1986	Switzerland	61.4
28	The Voice	Eimar Quinn	1996	Ireland	61.4
29	En Un Mondo Nuevo	Karina	1971	Spain	60.3
30	Hi	Ofra Haza	1983	Israel	59.7
	Making Your Mind Up	Buck's Fizz	1981	United Kingdom	59.7
32	Rock Bottom	Lynsey de Paul and Mike Moran	1977	United Kingdom	59.3
33	Theater	Katja Ebstein	1980	Germany	59.3
34	Insieme: 1992	Toto Cutugno	1990	Italy	59.1
35	Beg, Steal or Borrow	The New Seekers	1972	United Kingdom	58.8
36	Why Me?	Linda Martin	1992	Ireland	58.7
37	It's Nice To Be In Love Again	The Swarbriggs Plus Two	1977	Ireland	58.3
38	C'est Le Dernier Qui A Parle Qui	Amina	1991	France	57.9
	Fångad Av En Stormvind	Carola	1991	Sweden	57.9
40	Johnny Blue	Lena Valaitis	1981	Germany	57.9
41	Hallelujah	Milk and Honey	1979	Israel	57.9
42	Un Premier Amour	Isabelle Aubret	1962	France	57.8
43	Dors, Mon Amour	André Claveau	1958	France	57.7
44	To Nie Ja!	Edyta Gorniak	1994	Poland	57.6
45	Ne Partez Pas Sans Moi	Céline Dion	1988	Switzerland	57.1
46	La Det Swinge	Bobbysocks	1985	Norway	56.9
	Better The Devil You Know	Sonia	1993	United Kingdom	56.9
48	Go	Scott Fitzgerald	1988	United Kingdom	56.7
49	Nocturne	Secret Garden	1995	Norway	56.1
50	Dansevise	Grethe and Jørgen Ingmann	1963	Denmark	56.0

NOTE: The United Kingdom (with ten appearances on this list), Ireland (with nine) and France (with six) account for half of the songs in the top fifty.

★ ★

1998

SCORING CHART FOR YOU TO FILL IN

Host country: United Kingdom ★ *Venue:* National Indoor Arena, Birmingham
Date: 9 May ★ *Presenters:* Terry Wogan and Ulrika Jonsson
Voting structure: Each country awarded 12 to its top song, 10 to the second, 8 to the third and 7, 6, 5, 4, 3, 2 and 1 point for the next seven
Total entries: 25 ★ *Debut countries:* Former Yugoslavian Republic of Macedonia (FYROM)

1998	Your Score	Croatia	Greece	France	Spain	Switzerland	Slovakia	Poland	Israel	Germany	Malta	Hungary	Slovenia	Ireland	Portugal	Romania	UK	Cyprus	Netherlands	Sweden	Belgium	Finland	Norway	Estonia	Turkey	FYROM	**Position**
Croatia																											
Greece																											
France																											
Spain																											
Switzerland																											
Slovakia																											
Poland																											
Israel																											
Germany																											
Malta																											
Hungary																											
Slovenia																											
Ireland																											
Portugal																											
Romania																											
UK																											
Cyprus																											
Netherlands																											
Sweden																											
Belgium																											
Finland																											
Norway																											
Estonia																											
Turkey																											
FYROM																											